Discerning the Body

Discerning the Body

Searching for Jesus in the World

Jason Byassee

Foreword by
Martin E. Marty

CASCADE *Books* • Eugene, Oregon

DISCERNING THE BODY
Searching for Jesus in the World

Copyright © 2013 Jason Byassee. All rights reserved. Except for brief quotations in critical publications or reviews, no part of this book may be reproduced in any manner without prior written permission from the publisher. Write: Permissions, Wipf and Stock Publishers, 199 W. 8th Ave., Suite 3, Eugene, OR 97401.

Cascade Books
An Imprint of Wipf and Stock Publishers
199 W. 8th Ave., Suite 3
Eugene, OR 97401
www.wipfandstock.com

ISBN 13: 978-1-62032-376-2

Cataloging-in-Publication data:

Byassee, Jason.

    Discerning the body : searching for Jesus in the world / Jason Byassee ; foreword by Martin E. Marty.

    xviii + 242 p. ; 23 cm. —Includes bibliographical references.

    ISBN 13: 978-1-62032-376-2

    1. Christian life. 2. I. Marty, Martin E., 1928–. II. Title.

BV4501.3 .B93 2013

Manufactured in the U.S.A.

To the staff and people of Boone United Methodist Church.

Contents

Foreword by Martin E. Marty | xi
Introduction | xv

Part 1 Searching for Jesus in Local Congregations | 1
    Emerging Model: A Visit to Jacob's Well | 5
    The Church Downtown: Strategies for Urban Ministry | 12
    Africentric Church: A Visit to Chicago's Trinity UCC | 22
    Synchronized Worship: The Rise of the Multicampus Church | 31
    It's *Simul Justus*, Not the Tattoos: A Profile of Nadia Bolz-Weber and House for All Sinners and Saints | 37

Part 2 Searching for Jesus in Popular Evangelicalism | 47
    The New Monastics: Alternative Christian Communities | 51
    Be Happy: The Health and Wealth Gospel of Joel Osteen | 61
    En-raptured: Will We Be "Left Behind"? | 67
    Dinosaurs in the Garden: A Visit to the Creation Museum | 74
    Jeremiah Wright, Evangelicals' Brother in Christ | 80
    The Almost Formerly Important: Lessons of the Old Mainline for the New Mainline | 83

Part 3 Searching for Jesus in the Church in Africa | 85
    Perilous Presence: Christians in Uganda | 87
    Holy Space in Uganda | 94
    How the Church Grew in South Sudan | 98

Surprises in Sudan: Reading the Bible with Southern Sudanese Christians | 104
The Muse of Church Revival in Sudan | 110
Why Haven't They Left? Stability in the Church of Sudan | 112
University Presidents in the Congo: How to Stop a War | 114
Leadership as Dancing the Dance of All Your People | 116

Part 4 Searching for Jesus among Roman Catholics | 119

What about Mary? Protestants and Marian Devotion | 123
On the Grace-Filled Life | 131
Sanctuary: Mary, Methodists, and Immigration | 134
Joseph: Stepfather to God | 138
Mass Appeal? Attending a Latin Liturgy | 141
Dare to Discipline? John Kerry and Communion | 145
Going Catholic: Six Journeys to Rome | 149
Fathers and Sons at the Beach | 157

Part 5 Searching for Jesus in Popular Culture | 163

What You're Looking For: Worship at the U2charist | 165
Saint Lebowski | 168
Message of Light: An Interview with Seth Avett | 171
The Banjo Lesson: The Carolina Chocolate Drops | 177
The Difficulty and Glory of Collaboration | 179

Part 6 Searching for Jesus in Sports | 183

Holy Hoops: The Quasi-religious Basketball Rivalry between Duke and North Carolina | 185
Duke Basketball: You Are What You Do Regularly, Excellently | 189
Invisible, Sticky Leaders | 191
The Last Guy on the Bench: Casey Peters | 193
Duke Football: How to React to a Failure that's Not Your Fault? | 195
Marathons: Straining toward Holiness. Together. | 197
Marathons as Grace or Heresy? | 199

Part 7 Searching for Jesus in Christian Institutions | 203

   Hierarchy of Holiness | 205
   Outrageous Ambition in East Africa | 208
   Campuses of the Kingdom | 210
   Cells in the Body of Christ | 215
   Luring a Campus into the Faith | 217
   Academic Diversity through Church Affiliation | 220

Part 8 Searching for Jesus amidst the Task of Writing | 223

   Why Religious Journalism Is Boring | 225
   Paying Attention | 231
   Abounding in Hope | 236
   Joining the Communion of Saints and Writing the Unwritable Word | 240

Foreword

AUTHOR JASON BYASSEE POSSESSES many talents, achievements, modes of professional outreach, and, most important, a sense of vocation. But second most important to those of us who come across this book is that he has what critics call a "voice." The temptation for authors of columns—and this book is largely a collection of columns—is to indulge themselves and entertain us with short-term, scattershot, often unrelated snippets and randomly collected items. Those columnists, however, who operate with depth and who draw upon resources of wisdom gained from experience hold our attention, and their writings remain in our minds long after we have read them.

I once read that composer George Gershwin's musical inspiration and energies were usually expended on short pieces, songs, preludes, and the like. He did not write symphonies and produced only two concerti, a noted rhapsody, and a couple of other longer-than-three-minutes compositions. These varied greatly, their themes being sometimes romantic, sometimes comic, even at times cynical. But we recognize them as Gershwinesque, wrote a critic, because the composer had a "voice." Artists have visual analogues to a voice; we are never wearied by varied works of art from the hand of Monet or Raphael or Dürer because their products are united by a certain distinctive captured vision of reality. So with poets and authors: Walt Whitman said he "contained multitudes," but the writings were singular.

I won't embarrass Byassee by nominating him for a place in this hall of fame; he's too young yet, and we don't know how he'll turn out. But, as readers of his columns have known, and as readers of this book will discover, his voice is unmistakable as he directs it exquisitely to varied purposes. I think he has a horror of boring readers or hearers, and he has striven to make his work interesting. I wish I could think of a more appropriate word, but *interesting* serves my purpose best. He has the gift for lifting the uncommon up out of the commonplace.

Foreword

I trust that his parishioners hope their pastor is going nowhere but where he is, but we who have come to know him have to say, "wherever he goes," he now writes as a pastor. He manifests the interests, heart, soul, and agenda of a pastor whose focus is a local church, and thus, I am tempted to say, he has in mind "the one, holy, catholic and apostolic church," locally embodied. While I spent only a decade in parish ministry, I think and hope that the experience of those years imprinted itself on me wherever my vocation took me. Byassee is not going to be able to discard what he has become already, thanks to the closeness a parish minister knows as he or she keeps an eye on the Big Picture.

Important note: this is not a book for parish pastors, or not only for them. They are significantly outnumbered by Christians who do not hold pastoral office, and I don't think he'd like it if I limited the market to clergy. I also don't think this is only for Christians. If the general public gained insight into the claims of the Gospel as they are embodied by some of their fellow-citizens, that public might correct some impressions that the media can easily leave them with. Pastors deal with the issues we call "existential," with questions such as "Why are we here?" and "What is the purpose of life?" and "For whom should we care, and who will care for us?"

Different readers may assess Byassee's voice and interests in diverse ways, but after having worked with him (at *The Christian Century* magazine, where he worked on-site and I dropped in), read him, and conversed with him now and then, I'd offer this: he does not tolerate theological and ecclesiastical fools lightly. When given the choice between classical or—dare I mention it?—orthodox versions of Christianity and the latest inventions of sensation-seekers, he goes for the classic accent. He's sufficiently traveled, intellectually and physically, to know that it is futile to try to define the faith or the Christian community satisfactorily for all interests. For instance, he is and has to be informed about, drawn in some measure to, and adept at explaining the ever-emerging church (aka the Emergent Church), but he is not moved by those who claim, without having been given a new revelation, to have invented new cure-alls for what is troubling or confusing the faithful. He is bored by and a bit disdainful of those who claim too much for their discoveries and new manufactures. Yet his faith, hope, and charity do not permit him to close his eyes to what is new and fresh. This book is by an author with "eyes wide open."

While he has helped the reader by organizing the columns into eight topical parts, he has not attempted to provide a step-by-step instruction book for those who would weather the current Christian storms. He rather opens his eyes to his environs, brings the perspective of enduring faith to his observations, takes risks, writes, and then publishes what is before you.

Foreword

Sometimes explicitly and always at least implicitly, he is offering advice to fellow Christians. For instance, they should not be taken in by ideology. Readers can here find surprising if insinuated counsel retired from among the complex inheritances from the long (and recent) past. They will henceforth likely take a chance at mining the tried and true in theology and church life and will less likely fall for often untried and untrue options, which, though he uses the term sparingly, turn out to have been fads.

British philosopher Ernest Gellner once wrote that there are few things more dated than the modernism of the previous generation. Byassee is not likely soon to be dated, not because he has chosen to be crusty and antique-loving, but because he knows from study and experience—thank those parishioners again—that there are depths in Christian texts and life and faith that offer more than do today's quick resolutions. Byassee's book is an invitation to a conversation more than a challenge to argument. So, turn the page, please, and start conversing with someone who shows through his writings that he can listen as well as speak and write. He has a voice, but he also has ears to hear the Gospel and those who listen to it.

Martin E. Marty
The Fairfax M. Cone Distinguished Service Professor
at The University of Chicago and a (very) longtime editor of
and contributor to *The Christian Century*

Introduction

Two ancient Christian reflections guide my work in these pages. One comes from St. Irenaeus, speaking about Old Testament interpretation. To read Israel's scripture is like having the pieces of a mosaic arrayed, ready to create something beautiful. The Gnostics—ancient Christian heretics who deny the goodness of the body, Israel's covenants, and the whole of God's creation—take those glass pieces and arrange them to represent something disgusting, such as a dog or a fox (well, disgusting for the ancient world anyway). But to read scripture rightly is to take those tessarae and arrange them in the image of the true king.[1] Whatever we do with the scriptures' particularities will be determined by the image of the one we keep in mind, to whom those scriptures bear witness—the coming king to whom they point forward.

The other comes from St. Augustine, commenting on our Psalm 102, a lament psalm of the sort that reads particularly well in time of national disaster. Our modern versions tend to render Psalm 102:6 like this: "I am like an owl in desolate places." But Augustine's version translated that bird as a pelican. He's never seen a pelican, they don't live in his part of the world, so he has to do a little research. And he reads in Roman zoology annals that mother pelicans slay their young in the nest, then wound themselves and pour their blood on the young, who revive. Augustine is skeptical about the biology, for good reason! But if the story *is* true, "observe how apt a symbol it is of him who gave us life by his own blood."[2] God slays her (his?) young and then wounds him (her?) self and pours blood out to revive them. Augustine is often at his most creative when he is being most biblical (following Deut 32:39, "I kill and I make alive; I wound and I heal"). Scholars

---

1. Irenaeus, *Against Heresies* I.8.1, trans. Robert M. Grant (London: Routledge, 1997) 66.

2. Augustine, *Expositions of the Psalms*, ed. John E. Rotelle, trans. Maria Boulding, Works of Saint Augustine: A Translation for the 21st Century (Hyde Park, NY: New City, 2003) 5:53.

Introduction

have often noted the interestingly feminine images Augustine uses for Jesus, as a nursing mother, here as a killing and reviving mother pelican.[3]

Then this is how the image is supposed to work—as I was sharing this image with students at Garrett-Evangelical Theological Seminary, they started smirking to themselves. "What?" I asked, assuming the cynical age we live in was overwhelming my brilliant teachable moment. "Don't you see the pelican every day?" one asked. Sure enough, above both doorways of the seminary building is a pelican's nest carved in stone, tiny beaks just visible, a mother reigning over the roost, killing and giving life. The smirks were because the pelican had become familiar to them as a reference to Christ—I had no need to sell it so hard! On another occasion, slightly more momentous this time, I was preparing to ask my wife to marry me. We had done all the preliminaries: the ring was bought, the wine was drunk, we were sitting on the beach, she was waiting and I was terrified (not being above the chronic disconnection of our age). And what did I see but a flock of pelicans, flying in formation, a V crowning the sky. Now, that was either a banal coincidence or Jesus come to reassure us that there would be cruciform difficulty, and also resurrectional grace, in our union. And if you prefer the former, then as Barbara Brown Taylor likes to say, I wish you a boring life.

The point of both of these vignettes is the way ancient Christians went looking for Jesus in everything: in the Old Testament, in the creation, in the dramas of their own lives. They learned from the New Testament and Christian liturgy how to do this. As the Bible points to Jesus, so do all of our lives, if viewed aright. In fact, so does all creation, since the one who created it is saving it in Christ, drawing it to himself by the power of the Spirit. Much of creation, especially we creatures, is still in disarray and rebellion. But we cheat ourselves if we fail to see the mighty acts of redemption all around us all the time. The way it's supposed to work is this: now, after learning of St. Irenaeus' image, when we see a mosaic we're reminded of Jesus. When we see a pelican, we're reminded of Jesus. Creation is always meant to bear witness to its creator, fleshed in Jesus, poured out for its consolation. Now, a little bit of that creation is christologically marked for us. One day it will all be for everyone.

In one way the work in these pages is enormously disparate, covering topics from popular culture to politics to ancient Christianity to institutions and back again. This reflects the occasional nature of the publications I've been asked to write for. Magazines want a variety of topics, and *The Christian Century*, where I worked full time from 2004 to 2008, was willing to publish me on all manner of things, starting with theology and church

---

3. See Jean Bethke Elshtain, *Public Man, Private Woman: Women in Social and Political Thought*, 2nd ed. (Princeton: Princeton University Press, 1993).

history and radiating out into contemporary culture and church practice. *Faith & Leadership*, the Web magazine startup for which I worked at Duke Divinity School from 2008 to 2011, directed my writing in a more focused way to questions of institutional leadership, but even so I drew on sources as disparate as ancient and contemporary Judaism, the saintly Jean Vanier, Duke basketball, and grunge grass music. Other publications for which I've written run the theological gamut from the flagship liberal mainline *Century* to the flagship evangelical *Christianity Today* and the neoconservative and largely (but not entirely) Catholic *First Things*. Amid such variety, what holds these pieces together? It could be that my writing career simply reflects intellectual ADHD. Sure enough, the virtue of writing in this way is I can get intensely interested in a topic for a number of days or weeks and then move on to something else just as new and interesting.

Thinking further, I realized the red thread running through my work is, simply, the answer to every question ever asked in a children's sermon: Jesus. I've spent my literary career, such as it is, trying to discern the body of Jesus in the church and the world. And I've looked hard for Jesus in the church. *Where* in the church—from the mainline to the evangelical, from the Catholic to the Orthodox, from the borderline orthodox to the academic, from the creaky-jointed global North to the sprightly global South—can we discern Jesus' presence in his people's life together? The ancient church taught me to train an eye for Jesus in unlikely places like the oddest corners of Israel's scripture, the smallest liturgical act, the contours of world history. Stanley Hauerwas taught me to look for the church as the specific, fleshy place where God saves us, compromised though it often is, called to greater holiness as it will be till the eschaton. Jesus' coming marriage with his church is the most interesting thing there is. And if this is reflected, however slightly and unintentionally, in any place in human thought and culture, then Christians should pay attention to it and practice the delight of finding Christ precisely there.

The work is organized in sections according to topics. Each section will have a brief introduction situating the kind of article within it and showing its coherence to the rest of the work. In every case my work is partially journalistic. I wander around in the church and report on what I see that interests me. I usually have in mind as an audience fellow pastors and interested and attentive Christians more generally. In every case my work draws on my own academic background in study at Duke and teaching in a variety of institutions in the Chicago area while at *Christian Century* and subsequently in North Carolina. And I try to write from and for the whole people of God, including Israel according to the flesh, the church catholic (and Catholic), evangelicals and Orthodox—essentially everyone pursuing

Introduction

life with the God with whom Jacob wrestled by the Jabbok. If I have anything to offer it is that something has delighted me. I found something fascinating and wanted to hold it up in praise (or ridicule, but usually praise) for a wider congregational audience. St. Augustine once told a pastor who asked his advice on catechizing new Christians that the most important trick to teaching well was delight.[4] A teacher's delight is contagious. In writing these pieces I've been graced to find much in which to take delight, and I hope this is not only contagious, but Christly. G. K. Chesterton somewhere compares God to a child who, after every trick a grown-up does, says, "Do it again!" *ad nauseum*. Every day God says, "Do it again!" and the sun comes up.

I realized the need for a volume like this for selfish reasons when I was introduced as pastor at Boone United Methodist Church. Folks in this academic hamlet in the North Carolina mountains realized I had something of a writing career and they went looking. Some found my book on the small church—not particularly helpful for how I would pastor a batch of nearly fourteen hundred souls. Others found my books, academic and popular, on the early church. Their lack of comments to me suggests they didn't get far into those volumes. Others found my pieces on the Web, but they were left swimming—how to tell what's important, what's less so, what's at the heart of things? I wished then I had a volume I could hand them with my voice in it on topics they cared about, like Jesus and the church. I'm grateful to Cascade Books for that option now.

The other source was my own traveling and speaking to church groups around the country. These would ask which of my books to sell. When I was with pastors of small churches, the answer was obvious. When I was with anybody else, it was less so. I'm grateful now to have a volume between covers for such occasions. The danger of such occasional speaking work is its Gnostic character—you parachute in to talk to strangers, they say nice things about you (both you and they have a vested interest in your being praised), you dump your stuff on the audience and then leave. I've found, by contrast, an interest in the particularity of the people I've been invited to be with. Priests of small Episcopal churches in western Nebraska and north central Pennsylvania, pastors of small Presbyterian churches in Ohio and Michigan, batches of Methodist small church pastors in the Carolinas— they all have something in common: they're trying to preach the Word, to minister the sacraments, to forge a people in the image of Christ. They're often discouraged, occasionally astounded at Christ's generosity, and always—whether they can tell it or not—always beautiful. If my journalistic

---

4. See Augustine, *Instructing Beginners in Faith*, trans. Raymond Canning (Hyde Park, NY: New City, 2006).

Introduction

work has any coherence, it's this: I'm trying to show other parts of the body of Christ something interesting happening in one part of the body of Christ. I hope they can learn to see him in surprising places and have their ministry renewed. It's very hard to expect to be surprised by anything. But that's the Christian life—to expect to be surprised by Jesus.

I dedicate this volume to the staff and people of Boone United Methodist Church, whom I'm honored to serve as their pastor. They will hear me not talking like me in some places. Reporters pass on others' voices. I hope they will hear me in other ways—innovative faithfulness might be my favorite preaching and teaching theme. For most of them my work has been confounding, occasionally interesting, and once in a while, despite itself, the gospel. For my work now is preaching, bearing witness, leading a community, stitching together ligaments in the body of Christ in one place. Here's the book I wish I could have handed them when I arrived. If I've done anything of import among them it's in encouraging us to be Bonhoeffer's "Christ existing as community" in the Blue Ridge Mountains. What work could be a greater privilege?

Part 1

Searching for Jesus in Local Congregations

FOR THESE ARTICLES, I study a unique congregation, interview pastors and lay leaders, attend worship, try to notice what's unique, and then try to tell others elsewhere in the body of Christ what I see in that one place. Writing is a permission to be nosy. It can be dangerous. A pastor laboring away in what she takes to be a rocky field, difficult to plow, reads pieces like these and despairs: "Some people get *interesting* congregations." I understand that temptation. Some of these congregations have grown like some sort of biblical miracle. They have launched innovative ministries, garnered national media attention, and become the pride of their denomination. But their interest for me lies more in their ordinariness. Even pastors of growing congregations have to attend meetings about taking care of the building. They worry about their families, ponder how they should pray, worry over what they should hope for. They reflect on what they learned in seminary and how to profit from it further, what to discard and what to learn more about. They worry about how to integrate new media into ministry (or whether to try to do so at all). They also get bored and despair. There is wisdom in the desert fathers' admonition to "stay in your cell, and your cell will teach you everything." Wherever we are, our temptation is to wander off somewhere different, somewhere "better." One way of becoming fascinated anew with one's own place, or "cell," is to learn how others have done so in their setting. I want readers to find the hope

Part 1: Searching for Jesus in Local Congregations

I've seen in the doctrine of the communion of the saints, spread out not just through time, but also through space.

This is one reason I concentrate so highly on the local in these pieces. Chicago was an intellectual playground for a churchly journalist in the years I was there. The downtown churches I cover here are ones I walked by every day, got curious about, and then cooked up a story idea for an excuse to be nosy about the lives of people who lead them.

I got interested in Trinity UCC in between waves of national media interest. One had already taken place during the Democratic primaries in 2008 but had died down by the time this article appeared (in fact, at the time of its publication, it looked as though Obama's star had crested and the article appeared too late!). A later wave took place as Jeremiah Wright took to the airwaves. I remember sitting along Michigan Avenue with a staffer of Obama's during the campaign and him saying, "They're freaking out up the avenue. Wright's going out speaking, and there's not a thing they can do to stop him." Yet within Chicago's peculiar religious matrix, Trinity was a mainstay, trying to carve out space for a Christianity rooted in the black experience over against versions of Islam quite clearly rooted there and versions of black intellectualism for which religion was a bad idea, full stop. The irony of this piece for me was that Trinity had coveted media coverage in Chicago and beyond for years. All of a sudden they had it, but not the kind they wanted. It's sad to think Obama felt he had to cut his ties to such an interesting and vibrant congregation.

Other pieces are rooted in different particularities. It's hard to imagine House for All Sinners and Saints existing anywhere other than Denver, or Jacob's Well anyplace other than Kansas City. Each ministers to its own city's sort of urban hipsters and does so with integrity to Jesus. I wrote on JW when the Emerging Church Movement (ECM) was attracting interest from mainline churches like mine—often as speakers at conferences about how the mainline could staunch its decline. Unfortunately for the ECM, those invitations came as it was being drummed out of evangelicalism for dropping the things that movement cares about—Christocentricity, focus on the scriptures, passion for evangelism. Jacob's Well is the better place to evaluate the ECM than those national spokespersons, and by such an evaluation it's doing just fine. The profile of Nadia Bolz-Weber and House for All Sinners and Saints was written as part of the New Media Project at Union Theological Seminary in New York, focusing on how the church can draw on new technologies for its life together. Both churches interest me primarily for how they've managed to be traditional and innovative at the same time—to hold on to what's essential while adapting what is not. The mainline could use shock therapy in both directions. Even LifeChurch.tv is most interesting

Part 1: Searching for Jesus in Local Congregations

to me in its specificity as an outfit begun and captained from Edmond, Oklahoma. On my way out there to cover the story, a woman in the row in front of me on the plane got saved. She responded to a stranger's evangelistic entreaty, prayed to accept Jesus, and ten minutes later was yakking on her cell. It's Oklahoma—what do you expect but for people to get saved?! Here what primarily interests me is, once again, the traditionalism—LifeChurch finds itself battling with Disney more than with fellow churches, and is surprised to realize that sacraments don't do well online.

What holds these pieces together for me is a fascination with the local church, with the form of the pastoral life, and with the ways Jesus surprises us in each place. I was struck by how similar these pastors' lives are, even rooted in these particularities. These were all enormously talented people, granted. But their lives are tied up in preaching the gospel, loving the people of their congregations and neighborhoods, tending to the hurting, trying to make sense of a world that often makes no sense for a people dying for a story worth living for. The irony is that writing these pieces is partly what drove me to want to lead a local church again, as I do now at Boone United Methodist. But that work is what makes this sort of writing now impossible, since I can't attend worship elsewhere. I hope for others whose work will lead them deep into the lives of local congregations to remind the rest of us that God is always up to something, even in our own churches.

Emerging Model
A Visit to Jacob's Well[1]

THE WESTPORT NEIGHBORHOOD OF midtown Kansas City, Missouri, is a mix of avant-garde youth and aging hippies. If bumper stickers are any indication, political views range from the muscular left ("Veterans for Kerry") to the forthrightly left ("Peace is patriotic") to the crudely left ("Dump the son of a Bush!"). The first man I passed on the street had his shirt off and displayed pierced nipples. No doubt he was on his way to one of the area's many wine bars or tattoo parlors.

This neighborhood is also home to a thriving church called Jacob's Well, which attracts about one thousand people each week to its various services. The church is led by Tim Keel, who, along with author Brian McLaren, is a founder of the Emergent movement. I went to JW hoping that it could help me understand a phenomenon that remains elusive—the Emerging church.

The innovative JW is housed, ironically, in a classic church building that Presbyterians erected in 1930. The building is the envy of the numerous congregations in the neighborhood, including two that have exchanged their denominational labels for more jazzy names and logos—one Baptist (now River City Church) and one Evangelical Covenant (now City Church).

The classical space and biblically resonant name suit JW just fine, and they also say something about the Emerging Church Movement. If yesteryear's evangelical church was the equivalent of a starter castle in the exurbs, JW is more akin to a rehabilitated loft in a gentrifying city. Whereas evangelical churches (and increasing numbers of mainline ones) seek to attract young people by designing spaces stripped of Christian symbols or tradition, JW people seem to like the traditional feel of the sanctuary, with

---

1. Copyright © 2006 by *The Christian Century*. "Emerging Model: A Visit to Jacob's Well" by Jason Byassee is reprinted by permission from the September 19, 2006 issue of *The Christian Century*.

Part 1: Searching for Jesus in Local Congregations

its dark wood, stained glass, and high ceilings. While other churches would be thrilled by the numerical growth—one thousand attenders after seven years of existence—JW worries that the growth means it may not be intimate enough to nurture community and friendship. A recent sermon on stewardship insisted, apparently in all seriousness, that the church didn't need any more money or volunteers, so giving of time or money should come only out of genuine gratitude.

In short, JW is a rebuke to those churches that, in imitation of cutting-edge 1970s evangelicalism, deliberately strip themselves of historical symbols, creeds, and practices in an effort to grow. JW is succeeding by moving in precisely the opposite direction.

JW changed very little about the sanctuary when it bought the building in 2003 (with cash) after renting the space for four years. It moved the altar table out from the wall, removed choir pews to make room for a band, and took down the pulpit (Keel preaches at eye level). Other parts of the building were changed more dramatically. Walls were splashed with trendy purple or deep blue paint, and a parlor was turned into a prayer room with floor pillows and scented candles. A large Sunday school classroom was turned into a coffee bar and recreation room—now mostly for staff, since the congregation has long since outgrown it.

Emblazoned on that rec room wall is a quote from Stanley Hauerwas: "The work of Jesus was not a new set of ideals or principles for reforming or even revolutionizing society, but the establishment of a new community, a people that embodied forgiveness, sharing and self-sacrificing love in its rituals and discipline. In that sense, the visible church is not to be the bearer of Christ's message, but to be the message." How many churches have a quote from Hauerwas on a wall?

The opening prayer on the Sunday I visited was written by Walter Brueggemann. The interest of Emerging churches in people like Hauerwas, Brueggemann, Miroslav Volf, Nancey Murphy, and N. T. Wright indicates that while members may be sons and daughters of evangelicals or fundamentalists, they take their theological cues from mainline theologians.

Keel is drawn to theologians who articulate a post-Christendom perspective and who argue that Christians are most faithful when they are not seeking cultural or political power. Keel carries no weapons in the culture war, and he figures that his people, hardly stereotypical evangelicals, vote Democratic or Green as often as Republican. Recognizing that we live in a post-Christendom world means, for Keel, never assuming that his listeners have a basic knowledge of Christian thought, language, or practice. He cites the late British missiologist Lesslie Newbigin, one of the first to describe the West as a new mission field: "How can this strange story of God made man, of a crucified savior, of resurrection and new creation become credible? . . . I know of only one clue to the answering of that question, only one real hermeneutic of the gospel: congregations that believe it."

Sunday worship at JW reveals some of what the Emerging Church Movement (ECM) means by calling itself postevangelical. The music is led, conventionally enough, by a rock band that plays loudly enough to shake the wooden pews. But this is not happy-clappy "Jesus is my boyfriend" music. It's much more edgy, closer to grunge than to praise-chorus music. (Says Keel: "Grunge is what happens when the children of divorce get guitars.") The lyrics, many written by worship minister Mike Crawford, lift up pain as well as praise: "Jesus full of grace, / the humble you adore. / This world's a hungry place, / with no justice for the poor. / Jesus full of peace, / yet our hearts so full of war. / We take our pruning hooks / we beat them into swords."

The songs are new, and the words are flashed up on a plasma screen by PowerPoint, but the language is as old as scripture. Most songs, in fact, are paraphrases of scripture. And as loud as the music is, the singing is louder. Andy Crouch of *Christianity Today*, who is critical of much of the ECM, praises JW as "the best singing white church I've ever been to." JW's effort to make music participatory rather than performance-based struck a chord with Crouch, who also signaled his awareness that JW is rooted in its own particular neighborhood and could not be easily replicated elsewhere: "It made me want to move to Kansas City. Really."

Keel begins his sermon after the introductory music and prayer end. Few announcements or even greetings clutter the service. He offers questions he expects the congregation to answer. "I'm not just trying to be engaging," he says. "I really want to know what everyone else thinks." Regulars, who often mention Keel's preaching as a major reason for their attendance, remember times when he has taken his sermon in a different direction because of the feedback he's getting.

Keel's expository style reflects his evangelical heritage and his training at conservative Denver Seminary. He takes his listeners through an odd corner of 1 Samuel 4 in which the Israelites respond to defeat at the hands of the Philistines by fetching the Ark to ensure victory—after which they are defeated again, with far worse casualties. "Some passage, eh?" he jokes.

Keel observes that Israel treated the Ark as a totem, a magic object that would force God to give them success. "It reminds me of meaningless God-talk," he says to appreciative nods. "This is my pet peeve—just 'Godding' everything to pretend you have control when you don't." He draws a lesson for his congregation: "We can't assume that because God has blessed what we've done in the past here at Jacob's Well that he will again. We serve a living God, and are hardly the same as we were a year or two ago."

Part 1: Searching for Jesus in Local Congregations

This embrace of change worries the ECM's critics, who think that the movement's style is just one more churchly fad. Keel worries about Emergent being a fad too, and he criticizes the recurrent search for techniques of church growth, well aware that churches that have followed other trends—whether the Alpha course or *Purpose-Driven Life* studies—are likely to try out aspects of the Emergent movement. He assails the notion that (as he wrote in an essay in *The Relevant Church*) "if only we can (re)discover X (fill-in-the-blank: prayer, fasting, worship, community, drama, service) and implement it, then the Church will have Y (fill-in-the-blank: impact, relevance, meaning, validity, profile, etc.)."[2] Many of the ECM's leaders, including Keel, got their start in the Willow Creek–inspired Leadership Network, which they found to be a sort of factory geared to church growth rather than anything more authentically communal. Looking for a technique is "much easier, short-term, than living out the life of the gospel in community."

Jacob's Well reveals the theological and ecclesial fissures not only in evangelicalism, but in the ECM itself. Many in that group sound fed up with the church as a whole and make sport of bashing it. But Keel stresses, "I love the church. . . . Anyone wanting to manifest the kingdom of God proclaimed by Jesus must deal with and through the church, specifically the local church."

God loves not only the church today, but the church through time. Keel makes spiritual retreats to a local Benedictine monastery where he has a spiritual director. JW celebrates communion at every gathering not as an afterthought, but as a response to the word and the climax of worship. Its people take no membership count because they envision something like a monastic rule of life—attracting fewer members but higher commitment. On its Web site (jacobswellchurch.org), instead of articulating its own statement of faith, JW cites the Apostles' Creed.

Yet innovation is part of the atmosphere at JW because of its large community of artists and the artistic environment. Keel even talks about JW as an "artistic haven." There are so many musicians in the church that the members of the band behind Mike Crawford change every week. The prayer room doubles as a gallery, which hosts regular art shows and is part of a city program that brings art lovers—not usually a churchy crowd—into the professionally lit space. Art photographs adorn JW's Web site.

"Artists have a nose for propaganda," Keels says, and they often smell it on evangelicals. JW tries to make space for whatever art community members create and then design space or liturgy around it. This fits with Keel's and JW's theology of salvation: "What if instead of seeing salvation's story

---

2. Tim Keel, "Love Is of the Essence," in *The Relevant Church: A New Vision for Communities of Faith*, ed. Jennifer Ashley et al. (Lake Mary, FL: Relevant, 2005) 73.

as one of creation-fall-redemption, we saw it as creation-incarnation-re-creation?" he wonders aloud.

Such exploratory questions about core Christian teachings reflect an Emergent trait that disturbs critics who see the bogeyman of theological liberalism at work. D. A. Carson has launched a book-length attack on the movement, *Becoming Conversant with the Emerging Church*,[3] and former ECM leader Mark Driscoll and *Christianity Today* columnist Charles Colson have also inveighed against it. Their primary criticism is that Emergent is abandoning Christianity's claim to objective, universal truth.

It's true that Keel and others in the ECM avoid the language of objective truth. They believe that such language is defined by the categories of the Enlightenment, that there are different ways of reasoning, and that the church must make its claims to truth on a contested field without shouting in advance that others are wrong and it alone is right. Keel deplores the "bounded-set thinking" that such charges evidence—the urge to define "in" and "out" groups. He characterizes the ECM as pursuing "center-set thinking," in which Jesus is the center of a circle whose edges are fuzzy. "I see so many Christians with so much of their lives not in submission to Christ, and so many non-Christians with so much of their lives in submission to Christ."

Driscoll and others have argued that ECM churches show little growth through conversion and merely recycle sheep within the fold. Keel responds to this charge by telling me about a Hindu student who began coming to Jacob's Well for the art and leaving before the service began, but then started staying just for the music, and finally stayed for the whole service. "If most evangelicals follow a pattern of believe-behave-belong, we reverse that pattern and make it belong-behave-believe," said Keel. "We say, 'Try on these clothes, take up these practices, and see what happens.'"

Some aspects of JW—its post-Christendom political posture and its postliberal theological tone—are hardly unique. Even its effort at grunge worship and to be an artistic haven has imitators and precursors elsewhere. But Keel says, "I'd hate to think JW could be imitated elsewhere," since, as he sees it, churches need to be "environmentalists"—to take the temperature of their particular place and serve it accordingly. Nevertheless, students at the three seminaries in the Kansas City area and other people interested in church plants are paying attention to JW (two study groups were visiting the night I attended).

ECM members are often kidded for their body piercings and tattoos, but such displays simply reflect the demographic of these churches. "Twenty

---

3. *Becoming Conversant with the Emerging Church: Understanding a Movement and Its Implications* (Grand Rapids: Zondervan, 2005).

Part 1: Searching for Jesus in Local Congregations

percent of people aged twenty to fifty have a tattoo," Keel reports. He adds that tattoos are usually a marker for some experience of pain. Part of JW's success is that it doesn't hide from pain. Keel speaks regularly of his experience of his parents' divorce, and about the consequences of drug and alcohol abuse and sexual experimentation. He talks about being "naked in the pulpit" (the title of an essay of his). This is not exhibitionism, he insists, but being authentic about one's brokenness and ongoing need for healing.

Authenticity is a word one hears a lot at JW. Perhaps that (and a weekly Sunday evening service) is why JW has become a haven for a number of pastors, who come to the Sunday evening or a midweek service. "Pastors often feel they can't be human with their own churches," Keel laments as he shows me a thank-you card from a minister who said he had been ready to leave the ministry before encountering JW.

Another person who appreciates JW is Susan Cox-Johnson, a United Methodist district superintendent in Kansas City. She writes in the denominational publication *Circuit Rider* of how Broadway UMC had once been the largest church in its conference, largely because of the success of a Sunday school ministry. Under JW's inspiration she started a coffeehouse in the Broadway church, whose congregation is now graying.

Cox-Johnson believes that the ECM can help mainline churches reach out by reminding them of their own neglected resources, such as the Methodist emphasis on holy friendship, which these days can be nurtured in coffee shops.

ECM types are also kidded for their love of "cool"—their trendy hair and their up-to-the-minute pop-culture references. In this case, the shoe fits. In his sermon Keel made a reference to a movie, *Snakes on a Plane*, that had yet to open but was getting a lot of buzz on the Internet. He admits on his blog, "I love Apple products so much. . . . My wife has completely given up making photo albums. We take gads of digital pics and then load them onto iPhoto. From there I either import them into iMovie and burn a slide show through iDVD, or I make a slide show right in iPhoto, upload it onto my iDisk, then connect it to my Mac homepage for viewing. . . . If you want a sample of what I'm talking about, click here."

Keel grew up as something of a church mutt, spending time with Methodists, Presbyterians, charismatics, and Jesus People. He laments the day that Roanoke Presbyterian folded and sold JW the building. Worshiping with the Presbyterians, he says tenderly, "was like worshiping with our grandmothers."

Perhaps Keel's positive interaction with mainline churches explains his openness to things catholic and ecumenical. He is not tempted to speak as though the ECM is inventing the wheel, as many of his colleagues do, when it places women in leadership roles or advocates for social justice. Though he has his doubts about whether the ECM can "work" in the structures of a denomination—he says he was never tempted by the "golden handcuffs" of church-plant funding—he values interaction with mainline pastors such as Cox-Johnson. The Emerging Church as a movement has never sought to be a brand, much less a new denomination, but instead is a friendship network among members of several church bodies.

As one looks at the twentysomethings and thirtysomethings involved at JW, it seems as though Gen-Xers are reacting to their parents of the Me Generation by rebuilding the structures that their parents tore down, literally moving into a neighborhood and church like the ones in which their grandparents lived and worshiped. In JW's case, the emphasis is on the importance of the local, of community, of friendship. Keel writes, "I belong to these people, and they belong to me. Together we belong to Jesus. It doesn't stop there: because we belong to Jesus, we belong to other communities of people who belong to Jesus"—thus enunciating an ecclesiology that closely reflects John's Gospel.

JW has been praised for putting into practice the emphasis on community and on the kind of post-Christendom, mission-oriented faith that McLaren, Newbigin, and others have written about. The people I talked to at JW had never heard of Emergent or of McLaren. They're just going to church with their friends, unaware that their congregation is a model for how to be "post" many things (postevangelical, postliberal, postconservative, postmodern) precisely by sinking its roots deeper into the local, the particular, and the church catholic.

The Church Downtown

Strategies for Urban Ministry[1]

THE CITY IS CHANGING. For decades white people with money fled the city for the suburbs, leaving behind a mostly brown and black population that was often bereft of resources. But recently, in many cities, patterns of gentrification have reversed this trend. People with money have moved back to the city and rehabbed old housing stock, seeking to live where they work and play. As housing prices and property taxes go up, lower-income people are often driven out.

How is the church responding to this most recent change and ministering to the new set of urban dwellers? Chicago offers the examples of several churches that have responded to the swell of new urban elites who began coming in the 1980s and have not stopped.

First United Methodist Church—From Log Cabin to Skyscraper

Chicago once had a number of downtown "First Churches." Almost all of them packed up and left in the wake of urban changes in the late nineteenth and early twentieth century. But First United Methodist did not.

First United Methodist Church began at a meeting in a blacksmith's log-cabin shop in 1832—six years before the city of Chicago was incorporated. It thrived amid the nineteenth-century urban scene through the clever idea of having a mixed-use building: the church built more space than it needed for worship and rented some of the space to businesses.

---

1. Copyright © 2008 by *The Christian Century*. "The Church Downtown: Strategies for Urban Ministry" by Jason Byassee is reprinted by permission from the March 11, 2008 issue of *The Christian Century*.

The Church Downtown

That concept was expanded audaciously in 1922 when the congregation decided to build a skyscraper, putting the sanctuary and church offices on the first two floors, commercial space on floors three through twenty-four (Clarence Darrow's office was once on the sixth floor), and the parsonage in the loft. The church called itself the Chicago Temple—an odd usage of the term by Methodists, perhaps a sign of the grandness of their vision. The skyscraper, diagonal from City Hall in the Loop, Chicago's downtown, is almost indistinguishable from the buildings around it. Commuters can walk by it for years and never know it's a church.

Pastor Philip Blackwell calls it "a cathedral church" that serves two very different populations. It has a Sunday crowd of about one thousand worshipers who come from every zip code in the city and eighty suburbs. But the multiple staff would be busy if they had no regular congregation at all. The Chicago Temple offers midweek services for downtown workers (90 percent of whom are members of other churches), and it has a ministry to the many homeless people who spend days and nights in the Loop. Claude King, the pastor who leads the ministry to the homeless, looks like he could handle himself in a fight—and indeed while I visited the church he was called to the lobby to pacify a brewing confrontation.

One simple, powerful ministry of the Temple is its open-door policy: it leaves the air conditioning or the heat on in the sanctuary and keeps the sanctuary open for prayer. Homeless people are almost always in the pews, surrounded by wooden angels, stained glass, and oceans of dark wood. Many of them eventually join the church, or at least come forward for communion. "They're pretty hungry," observes Blackwell, who has a quick wit and a young, impish face under a white crown of hair. His ministry is of an intellectual bent. He is proud of the church's new science and theology study group that will be part of a citywide program, sponsored by the Museum of Science and Industry, called "Science Chicago," meant to enhance appreciation for the discipline.

Churches like the Chicago Temple don't thrive unless they improvise. The Temple's most recent innovation is a theater. When the time came to renovate the church basement, the church spent a few hundred thousand dollars to create a venue for the Silk Road Theater Company, which uses the space for free.

Silk Road Theater was founded in the wake of the 9/11 attacks in an effort to engage the cultures of the East with sympathy rather than rancor. Its founders are a Muslim and a Syrian Orthodox Christian. Some 1.5 million people with origins in the Silk Road region live in Chicago. The theater has received glowing reviews for its staging of such plays as *Merchant on Venice*, which turns Shakespeare's play about Christians and Jews into a story about

Muslims and Hindus, and *Golden Child*, by David Hwang, about the cultural clash between Christian missionaries and the Chinese. "Christianity is a Silk Road story," Blackwell said, "and we need a Middle Eastern context to understand the Bible." The theater recently was honored by the Chicago Commission on Human Relations for its "achievements in promoting cross-cultural interaction."

Silk Road is not an evangelistic effort, though there is a notice in the playbills welcoming patrons to the "historic Chicago temple" and a few people have migrated from the theater to the pews on Sunday. The theater company has complete artistic freedom. The point of the church hosting a theater is simply to host a first-rate company.

Silk Road director Jamil Khoury says the church trusts his company to take on such sensitive subjects as homosexuality and the clash of civilizations. "Theater people often have baggage with the church," Khoury says, so they're pleasantly surprised to find a church taking theater so seriously and making space for it so generously. Chicago Temple's hospitality to the theater may suggest a way to reach a population that is new to the city and is hip to the cultural scene but not to the faith. And what do old downtown churches have, in many cases, but plenty of underused, aesthetically pleasing space?

Old St. Patrick's—A Celtic Christian "Thin Place"

A few blocks west of the Temple, across the Chicago River, is another old downtown church—the oldest public building in Chicago. When Father Jack Wall arrived at Old St. Patrick's in 1983, the church had only four parishioners. Its heyday as a harbor for Irish immigrants was long gone. An expressway built in the 1950s had lopped off half its property, and not even the West Loop's once famous flophouses were around anymore. His parish was filled with warehouses. "My parents were worried for me," he recalled. "But it was the safest police district in the city. There were simply no people."

When Father Wall retired from Old St. Pat's last year, the church had 3,500 families on its rolls, and it counted 5,300 more people as affiliated with the church.

What happened? Some of it had to do with being in the right place when gentrification occurred. Another element is the building's stunning beauty—Celtic art runs from the statue of St. Patrick in the front and across gorgeous green and gold walls, in mazelike patterns that flow even under the water of the baptismal font. It is a Celtic Christian "thin place," especially after extensive renovation in the late 1990s.

But part of the turnaround is clearly due to Wall's own charisma. He's dashingly handsome, with an intent gaze and laugh marks around his eyes. As a young priest at another parish in the city, he used to wonder about the nearly moribund Old St. Pat's: "Could this church start all over?" When he saw the church's unusual twin spires, one a steeple in the Western tradition, the other an onion-shaped dome recalling the styles of the Christian East, he was reminded of a crossroads. He imagined a church that would draw people back to the city, a church based not on ethnicity or neighborhood but on intentional outreach. (The church's recent history is told in several places, including Lowell Livezey's *Public Religion and Urban Transformation*.[2])

The church eyed busy professionals who would be attracted by programs that had definite start and end times and that would fit around commuters' schedules. These programs had to be good. A glance at the church's monthly calendar indicates the kinds of programs the church developed: bike-to-church Sunday, wine tasting at a trendy restaurant, an Oktoberfest gathering, a stress-reduction program.

The church tapped into the Midwestern tradition of the block party and started what it billed as the "world's largest block party," a several-day party and fund-raiser. Though it has now become more of a secular event, the block party still brings in major revenue with the help of terrific bands and loads of kegs. Stories circulate about how many couples in the parish first met at the block party.

Wall found that young professionals "wanted to know how what they did mattered." They were also thinking about marriage. Wall recalled that at the beginning of his tenure, when people would call the parish to ask about getting married there, "The first response would be, 'Are you a member?'—not [a word of] congratulations or celebration." The church decided to make weddings the occasion to do evangelism and formation.

A wave of children soon followed. St. Pat's responded by opening the first new Catholic grammar school in Chicago in twenty-five years. From its storefront beginning it has grown to a school of seven hundred children on two campuses.

Developing the programs and the sacramental and educational emphases was not a matter of meeting needs, according to Father Wall. "When you're down to four parishioners, the last thing you do is ask them their needs so you can meet them." The church reoriented itself around mission. People do not want to be members of institutions that will meet their needs, Wall said, but they do want to be part of a mission, to have an experience

---

2. *Public Religion and Urban Transformation: Faith in the City*, ed. Lowell Livezey (New York: New York University Press, 2000).

of the church in action. Wall was surprised to find that it wasn't just young urban professionals who were coming to Old St. Pat's; the yuppies were bringing their parents, who were disaffected with their suburban parishes or with Catholic life altogether. "They were re-creating the Sabbath," Wall says.

One of the parishioners who wanted to know how what he did mattered was Tom Owens. Inspired by the example of Mother Teresa, he started using his connections to get work for the unemployed and health care for those who needed it. Out of that effort was born the Cara program (the word *cara* in Old Irish means "friend"), which moves some two hundred people a year from the streets into jobs with benefits. Since its founding in 1991 some 1,900 people have benefited from the Cara ministry. This is Vatican II ecclesiology at its best—the ministry of the baptized, rather than of the clergy *alone*.

When I asked Wall to explain the church's success, he said that Old St. Pat's is rooted in "communion with God—discipleship—and so we're moved to create communities." The church is not a club, it's a mission, an event that takes place as it reaches out to others. "God only tells us who we are as we are a gift beyond ourselves and as we receive gifts from others," he said.

LaSalle Street Church—"To Do This One Thing Well"

LaSalle Street Church in the Near North neighborhood looks like a venerable downtown First Church, but it actually began in the 1960s when evangelicals from institutions like Wheaton College and Moody Bible Institute sought to create a grittier, more streetwise form of church life. (The building was bought from another congregation.) The church certainly doesn't feel like the average evangelical church—it has none of the suburban sleekness one would find at Willow Creek, and no narrowness in doctrine. The senior pastor is a woman, Laura Truax, and the congregation is scruffy around the edges, attracting members from the nearby housing projects as well as from the wealthy Gold Coast and many other parts of the city. It is notoriously difficult for white do-gooder churches of any stripe to be more multicultural (Old St. Pat's has struggled with this problem mightily). LaSalle has done it. Though predominantly white, it includes African Americans and Latinos.

One sign of its character is its homeless ministry, called Breaking Bread. In 2003 someone in the church office saw a homeless man sleeping in the bushes beside the building. The staff member opened a window, offered the man coffee and a roll, and proceeded to learn about the man's mental illness, lost job, and drug problem. Pastor Truax used the incident to challenge the congregation: Could church members let homeless people sleep right underneath their noses and not do something about it?

Breaking Bread is meant to be more than a soup kitchen. It aims to "invite strangers as family to the table," creating community with the homeless, serving them with dignity. Pastor Oreon Trickey, director of Breaking Bread, describes the ministry with a line from Psalm 68:6: "God puts the solitary into families." Evangelical enthusiasm and a streetwise sensibility radiate through her 6'4" frame and spikey hairdo.

Breaking Bread offers a restaurant-style meal to seventy to eighty homeless people once a week. Salad is on the table when guests come in. Full plates are brought out by volunteer waiters. Real silverware and plates are used. Many of the volunteer workers are themselves homeless. When they come in each Wednesday they "visibly relax," Trickey says. Some will get up and sing, "and no one tells them 'Sit down! Shut up!' They can be themselves."

Keith Richardson, Breaking Bread's cook, was himself homeless for thirteen years. He is summoned if there's a dispute in the dining area because he can "talk folks down," Trickey says. Richardson describes his work as "giving back to people I used to hang out with. I understand, I've been there, I have a bond with them." Richardson also knows how they like to eat: "I blackify everything," he says. "You can't just make what's in the Kraft box, you got to put eggs in the macaroni."

Breaking Bread is keen to not try too much more. The temptation, Trickey says, is to think, "This is great, let's make it bigger!" She worries that professionalization would set in and the church's role would focus more on grant writing and paperwork. "You can compromise your intimacy and depth. Just because you can do more doesn't mean you should. We prefer to do this one thing well."

Urban ministry has changed even in the four and a half years of Breaking Bread's life. The nearby public housing project towers have come down, replaced by mixed-income housing. There are fewer visibly poor people in the neighborhood now. Those who remain are under pressure from the city not to sit on front porches lest the neighborhood seem less safe for the professionals who are moving in. But the poor are still there. "And as long as we offer services, they will come," Trickey says. "The poor we will always have with us."

And some will come to church. Trickey, who is also the church's outreach coordinator, tries to integrate visitors on Sundays into church life. She spots several guests from Breaking Bread at each service. Trickey hopes a volunteer from Breaking Bread will also be there on Sunday to greet them. "Those in the homeless system have heard enough sermons," Trickey says. "What they need is relationship."

Part 1: Searching for Jesus in Local Congregations

Willow Creek Community Church—"A Sense of True Community"

Nothing suggests suburban ministry like Willow Creek Community Church, the influential megachurch that attracts twenty thousand people each weekend to its sprawling campus in South Barrington, Illinois. But after years of insisting that people who come to church should have their own needs met, founder Bill Hybels sings a bit of a different tune, learned from friends like U2's Bono: Christians should serve the needs of people outside the church. Willow Creek Chicago is part of this new effort to advocate for social justice and extend "a sense of true community," as the Web site proclaims, to Chicagoans in the quickly gentrifying South Loop area.

Renting space in the magnificent Auditorium Theater, with its golden mosaics and turn-of-the-century opulence, Willow Creek Chicago has about 1,200 attenders after only a year of operation. A greeter told me, "We visited 150 sites and this one worked the best. It seats 4,500—so we have room to grow." A Hollywood-quality video montage celebrating the church's one-year anniversary boasted of 51,000 church attenders, 9,000 worship hours, 312 songs, 40 baptisms, 440 people in small groups, community care for 50 people, 5 relief trucks sent to Louisiana after Hurricane Katrina, 850 prayer requests responded to, and 320 converts made after services.

Willow Chicago certainly feels different from Willow Barrington. For one, it has been intentionally multiethnic from the start. The music when I visited had an African-American or even Caribbean vibe, not the laced-up guitar sound of most megachurches. I counted twenty choir members, six lead singers, a six-piece string section, four guitars, two synthesizers, and two bongo drummers. The lead singers constituted such a multiethnic combination that I wondered if quotas were in place. An unusually rhythmic version of the evangelical mainstay "Lord, I Lift Your Name on High" was followed by a couple dancing the salsa.

The pastor, Steve Wu, was CEO of two companies before he quit to go into full-time ministry. He projects humility and a sense of confidence, and his comic timing is flawless. He is also an example of the church's ability to weave multiple ethnicities into community. Drawing a stick figure on a marker board to make a point, he drew slanted, Asian eyes, and then feigned surprise when the congregation started laughing. "They're just eyes!" he said. I'm surprised to learn from a church spokesperson, Mary-Beth Morehouse, that Wu is divorced. "He can relate to those who've been through that," she tells me, "and help them to be equally yoked next time." The hundreds around me seem undisturbed when Wu's sermon ticks past forty-five minutes.

A common criticism of Willow is that it's a show more than anything and that its studied nonuse of Christian symbols or liturgical gestures is a too-easy accommodation to modernity, the market, and individualistic Christianity. But at Willow Chicago there is no effort to hide that this is, indeed, a church, if an unusual one.

Another common criticism is that visitors to Willow can't possibly hope to get involved in the worship ministry—who expects to go from being an audience member to part of the cast of a Broadway play? But when I mentioned this problem to lead singer David Thompson, he dismissed it. He said he had tried several Presbyterian churches when he moved to Chicago, and only Willow asked him to use his talents in worship.

Willow Chicago makes a clear effort to reach the city. When I tell Morehouse I'm interested in gentrification, she replies, "We're against it!" She goes on to talk about Willow's intention to "transform the city a bit at a time." The chief problem the church sees is loneliness. Evangelicals can't stand to live in buildings where they don't know their neighbors—how could they ever evangelize someone they've not met? So Willow has launched "Neighborhood Life," a social outreach program that allows Creekers to meet their neighbors—"not to convert anybody," a greeter assured me, but just to get to know them.

Given Willow's effort to be city-savvy, I almost swallowed my gum when I heard where the one-year anniversary party would be held: the Congress Hotel. Workers have been on strike for four years at the Congress, seeking better wages and health benefits. Hotel owners have steadfastly refused to negotiate. Religious groups have been among those supporting the strike. Every Sunday, Creekers were crossing the picket line to enter the hotel, using it as a fellowship hall. (Willow Chicago has since stopped using the hotel, though Morehouse described the strike to me as "a pretty pathetic situation" and said, "These people need to either find better counsel to argue their case or move on to employment elsewhere.") A church purporting to care about social justice and to be sensitive to the needs of the city might start with a willingness to stand up for workers.

Wicker Park Grace—A Good, Small, Delicate Thing

Wicker Park is a working-class neighborhood a few miles northwest of the Loop. Its proximity to downtown has made it ripe for gentrification. New bars, coffeehouses, and restaurants have popped up as young professionals have moved in and rehabbed the housing stock, which in turn has raised the cost of renting or buying housing.

Part 1: Searching for Jesus in Local Congregations

Ministering in this neighborhood is Wicker Park Grace, which is part of the Emerging Church Movement. Grace is explicitly reacting against the slickness of the megachurch style and against the theological smugness that it detects in much of the evangelical world. Pastor Nanette Sawyer put off my initial request for an interview, saying, "It seems like you want a story about all the beautiful people. We're more like the island of misfit toys."

Once I talked her into meeting with me, she urged me to come soon so I wouldn't miss a neighborhood art show. The art council building that the church uses was hosting an exhibit of an Ecuadoran artist's work. The exhibit was just beside the coffee shop that the council opens for special events and that the church uses for services. The whole vibe was crunchy and welcoming, like entering a familiar old garage with someone else's cool stuff in it.

If Willow Chicago matches Steve Wu's personality as a former CEO, Wicker Park Grace matches Sawyer's mystical and artistic streak. It holds worship on Saturday evenings either with a Taizé-style prayer service or with a jazz vespers. Sawyer teaches more than she preaches, and the service is mostly filled with directed prayer and silence.

The key mark of the church for her is hospitality (her book on the topic is *Hospitality, the Sacred Art*[3]). Her ministry is shaped by her experience at a little Presbyterian church in South Boston that welcomed her while she was a student at Harvard Divinity School. The church "made me feel safe and valuable and free to be honest and authentic on the spiritual journey I was on," she recalls. So she now invites others.

About thirty people gather for vesper services, and about 140 are on the church's e-mail list. When it comes to numbers, Sawyer is a bit less ambitious than Willow Creek: "We'd like to have one hundred or so." She has no interest in buildings, only in art.

Her church is made up of the artists who moved into the neighborhood when it was still cheap to live there. Funky shops followed, and then came the trend-following gentry. Condos are going up right outside Sawyer's office, and the arts council is being displaced from its building—the owner is looking to raise rents above what artists and churches can pay. The church will be moving to a space above a Target store. "Don't worry, we'll artify it!" Sawyer promises.

Sawyer sounds like she has Willow in mind as her negative example when she describes Wicker Park Grace's philosophy: "Don't create a show for worship to be purchased by consumers. We want to create a community for participants."

---

3. *Hospitality, the Sacred Art: Discovering the Hidden Spiritual Power of Invitation and Welcome* (Woodstock, VT: SkyLight Paths, 2008).

The way artists have contributed is most obvious in Wicker Park's Stations of the Cross exhibit during Holy Week. These artistic renderings of Jesus' steps on the way to his death have brought the neighborhood out and captured local media attention. Jesus' trial is portrayed with the iconic image of early twentieth-century lynchings in the American South. A rendering of Veronica's veil has a papier-mâché hand reaching out to the viewer. Jesus' burial scene includes what looks like an actual death shroud over a face. The resurrection is portrayed as a glorious montage of eyes and flowers and light, in an Eastern Orthodox iconic vein.

The use of art is not a method for church growth at Wicker Park—if anything it seems designed to keep things small. Poetry fills the services, with poems by Christian saints like St. John of the Cross ("'What is grace,' I asked God. And he said, 'All that happens'") and the Indian philosopher Sri Chinmoy ("Yesterday I lived inside My mind's disastrous uncertainty-sea. Today I am living inside My heart's rapturous divinity-ocean"). Wicker Park Grace is a good, small, delicate thing, riding the tides of gentrification and gathering up refugees from other churches, promising a more peaceful, gentle way—even while perched above Target.

Meeting these churches and their pastors leaves one impressed with the enormous, diverse intellectual energy needed to minister in the changing city. No one church can do everything in response to massive and various human needs. The successful ones concentrate on doing a few things—connecting to people through hospitality, art, companionship, theater, food, or service. Theological distinctions seem to fade amid the challenges of the city. Mainline pastors, Catholic priests, and evangelical ministers are all improvising, trying new things, risking failure, scattering seed, and seeing what fruit might spring up.

Africentric Church

A Visit to Chicago's Trinity UCC[1]

ONE OF THE BRIGHTEST points in Barack Obama's rising political star has been his ability to talk about Jesus without faking it. Beginning with his rousing "Audacity of Hope" speech at the 2004 Democratic National Convention and continuing with his book of the same name, Obama has shown that he can speak about his Christian faith in ways that are authentic and broadly appealing.

Little wonder that his enemies have tried to turn that strength into a liability. Right-wing bloggers and TV pundits have been targeting Obama's church, Trinity United Church of Christ in Chicago, and its pastor, Jeremiah Wright, complaining that its self-proclaimed Africentric Christianity is separatist or even racist. Obama's campaign has itself pulled back a bit from being identified with Wright. In February it revoked an invitation to have him give the opening prayer when Obama announced his run for the presidency.

Africentrism (that's the term Trinity prefers to Afrocentrism) is wholeheartedly embraced at Trinity. One of the church's mottos is "Unashamedly Black and Unapologetically Christian." Its choir is regularly decked out in brightly colored African dress, as is Wright when he preaches. The church emphasizes its connection to the African diaspora: it sponsors trips to western and southern Africa, the Caribbean, and Latin American countries with significant African populations. Julia Speller, a leader at Trinity and author of *Walkin' the Talk: Keepin' the Faith in Africentric Congregations*,[2] notes in her book that the church offers courses in Swahili and that its youth

---

1. Copyright © 2007 by *The Christian Century*. "Africentric Church: A Visit to Chicago's Trinity UCC" by Jason Byassee is reprinted by permission from the May 29, 2007 issue of *The Christian Century*.

2. *Walkin' the Talk: Keepin' the Faith in Africentric Congregations* (Cleveland: Pilgrim, 2005).

programs, Intonjane and Isuthu, take their names from Swahili words for coming into manhood and womanhood. The congregation celebrates the Kwanzaa holiday and Umoja Karamu, a Thanksgiving Day service that narrates the story of the black family from its West African origins to today with dancing, drumming, and storytelling.

Bible courses at Trinity emphasize the African roots of Christianity, focusing on the account of the Exodus and such passages as the psalmist's promise that Ethiopia would stretch out its hands to God (Ps 68:31), and the conversion of the Ethiopian eunuch in Acts 8. In his preaching Wright goes out of his way to describe Moses as "an African prince" and his wife as a "raven-black" beauty. He declares that Jesus himself had "nappy hair" and "bronze skin" (he cites Rev 1:14–15). Otis Moss III, who will succeed Wright upon his retirement this summer, says that the church is proud of its "Africanity," proud that "when we talk about Sudan, we have Sudanese present."

African Americans have generated distinctly black forms of Christianity since they arrived on these shores. The significance of these forms has been appreciated in mainline seminaries and churches for at least two generations. Trinity is well within the mainstream of the black church, and is remarkable in the mainline world only for its size and influence and for its handful of celebrity members, like Oprah Winfrey and hip-hop artist Common.

Critics have pounced especially on the church's "Black Value System," by which members affirm their commitment to God, the "black community," the "black family," and the "black work ethic," and disavow "the pursuit of 'middle-classness.'" One hatchet-job report in *Investor's Business Daily*, pointing to the Black Value System (a statement written not by Wright but by church members in the early 1980s), concluded that there is "little room for white Christians at Obama's church." Black conservative pundit Erik Rush said the church has embraced "things African above things American," and he claimed that this should be as alarming as a Republican presidential candidate "belonging to the Aryan Brethren Church of Christ." Tucker Carlson of MSNBC described Trinity as having a "racially exclusive theology" that "contradicts the basic tenets of Christianity." Sean Hannity of Fox News confronted Wright on TV and asked how a black value system is any more acceptable than a white value system. Hannity also suggested that Trinity's emphasis on black values contradicts Martin Luther King's famous hope that people would be judged "not by the color of their skin, but by the content of their character."

Such charges are really aimed at Obama rather than Wright or Trinity. By trying to link Obama to black radicals, his critics attack one of Obama's political assets: his seeming ability—shared by Colin Powell, Oprah Winfrey, and Michael Jordan—to "transcend" race. Because Obama is able to do this, he invites the white support that Al Sharpton and Jesse Jackson lack (which perhaps explains the decided coolness of some black leaders toward Obama's candidacy).

Wright's critics completely ignore America's history of racism as well as the impact of the civil rights movement and the struggles of the black church to communicate the gospel's relevance in the black community. Perhaps, as one blogger suggests, the attacks on Wright and Trinity are not even "meant to stand up to scrutiny." They are merely designed to tie Obama to images of "the black bogeyman." As with the Swiftboating of John Kerry, it does not matter that the claims are false as long as they are out there.

A sympathetic profile of Obama in *Rolling Stone* quoted this jeremiad from one of Wright's sermons: "Racism is how this country was founded and how this country is still run! . . . We believe in white supremacy and black inferiority and believe it more than we believe in God . . . And. And. And! GAWD! Has GOT! To be SICK! OF THIS SHIT!" This may be the kind of passion that Obama now finds a bit embarrassing. The sermon was actually delivered as part of the inauguration of a new dean of the chapel at Howard University, whom Wright was encouraging to take on a prophetic role, not just a priestly one. But all that was posted on YouTube was a video of Wright shouting the words above.

Ironically, Wright says that in that part of the sermon he was quoting white evangelical preacher Tony Campolo, who has long railed about social ills in front of evangelical audiences. One of Campolo's signature rhetorical gestures is to use colorful language and tell his listeners that he fears they are "more concerned that I said 'shit'" than with racism in America. When Campolo makes this move, he's regarded as a prophetic figure. When Wright does it, his opponents call him a militant.

Trinity did not set out to be an Africentric church when it was founded. The goal of United Church of Christ leaders was to create an integrated church at a time when whites were not much interested in integration. But the UCC was also interested in finding "the right kind of black people," according to Speller—those who were middle class and "high potential" enough to integrate easily into the majority-white denomination. Congregationalist missionaries who established black colleges and universities throughout the South in the late nineteenth century insisted that educated blacks eliminate displays of emotion in singing and preaching. That's why graduates of Morehouse College and Howard University (where no gospel music was allowed until the late 1960s, according to Wright) abandoned black ways of worship.

In a 2006 essay, Wright summarized the early 1960s vision of integration: "Blacks should adopt a white lifestyle, a white way of worship,

Africentric Church

European values, and European American ways of viewing reality."[3] One of the UCC's few black ministers in the 1960s actually said from the pulpit, "We will tolerate no 'niggerisms' in our services." This meant, Wright explains, that "no one could shout.... There would be no hand waving. There would be no displays of emotion."

Wright dates the collapse of this vision to 1968. The assassination of Martin Luther King Jr. "was enough to make a negro turn black," he says, borrowing a phrase. By this point, a large segment of the black community had turned against King's Christian, nonviolent challenge to racial segregation. Chicago was an organizing center for militant black religious groups like the Nation of Islam and the Black Hebrew Israelites. Ironically, these groups, with whom conservatives today would like to lump Obama and Wright, are the very ones against which the young Jeremiah Wright was arguing while in graduate school in the 1960s—trying to make the case that Christianity is not a white racist religion.

It was in this climate of radical black activism that Wright set out to show what a church steeped in Christianity's long-neglected Africanity could look like. It took courage, Speller points out, for a black pastor to work "without apology" in a white denomination that seemed hopelessly corrupt to black nationalists. The militants didn't understand "the radicality of genuine Christianity," observes James Cone, a theologian at Union Theological Seminary in New York and a longtime colleague of Wright's, who made a similar triangulating move.

When Wright arrived at Trinity in 1971, he helped the congregation ask, "Are we going to be a black church in the black community . . . or are we going to continue to be a white church in blackface?" Wright introduced revival hymns like "Nothing but the Blood" and "What a Fellowship." Then he added an altar call to the service. Drums, tambourines, and even a washboard became part of the music. A youth choir asked permission to sing gospel music, and on its first Sunday the group "came in 'stepping' like members of an Omega Psi Phi [a traditional black fraternity] step show" and wearing red and green dashikis. Adults then started asking if they could join the youth choir. Today nothing announces the church's commitment to unapologetic black Christianity more than its huge choir, which sways and sings in African dress, leading the hand-waving and the "Amens."

These years also spawned the church's other motto: "In the heart of the community, ever seeking to win the community's heart." Trinity's location on Chicago's South Side is crucial to understanding its history and mission.

3. "Growing the African American Church through Worship and Preaching," in *Growing the African American Church*, ed. Carlyle Fielding Stewart (Nashville: Abingdon, 2006) 63–81.

Part 1: Searching for Jesus in Local Congregations

Wright has written that it is hard to imagine a church like Trinity "taking place in Maine."[4] In Trinity's neighborhood, children on their way home from elementary school are recruited by the Nation of Islam. The church sits just blocks from an enormous federal housing project built in the 1940s (home to a population that the original self-consciously middle-class congregation tried to overlook).

Trinity's rootedness in its neighborhood does not prevent it from having a global impact. Chicago's many seminaries regularly send students to intern at Trinity or just to observe its ministry. Wright has sent dozens of students into ministry, many of them women. UCC youth groups from throughout Illinois travel to Trinity to learn about evangelism and racial justice. "They have a ball," Moss said of the wide-eyed white kids visiting Trinity most Sundays. "They say, 'Is this a UCC church?'"

Moss sees Trinity's Africentrism as crucial to its success. "Churches that are, say, Lutheran first, but then just happen to be black secondarily don't grow. We're a black church first—one that just happens historically to be UCC." Moss is troubled when I remind him that Trinity is criticized as being "separatist." Trinity made a conscious decision to serve the community when whites were fleeing to the suburbs. "People who won't even come to the 'hood criticize us for being in the 'hood," he said. Understanding Trinity's social context helps one understand the church's critique of middleclassness. With increased access to prosperity and social status, blacks can imitate the white families who fled the area in the 1950s for the greener pastures of the suburbs.

Obama's first book, *Dreams from My Father*, recounts an exchange he had with Wright over black middleclassness. A church secretary was planning a move to the suburbs so her son could have a better life. Wright's response was: "That boy of hers is gonna get out there and won't have a clue about where, or who, he is." Obama defended the secretary, suggesting that the boy would be safer outside the inner city. Wright replied, "Life's not safe for a black man in this country, Barack. Never has been. Probably never will be." Black flight, Wright seemed to be saying, is no better for those who flee than for those who are left behind.

When the first criticisms of Obama's church came to the senator's attention, he seemed genuinely perplexed. He converted to Christianity at Trinity, responding to one of Wright's altar calls, weeping beneath an old wooden cross as he promised to follow Jesus. He told the *Chicago Tribune*: "I would be puzzled that they would object or quibble with the bulk of a

---

4. "Doing Black Theology in the Black Church," in *Living Stones in the Household of God: The Legacy and Future of Black Theology*, ed. Linda E. Thomas (Minneapolis: Fortress, 2004) 23.

document [the Black Value System] that basically espouses profoundly conservative values of self-reliance and self-help."

Dwight Hopkins, a member of Trinity and a professor at the University of Chicago Divinity School, argues that the church is within the mainstream of black churches and as such is socially conservative. Its emphasis on education harkens back to the days when black parents worked two or three jobs to educate their children, since schooling was one thing "they can't take from you." Moss, noting the church's tutoring, SAT preparation, and scholarship programs, said, "We place more African-American students in college than any other organization in Chicago." Hopkins pointed to the church's annual marriage retreat, in which "five hundred black couples study the Bible's views on marriage together," as more evidence of the church's focus on traditional concerns: the Bible and the family. Obama himself believes that he could explain the Black Value System to people in Iowa and "get a few Amens."

Trinity's critics speak as though it is a political organization constantly advocating for social change, like Operation PUSH or the National Action Network. But it is neither more nor less than a church. "Trinity's activism is a write-your-elected-official activism, not one that mobilizes thousands to picket," Hopkins said. The only signs of politics that I saw in Trinity's packed worship bulletin the day I visited were a list of polling places in advance of an upcoming citywide election and a reminder to "boycott Wal-Mart." Not exactly the stuff of revolution.

There is no denying, however, that a strand of radical black political theology influences Trinity. James Cone, the pioneer of black liberation theology, is a much-admired figure at Trinity. Cone told me that when he's asked where his theology is institutionally embodied, he always mentions Trinity. Cone's groundbreaking 1969 book *Black Theology and Black Power*[5] announced: "The time has come for white America to be silent and listen to black people.... All white men are responsible for white oppression.... Theologically, Malcolm X was not far wrong when he called the white man 'the devil'... Any advice from whites to blacks on how to deal with white oppression is automatically under suspicion as a clever device to further enslavement." Contending that the structures of a still-racist society need to be dismantled, Cone is impatient with claims that the race situation in America has improved. In a 2004 essay he wrote, "Black suffering is getting worse, not better.... White supremacy is so clever and evasive that we can hardly name it. It claims not to exist, even though black people are dying daily from its poison."[6]

---

5. *Black Theology and Black Power* (New York: Seabury, 1969).
6. "Calling the Oppressors to Account: God and Black Suffering," in *Living Stones*

Part 1: Searching for Jesus in Local Congregations

Wright agrees. When I asked him whether white Americans are right to maintain that the racial situation has improved since the days when Africentric Christianity was born, Wright pointed to the racist remarks by radio host Don Imus: "And you say things have improved?"

When I asked Otis Moss and Dwight Hopkins about the attacks on Trinity, they both noted that ethnic versions of Christianity are commonplace among white Christians—Greek Orthodoxy, Irish Catholicism, German Lutheranism. Why, they wonder, is that kind of ethnocentrism permissible for whites, but Africentric Christianity is not legitimate for blacks?

Wright's preaching regularly draws attention to standards of beauty in America that drive black women to use beauty products and hairstyling to make themselves appear more white. "The church should be the place where children of color see themselves in a positive light," Moss has written.[7] It is hard to see any Christian disagreeing with these tenets of black Christianity.

"We are descendants of Africa, not Europe," Wright has written. "We have a culture that is African in origin—not European. The Bible we preach from came from a culture that was not English or European."[8] In his teaching Wright refers to the Holy Land as "northeast Africa," pointing out that such a designation is not less absurd than calling the land of Israel and Jesus "the Middle East." For Wright the church's theology needs to be reworked along African rather than European lines. Moss quotes theologian James Evans, who sees links between the incarnation and black Christianity: "The two stubborn facts of African-American Christian existence are that God has revealed God's self to the black community and that this revelation is inseparable from the historic struggle of black people for liberation."

Black intellectuals have often insisted that white identity itself has been built on black oppression. Moss quoted James Baldwin to me: "If I'm not who you think I am then you're not who you think you are." When James Cone says that "Jesus is a black man" or "racism is America's original sin," the very vehemence of white Christians' negative reaction shows how alive these issues still are.

But the naming of sin is never the last word in black preaching. James Baldwin also wrote in a famous letter to his nephew that "you must

---

in the Household of God: The Legacy and Future of Black Theology, ed. Linda E. Thomas (Minneapolis: Fortress, 2004) 10.

7. "Real Big: The Hip Hop Pastor as Postmodern Prophet," in The Gospel Remix: Reaching the Hip Hop Generation, ed. Ralph C. Watkins (Valley Forge: Judson, 2007) 126.

8. "The Continuing Legacy of Samuel DeWitt Proctor," in Blow the Trumpet in Zion! Global Vision and Action for the 21st-Century Black Church, ed. Iva E. Carruthers, Frederick D. Haynes, and Jeremiah A. Wright Jr. (Minneapolis: Fortress, 2005) 9.

accept [white people] and accept them with love. . . . They are, in effect, still trapped in a history which they do not understand. . . . We cannot be free until they are free."⁹

Moss summarized the history of the black church this way: "We have always worshiped with one foot in the soil of our present pain and another foot in our future hope."[10] After our interview, he offhandedly mentioned Sojourner Truth. "She was a slave, she was raped multiple times, she could've said, 'God can't use me.' But she didn't." The black church doesn't just talk about the Exodus, or even describe the black church's own Exodus. It relives the Exodus, right there on Sunday morning.

Indeed, Trinity is a complex place. It incorporates not only the classic texts of black theology but shows the influence of the Pentecostal tradition's emphasis on spiritual gifts and healing and the black church's emphasis on personal revival. At the service I attended the music leader dragged out the last hymn, slowly intoning, "There's still one more" as the congregation waited for a last soul to join the dozen or so already assembled at the front, seeking salvation.

At the same time, Wright pushes back against prosperity preachers like T. D. Jakes and Creflo Dollar. Such "prosperity pimps" preach that capitalism is "synonymous with Christianity," he complains.[11] Wright also counters the black church's traditional conservatism on issues like homosexuality and gender. Trinity has a singles class called "Same Gender Loving," and Wright has encouraged women into pastoral ministry throughout his career. Trinity's own disavowal of middleclassness sits uneasily with its thousands of middle-class to upper-class members, whose BMWs and Audis create traffic jams on 95th Street every Sunday morning and evening.

Wright's particular genius is his ability to hold all these emphases together. He's a black pastor of a black church that is the largest congregation in a mostly white denomination. He's the spiritual shepherd of black nationalists and Christian pacifists. He remarked in one sermon that both his "intellectual friends" and his "nationalist friends" wish he wouldn't talk so much about heaven, since Christian talk of heaven seems to denigrate the quest for justice on earth. His litany in response ran through the whole of the scripture in the best tradition of black preaching: "If I drop heaven, I'm going to lose the first verse in my Bible. . . . If I drop heaven, I'm going to lose two of my Ten Commandments. . . . If I get rid of heaven, I'm going to

---

9. "My Dungeon Shook: Letter to My Nephew on the One-Hundreth Anniversary of the Emancipation," in *The Price of the Ticket: Collected Nonfiction, 1948–1985* (New York: St. Martin's, 1985) 336.

10. "Real Big," 124.

11. "The Continuing Legacy of Samuel DeWitt Proctor," 8.

get rid of what happened when Jesus was baptized.... If I drop heaven, I'm going to have to stop praying my favorite prayer, 'Our Father' ... If I drop heaven, I'm going to have to do away with the Second Coming; I'm going to have to get rid of Pentecost. I'm going to have to throw Revelation out of my Bible.... Don't make me drop heaven."[12]

I asked Wright what response white churches should make to his Africentric gospel. He referred to a crash course on inner-city ministry he used to teach to white seminarians. He would close the course by telling them that the final exam was this: when their friends or family or parishioners exhibited racism, the students should speak up. If they didn't, they failed the course. And only they and God would know.

One of the actions for which Wright has been criticized politically is a trip he took to Cuba in the early 1980s. His Spanish-language translator for the trip was a young woman who needed his sermon manuscript in advance, since she had never learned a religious vocabulary. He didn't have a manuscript to send, so when he met her, he instructed her in the basics of the faith. During his sermon, he realized that the congregation was reacting to the translator—waving handkerchiefs, shouting, "Go ahead, baby! Go ahead, baby!" Wright realized that "she wasn't translating one word I was saying. She had accepted the Lord Jesus Christ and was over there praising him."[13]

The miracle (no lesser word is appropriate) of the black church is that the sons and daughters of Africa embrace rather than eschew the faith they first learned from their white slavemasters, and that they have renewed it again and again out of their own struggles. Conservatives may find the Africentric church too political, and liberals may squirm over its revivalist emotion. But the black church continues to makes converts in unlikely places, reflecting a God who makes a way where there is no way.

---

12. *What Makes You So Strong? Sermons of Joy and Strength from Jeremiah A. Wright, Jr.*, ed. Jini Kilgore Ross (Valley Forge, PA: Judson, 1993) 57–58.

13. See ibid.

Synchronized Worship
The Rise of the Multicampus Church[1]

Every week tens of thousands of people attend virtual worship services that use an online ministry called LifeChurch.tv. A hundred churches worldwide are part of the LifeChurch network, and twenty-three thousand additional churches have downloaded LifeChurch resources—for free—from open.life-church.tv. LifeChurch also has a multisite church network of its own, with thirteen separate campuses connected by satellite.

Perhaps you find this kind of ministry disturbing. The faith represented by LifeChurch is largely disembodied, you might suspect—nothing more than virtual Christianity.

But the reality is more complex. And it's undeniable that multisite models of church are mushrooming. Willow Creek Church and North Point Community Church are two of the more famous, and there are a thousand others. What if LifeChurch is simply ahead of the curve? What if network-based, satellite-fed congregations—supported by technologically savvy staff, professional-quality music, and an effective Internet presence—represent the Christianity of the future?

Craig Groeschel, founder and senior pastor of LifeChurch, certainly thinks that his thirteen-year-old ministry represents the wave of the future. Such innovations may be "despised and rejected by many," he writes, but "I'm guessing they will be generally accepted in less than five years."

Groeschel's face and voice are beamed via satellite all over the world. When he makes a joke in Edmond, Oklahoma, site of LifeChurch's original campus, he gets laughs in Albany, New York. When he asks people to raise their hands in response to a query, hands go up in Hendersonville,

---

1. Copyright © 2010 by *The Christian Century*. "Synchronized Worship: The Rise of the Multicampus Church" by Jason Byassee is reprinted by permission from the January 26, 2010 issue of *The Christian Century*.

Tennessee. When he hammers home the points of his message with *USA Today* simplicity and precision, worshipers in Australia nod in recognition.

It all seems very twenty-first century. But Groeschel's model of ministry is rooted in the example of John Wesley. Groeschel told me that he is intrigued by Wesley's circuit-riding ministry, "which perhaps planted the seed that would grow into the multisite idea."

Groeschel grew up in United Methodist churches. After attending Phillips Theological Seminary, a Disciples of Christ school in Tulsa, he served at Oklahoma City's First United Methodist Church. He was a pastor there in 1995 when Timothy McVeigh bombed the city's federal building and the church's sanctuary became a makeshift hospital and morgue.

But Groeschel left the UMC in frustration when he and others wanted to launch a new site in another part of Oklahoma City and the denomination refused to sanction it. LifeChurch began in a garage as a church plant of the Evangelical Covenant Church and remains affiliated with that denomination.

LifeChurch's hallmark is its sophisticated technological and Internet presence. At LifeChurch.tv, participants can hear sermons at any time, attend church online, and click on a "virtual lobby" where they can interact with other participants. During the sermon, instant messages appear on screen from other listeners who are responding to the messages in real time and getting responses from online LifeChurch pastors.

LifeChurch also sponsors the virtual world of Second Life, which includes a site called Experience Island where people can connect on spiritual matters. In addition, LifeChurch has a site called mysecret.tv, which offers an online confessional, and an iPhone application called YouVersion that allows users to download individualized biblical content. You can also engage in micro-missions and discuss your experience with others online.

LifeChurch is not only an online presence. Thirteen LifeChurch campuses share Groeschel's preaching live via satellite. A giant digital clock in the back of each of these churches—visible to the pastors but not to the congregation—makes sure that everything in the service happens according to script, down to the second. A switch is flipped exactly nineteen minutes and thirty seconds into the service: that's when Groeschel's sermon in Edmond goes global via satellite.

Groeschel never lets a worship experience go by without offering an invitation to follow Jesus. "Even though I grew up attending church," he told me, "I was never challenged to repent of my sins and trust Christ as my Savior." His preaching corrects that oversight.

But unlike many technology-infatuated churches, LifeChurch does not only emphasize conversion. LifeChurch's mission statement is "to lead people to become more fully devoted followers of Christ." The network offers messages that are more challenging than those of most other Web- or television-based preaching.

One recent sermon, for example, dealt with money—not how to get more of it, but how to keep less. Groeschel told his listeners that those who make more than $40,000 a year are, compared to the rest of the world's people, already rich, and they need to ask themselves: What does the Bible ask of rich people? How can we stop consuming in order to give more away to those in need?

LifeChurch is not dogmatic about its approach and bends over backward to help other churches. Former dot-com executive Bobby Gruenewald, LifeChurch's "pastor and innovation leader" (yes, that's his title), insists that LifeChurch wants to help its mainline colleagues, "even if it's just with a little technology. We want to see the church thrive."

In his most recent book, *It*,[2] Groeschel speaks of taking up offerings to send to other churches. He confesses to feeling envious of other churches' success and encourages readers to pray for the churches that they drive by on the way to their own.

While perhaps right of center, LifeChurch seems to have no need to stress a claim of doctrinal or political purity. Tome Dawson, pastor at the South Tulsa LifeChurch campus, told me flatly, "Our competition is not other churches. Our competition is Disney"—and a myriad of other forms of entertainment.

For Gruenewald, Internet technology is simply "amoral." What matters is how it is used. While he knows that the Web poses dangers, he argues that the greater danger comes from the church being disengaged from technology. "The absence of the church just allows [sin] to go on unhindered."

The Internet, he believes, allows for a new level of unity in the body of Christ. The fact that the LifeChurch network church in Ada, Oklahoma (population 1,000), gets the same online content as do the bigger churches is a good thing. "It's beautiful," Gruenewald said.

One of the problems that an online ministry faces is how to administer the sacraments. It's not easy to dunk somebody in cyberspace. When a woman in Maine converted online, LifeChurch leaders flew there to conduct her baptism. At other times, they will encourage a new believer to seek out a local church to receive sacraments. They have also mailed communion elements to an online worshiper and arranged for someone from LifeChurch to commune via Webcam.

---

2. *It: How Churches and Leaders Can Get It and Keep It* (Grand Rapids: Zondervan, 2008).

Part 1: Searching for Jesus in Local Congregations

While sacraments are a challenge for an online ministry, disembodied preaching seems to work fine. Groeschel observed that at one time one of LifeChurch's campuses struggled while others thrived. "Guess which one got smaller? The one where I taught 'live and in person.' All the campuses that experienced weekly video teaching grew. If you don't like video teaching, put *that* in your pipe and smoke it."

I visited three LifeChurch campuses in Tulsa, the largest of which claims to have some three thousand partners (Lifespeak for members). The campus in the far south of the city started in 2008 with seven hundred members drawn from the midtown church. Then about five hundred others from midtown peeled off to start a campus in Owasso, in northeastern Tulsa. LifeChurch expands rapidly out of a determination not to get too big in any one setting.

A preference for a relatively intimate atmosphere is one of the major reasons for having multisite campuses. The resources of a church of ten thousand or more are astounding, but the size of the crowd can be overwhelming. Nobody goes to a stadium for intimacy. And the cost of building a Saddleback-sized auditorium is daunting. Satellite-based preaching allows the largest LifeChurch I visited to have half a dozen worship experiences per weekend. Each service can accommodate five hundred people. And each attendee gets a "fresh" preacher on screen, not one who is on his sixth or seventh sermon of the weekend. So each campus has the intimacy of a medium-sized congregation, with the resources of a megachurch—including top-quality video images and sound.

I heard part of a sermon series on Elijah, which included the visual image of a raven beamed onto three enormous overhead projectors. Sound effects of the raven cawing and flapping set the stage for talk about the misery of the drought referred to in the book of Kings.

Announcements were either part of a video—produced with the snappiness of a TV commercial—or handled deftly by the campus pastor. "You have to be a better communicator here," one leader told me, "because you get only ninety seconds."

Each campus can be relatively light in numbers of staff because of the massive online presence and direction that come from the LifeChurch office in Edmond.

When I asked folks at the LifeChurch campuses in Tulsa what brought them there, nobody mentioned the online preaching. One member, who had grown up in a small church, admitted that the idea of a screen preacher was a negative for him at first. "It didn't seem very relational," he said. But others talked about encountering a warm atmosphere. A young African-American woman said, "We're all like family here. We live in this area [suburban south Tulsa]. It's very welcoming."

"It's so young and inviting here," a middle-aged white woman said as she set out donut holes and fruit. Many families come because of LifeChurch's video program for youth, LifeKIDs. One young white man presented a reason for attendance at LifeChurch that illuminates Oklahoma's evangelical context: "All of the other young churches in town are charismatic."

Since the network's preaching is done almost entirely by satellite and video, the pastors at the various campuses do not focus on preaching. Dawson speaks with some frustration about not getting to preach regularly. "We talk a lot about sacrifice here: giving up something you love for something you love more." But he feels that not having to spend twenty-five or thirty hours a week preparing a sermon frees him up for relationships.

I happened to visit on a Sunday when the campus preachers were scheduled to speak. The three preachers' talking points were all identical, clearly handed down from a central office. But their stories, jokes, and illustrations varied. At times they even clashed.

In South Tulsa, Dawson told a story of answered prayer—how a teenage girl survived a suicide attempt and was in church the next weekend. But at the Owasso campus, Eddie Stephens spoke of his wife's cancer and his twenty-year-old daughter's pregnancy—and his experience of unanswered prayer. A leader in Edmond watches all the worship services and may offer immediate feedback. This can be jarring: campus pastors may get a text message as soon as they sit down after speaking. Ken Behr, campus pastor in Hendersonville, values the feedback, since it is likely to be constructive: "Wouldn't you rather hear from the guy who knows what he's talking about?"

Michael Bartley, a Wesley Foundation minister in Tulsa who operates in the shadow of LifeChurch, sees a darker side to the network. "I know of four funerals of young people from LifeChurch.tv that were done by [ministers outside LifeChurch] simply because they could not be fit within LifeChurch's schedules," he says. He reports doing about fifty weddings a year for young people who "attend LifeChurch but feel little connection to it."

Jonathan Bartlett, a seminary student with a background in the Vineyard movement, says he sees little place in LifeChurch for strong lay leaders. "Their whole pitch for leaders of LifeGroups is 'It's easy.' LifeChurch is made up of people who liked youth group in high school, but then grew up and found nothing like it—until this."

But if Groeschel is right, all churches are headed in the direction of LifeChurch. Will congregations be cast in the role of providing pastoral care and sacraments to those who want the professional show provided by a church like LifeChurch? Will congregations become satellites of centralized ministries? Will most preaching be done via satellite television? If so, what will become of one particularly mainline gift: the credentialed, educated, warm-blooded pastor who meets the congregation in person?

The medium and the message are not inseparable. Some kinds of theology can be put into practice digitally and some cannot. But LifeChurch stands as a strong reminder that technology is shaping ministry—and that if we are going to use a new technology, we had better use it well.

It's *Simul Justus*, Not the Tattoos

*A Profile of Nadia Bolz-Weber
and House for All Sinners and Saints*[1]

MOST MEDIA ACCOUNTS OF Nadia Bolz-Weber and the House for All Sinners and Saints in Denver, Colorado, focus on her tattoos. She has the liturgical year tattooed on one arm, from creation to Pentecost; another features Lazarus still wrapped but very much alive. She got that one while struggling to write a sermon on Jesus' raised friend. The tattoos on a 6'1" woman with a taste for punk, a bad-girl past, and a gay-inclusive church make for easy picking for secular media. She's been featured on the front page of the *Denver Post*, on the evening news in that city, and was tapped to do the city's Easter sunrise service, preaching to ten thousand people in Denver's gorgeous Red Rock Amphitheater. Trying to muster up an angle on this impossible-to-ignore form of self-expression, I ask whether the tattoos are like social media—putting on the outside what's inside. "Maybe," she says, pensive. "Except for the impermanence. With social media you're out of the loop in a second if you don't catch the meme right when it's out."

In contrast to much of the superficial media coverage, what's most interesting about Bolz-Weber is her deep traditionalism. "Secular media doesn't understand the difference between orthodox and conservative," she tells me through a toothy smile, blue-green eyes blazing over thick-rimmed, fifties-era glasses. "House," as the community calls itself, is almost medieval in its liturgy. There are no instruments, just *a cappella* chanting and pillows for kneelers at a prayer station. The Eucharist is served weekly, and Eastern

---

[1]. This article was written as part of a case study on House for All Sinners and Saints for the New Media Project at Union Theological Seminary in October 2011. The full report of this case study and more information about all the case study research are available on the Web site of the New Media Project. See http://www.newmediaprojecta-tunion.org/pages/Case-Studies/default.aspx.

church icons drape the interior, the stoles, the church's Web site and literature. Latin hymns fill the communion liturgy the Sunday evening I attend, and Bolz-Weber is proud to be using Franz Schubert's setting for the mass. This is not high church fussiness; it is liturgical and churchly orthodoxy for scruffy hipsters. "I'm a liberal with a low anthropology," she explains. "There are about two dozen of us on earth." One member tells me that he comes for the church's "profound Christocentric passion that's not exclusionary." One theme in the church's preaching and liturgy is the depth of human sin. "I come here every week to get thrown on my ass," another parishioner says. Bolz-Weber uses some of the heaviest clerical language I've ever heard in a Protestant church for the absolution: "As an ordained minister of the church of Jesus Christ and by his authority, I declare that your sins are forgiven," she says. Bolz-Weber explains that many of her fellow social progressives want to jettison the Bible and Jesus in order to be more inclusive. "But why should we jettison the only things we have going for us?" she asks.

Bolz-Weber's and House's use of social media, by contrast, is hardly thought about at all. It's as commonplace as wallpaper. Every time I ask Bolz-Weber or a church member a question about social media, they have to stop and think about it. They usually come up with something, but it takes a while. "It's not like we have a strategy," one member tells me. "There's no social media committee," another says, laughing. Another updates her Facebook status during our group interview to make fun of my questions. "I'm doing Facebook for the Lord," she says, drawing clicks of her friends' "like" buttons. Bolz-Weber tells of being on the stage at the citywide Easter sunrise service wallowing through seven suburban women's off-key special music. She'd asked church members to text her while she was waiting to preach. They didn't. "Why the fuck weren't you entertaining me up there?" she asks. "I was dying!" The Millennials who make up the church use social media the way they use oxygen. If asked, they can discuss it. If deprived of it, they would suffer. Otherwise they don't think about it. "It's 2011," one says to me. "You can get a whole degree online. Why wouldn't we use this stuff?" If we think about social media alongside a congregation like House, we will not wring our hands about it, nor will we worship it as the church's salvation. Instead, we'll use it, attentive to the ways tools always shape and occasionally misshape us, but without anxiety or undue adulation.

Some historical context on House may be helpful. House for All Sinners and Saints is a church plant of the Evangelical Lutheran Church in America (ELCA) that began in 2008. Bolz-Weber planted it while a student at Iliff School of Theology, figuring that if there were ever going to be a church to her taste, she'd have to start it. She has the ear of her denomination's presiding bishop ("At synod no one could find Bishop Hanson, so I said I'd just texted him, and all the bishops' heads went 'woosh!' right toward me"), travels for speaking engagements sometimes twice a week, and is inundated with requests, from seminarians to synods, to study her church. All a bit odd for a church of some fifty regulars. Yet Bolz-Weber did preach at Red Rock to ten thousand and did preach at the Greenbelt Festival in the UK this summer to twenty thousand. And with close friends and collaborators like Sara Miles and Phyllis Tickle, one senses she could write her own ticket on the book publishing market.

Hers was not always a star on the rise in the ecclesial world. She describes herself as an angry, self-endangering teenager who was happy dying before age thirty and treating her body accordingly. She was a hipster before it was cool, getting tattoos as a teen and a nose ring before anyone had ever seen them. She says, "People asked how I blew my nose. I never thought the mainstream would catch up with me." But then something happened. "God picked me up off that path, said 'How cute!' and put me on another." She got off alcohol and drugs and met her future husband, Matthew, who was studying to be an ELCA pastor. She had been attending a Unitarian Universalist church but found they think too highly of human nature. "It makes me wonder if they read the newspaper," she notes. She often taps her chest and says, "It's dark in there." She found the Lutheran tradition was the only one that gave language to what she'd experienced. "When I learned about *simul justus et peccator* I was like, 'Oh yeah, we *are* all sinners and saints at the same time.'" The name for her future church was born.

House does receive benefits that other church plants in the ELCA do not. Though they are three years in, they are not being weaned from synod support, as church plants in, say, suburban communities would be. Two-thirds of her salary package comes from the denomination. Bolz-Weber describes the church as having recognized the importance of House's ministry to the whole denomination and beyond. Her being tapped to speak at ELCA synod meetings is just one example of the way the denomination not only supports her work but also lifts her up as a model.

Part of House's mission is gay inclusion. One parishioner, Stuart, has the playful title of "Minister of Fabulous." When I ask why he worships at House, he quickly answers, "They accept me here. An evangelical church told me parents would pull their kids out if I worked with the children's programs." Stuart entered a drag beauty contest and won. Half of the church was there cheering him on. "People asked how we knew him, and we said, 'We go to church with him!'" Another man named Asher recently transitioned from female to male. "We had a naming rite for him at Baptism of the Lord Sunday," Bolz-Weber tells me. "It was beautiful." Part of House's gift

Part 1: Searching for Jesus in Local Congregations

is that it reaches people whom much of the rest of the church, even those trying to be gay inclusive, never could reach.

They do it by making gay inclusion *not* their focus. Their focus is on Jesus, how screwed up his people are, and so how spacious and proactive his grace is. Bolz-Weber admits in church the Sunday I'm there that she is recycling a sermon from the year before. She first shows the humor of the former standup comedian she is, "Isn't that green of me?" and then confesses, "I've been traveling, it's been really tough lately, so I spent the last three days playing with my kids, which I'm also called to." Then she unleashes a gorgeous meditation on Psalm 23, asking if we can get underneath the hackneyed familiarity. As a child in the Church of Christ, she thought the King James formulation meant that the Lord is a shepherd *whom I do not want!* And why wouldn't she? God is portrayed as an angry guy "with a really great surveillance system." But, she says, she eventually came to realize that "this is a shepherd worth wanting." One reason, she says, is that he teaches us how to rest. For example, House recently learned it would have to move from its home of three years. Bolz-Weber panicked. "I raged, screamed, ate chocolate, yelled at my husband, yelled at a few more friends, cried, prayed, ate some more chocolate," and then did the "American elbow grease thing" and got to work. They had new digs a short time later (they shared the need on Facebook, and within days an Episcopal church offered space). "It was like a bitch slap from the Holy Spirit," she says. "Did all that anxiety actually turn out to be effective?" Can't we learn to rest in God in the moment, and not just to look back retrospectively and realize the anxiety was unnecessary, she asks?

This is Bolz-Weber's preaching at its purest—confessional, funny, aimed at conversion. She's out for your soul.

I ask Bolz-Weber whom she draws upon as a theologian. "The dirty little secret is that I don't read shit." She is accused of being a Barthian and of drawing on Tillich. I heard lots of Luther with a Willimon-like snark. She says she draws on those who read original texts, especially in a weekly lectionary group where she cherry picks from what others say. She loves Luther's insistence that we never outgrow our need for grace—that the movement of faith is always from God toward us rather than the reverse. Her conversion involved a slow, passionate immersion into the liturgy, followed by a subsequent one into the scriptures. She also draws on laypeople for her preaching, often posting teasers on Facebook the week before a sermon, or questions she wants to address. One recent Facebook status update asking what people thought of John 3:16 brought a chorus of stories about how the verse has been used to condemn people. She was not at all happy: "I was like, 'Shit, I wanted to preach on Nicodemus!'" (House's language, including its pastor, tends to the profane. This is not Stanley Hauerwas' profanity, calculated to shock. It's just how Bolz-Weber and her peeps talk.) So Bolz-Weber borrowed ideas from a pastor friend to preach a message about how most religious groups tell a gospel in which there is an in-group and an out-group, and those listening are in. The good news is that for Jesus, there is no more in or out.

In the sermon I hear, she turns from gospel to technology. "We all know how to change our Netflix queues on our phones," she says. "But how many of us know how to *rest*? How to languish in the Lord's presence? We could all check our email right now (in fact, I won't ask *how many* of us are checking our email right now!), but we all need to learn how to rest. The Dow Jones won't set a table for us in the presence of our enemies." The implication is clear—Jesus will.

She concludes worship with another innovative idea from church members based on the first lection from Acts 2 about the disciples sharing possessions ("You know, that idyllic hippie stage in the church that lasted for like twenty minutes?"). Members have brought possessions from their homes to sell on eBay. They're going to take the money earned and start a deacon's fund for members who need help with groceries or bills. "That way there's no difference between giver and receiver," she explains later. "Everyone has stuff they can sell." They will take pictures to post to Flickr and talk about what they've learned on Facebook, and they fully expect to hear from other churches who have been inspired by their ideas. "We're like a laboratory," she says. "No one here can say, 'We've never done it that way before,' or 'That'll cost us money,' since we don't have any. We get to play and put what we learn out there on the Web."

Are they ever on the Web. Their Web site looks expensive, but it's not. "A friend did it for me for $1,000," Bolz-Weber says. She has more than twenty-five hundred Facebook friends and her Facebook profile is a major way new people find their way to visiting House. When the group holds its Theology Pub, it announces meetings on Meetup.com, a public forum. Anyone can see the invitation, even those not involved in the church.

No community ministries at House *could* exist entirely online. But almost nothing they do could exist without the Internet either. Members told me about a hymn sing that took place in the pub. Participants wept to be singing "old time religion" songs over cold suds. Yet only some small portion of those singing came from the church. Others saw the meeting planned on Meetup.com and came too. Still others happened to be at the (largely gay) bar that day, heard the singing, and wanted to join in. Online and embodied communities are not here playing a zero-sum game. They supplement and depend upon one another. "We've only had like three Sundays since our founding without visitors," Bolz-Weber said. "When it's just us, it's such a letdown. It's like kissing your best friend." In other words, House is used to having porous borders, and technology helps those borders remain porous. "We live our life online, and lots of outsiders consume and comment on what we do," one member tells me. The message that there is no in or out is not just promulgated, but demonstrated, via social media.

While several members tell me they embrace House for its inclusivity, more say they do so because of its sense of community. "This place is by and for and within and into community," one says, piling up prepositions. Their way of doing community is online. Members go to events, post photos, and all are vicariously present. "My parents say we seem to have a lot of fun," one member says. They post where they are on CheckIn.com and others come and hang out with them.

Bolz-Weber describes herself as conducting much of her pastoral care online or via text. While one can't go into great depth in 140 characters, one can say something, and such connection can lead to further in-depth interaction. Social media furthers the church's effort at prayer. Bolz-Weber tells a story of the church starting a Google prayer group, so that members can log on and tell their ill companion she's being prayed for. That way one can watch as a prayer chain forms visibly before her eyes. Bolz-Weber blogged about this experience, showing that pastoral care is communal, not simply individual, and can come in short increments—in precisely the sort of attention span–deprived bursts in which newer generations specialize.

Bolz-Weber says she couldn't send a physical piece of mail to her parishioners if she wanted to because she knows none of their addresses. When I ask how often she's online, she says simply, "All the time. I'm never not on it." There is an exception to that—during worship I catch no one checking his or her phone. The contemplative ten minutes after the sermon known as "open space" (ten minutes! Among Gen Xers and Millennials!) is a space in which the quiet is holy and thick. Before service, everyone is on his or her phone, but during open space not one is. Bolz-Weber agrees, but then points out she checked her phone three times during a meeting earlier that very day. House's way of doing community is virtual, leading to embodiment and back, because that is how their age cohort does community. Bolz-Weber recommends Pew Research Center's poll to determine how Millennial one is (she scored a 96, "which means I'm a forty-two-year old teenager," she says). Find out who in your church is a Millennial native and also loves God, and let them create the future for you. "Don't market a product to them like you would to their boomer parents, because they will fucking resent you," she said.

It's Simul Justus, Not the Tattoos

As some of Bolz-Weber's comments have suggested already, she and her community are not unaware of the dangers of social networking. Parishioners tease her that they have seen her instant messaging her husband *while in the same room with him*. She agrees: "Social media are more dangerous to families than they are to churches."

As I arrive, Bolz-Weber is embroiled in the controversy over the refusal by *Sojourners* to sell ad space to a gay advocacy group. Bolz-Weber's name is on the magazine's list of contributors, but she will not join a boycott against them, citing their advocacy on behalf of the poor. Commenters on her blog accuse her of being no better than someone who compromises over race or gender. "That's just bullying," she says. When bullying happens internal to House, it can also come online, as with one member caring for a homeless man who regularly bemoans via email that the church doesn't do enough for them. "I'm actually proud of how we've helped them," Bolz-Weber says. "And I'm not going to let someone toxic become a black hole of need and manipulate others." So she played the bad cop and asked the woman to desist. Social media also create new ways for people to feel left out—for example, seeing those Flickr pictures of an event one wanted to be invited to but wasn't. Before social media, one might not have ever known.

Sometimes social media use is more mixed in its fruit. Bolz-Weber posted a sermon after bin Laden's killing about Jesus' command to love your enemies. Her father, still a Church of Christ member, printed it off her blog and read it to his men's prayer breakfast. You could hear a pin drop, he said. "Of course, I didn't say who wrote it," he added, which caused Bolz-Weber to feel betrayed. Her father said he'd fight the battle over women's ordination another time, and Bolz-Weber was glad that a group of wealthy conservative white men heard Jesus' message at that time. But she still felt the hurt.

In fact, Bolz-Weber blogged about the incident with her father in a response to the criticism she received for not boycotting *Sojourners*. The lesson: sometimes we work for change from within the system and that's okay. Bolz-Weber's father was, in turn, upset by her discussing their disagreement online. Such is the challenge of a sharing and open digital culture. But for Bolz-Weber the relationships always win out: "He is so unbelievably supportive of me and this ministry. I'm not sure he's ever failed to tell me how proud he is of me every time I see him."

Either of these events could have happened before the advent of social media. But they would have taken much longer to develop. Anger could not have crested into snarky rage at her or others. She wouldn't have felt so hurt so quickly, and others (including one transgender member of her community) wouldn't have had to leap into the fray in her defense. Bolz-Weber ruefully points out that if someone wanted to attack her for something, they

Part 1: Searching for Jesus in Local Congregations

should do it for "failing to give a shit about the poor." Later in our interview, someone mentions the church's practice of taking a homecooked meal once a month to Rainbow Alley, a drop-in center for LGBTQ youth. The kids are psyched when House comes, because most providers don't cook over their own stoves, they just bring store-bought food. Someone teases Bolz-Weber, "And you don't do enough for gay people."

The thing is, Bolz-Weber has a theology big enough to encompass all these events. She believes in the darkness of the human heart. She believes in the depths to which Christ plunged to save us, even to hell itself. And she believes that even after our union with him in baptism and Eucharist, we remain ever in need of grace. Social media can project House's laboratory findings around the world and increase its impact on others of like mind or goal, no doubt. It can amplify Bolz-Weber's humor. It can create new space in which to belittle and abuse. Someone who believes in the foulness of human hearts would expect no less.

House has several mottos for itself, all of which are imminently Tweetable. "We are anti-excellence, pro-participation," one says. Bulletins passed out often have jobs scrawled across their top; the recipient of a job then gets to lead in the call to worship, or the passing of the peace, or the prayer after communion. They don't have to be good at it. They just have to lead their friends for a minute. Several voices catch as they mouth the ancient and beautiful words. Bolz-Weber sees this drive toward participation, flattening, and democratization as a similarity between House and the effects of social media on the rest of us. Yet it is still she who pronounces absolution, who chants the eucharistic liturgy, who wears the clergy shirt. "It's not that I'm special, I'm just set apart not to have the same freedom as everyone else," she says. "I'm not free to flirt with people here, to have my emotional needs be met by people here, I'm not free to preach anything else but Christ and him crucified." Flattening has its limits.

Another slogan on House T-shirts is this: "Radical Protestants: Nailing shit to the church door since 1517." House is a model example for what Leadership Education at Duke Divinity calls "Traditioned Innovation," a concept in which innovation is never a matter of creation *ex nihilo*, but of finding in the tradition neglected resources to meet new challenges.

In Bolz-Weber's words, "You have to be rooted in tradition in order to innovate with integrity." She notes that evangelicalism in this country is often "twenty minutes old and two inches deep. We rarely see anything more than fifty years old." Yet we have an almost innate need to belong to something bigger, older, more mysterious than ourselves, she says ("Sort of in a Joseph Campbell sort of way, you know?"). As a pastor she needs a bishop looking over her shoulder, not to tell her what to do, but to make sure her hurricane of a personality isn't the source of her authority. The church's tradition is that. "The last thing I need is to get to make shit up as I go," she says.

But innovate she does. LGBTQ inclusion is not the half of it. An icon of mother and child sits at the front of the entrance. It's made of pieces of Christmas advertising, forming a mosaic of remarkable beauty and power. Using eBay to enact Acts 2 is a beautiful stroke of genius. Her own efforts to meet Millennials where they are include giving them power to create. "They are producers, not simply consumers," Bolz-Weber says. In one example, Bolz-Weber invited church members to create something new for Ash Wednesday. Several spent half the day Saturday doing just that. "If I asked them to join a liturgy guild that meets half of Saturday, they never would have," she says. But she gave them freedom and space and they created something beautiful. So it is with social media. This is a flattened world, as Thomas Friedman taught us all too well.[2] Authority is given away and those who try to squeeze it lose it. Another example: House's Easter Vigil was "off the hook," she brags, because she asked members to enact the scripture. Some did drama, others filmed movies, the choir sang original music for the Zephaniah piece, still others performed skits so funny that members laughed until they cried. She gave them space to innovate, and they did.

But notice how little of this innovation has to do solely with the Internet. It's embodied, as House's glorious liturgy makes unmistakable. "Social media can lead to Gnostic problems," Bolz-Weber grants, "but not here." House is too grounded in community to allow that to happen. They would never worship online. She's not in favor of seminaries teaching online either. "I want a PhD who knows more than me giving a lecture, not some fucking group project foisting people's ignorance on one another," she said. She does admit that when she was more of a blogger she regularly had online friendships become friendships in real life. Even then her enthusiasm is tepid.

Social media is just part of the ether now. It's the air that Millennial culture breathes. It's not a means to market anything to them, to get them to come back to church. But if you want to communicate with them you'd better use those tools. And if you want them to embrace church, then turn power over to them and give them the space—"and some theological education," she adds—to do something both ancient and new. They might even use social media to do it.

---

2. *The World Is Flat* (New York: Farrar, Straus & Giroux, 2005).

Part 2

Searching for Jesus in Popular Evangelicalism

My own background is among evangelicals. I had a Baptist-style conversion at a summer camp, first spoke in public in a bible church youth group, first led other people in an FCA fellowship in high school, and started to develop a sense of a ministerial identity in an InterVarsity Christian Fellowship chapter in college. I understand evangelicalese, even if I don't generally speak it fluently anymore.

Since much of my work was at *Christian Century* I wrote for an audience that often does not speak evangelicalese—or more extreme, understands itself simply to be *not* evangelical. Mainline Christians often don't know what they think about Jesus, the Bible, eschatology, or any of the other good stuff. But they know they're liberals politically, and whatever the other side supports, they're against (conservatives do the same, naturally). Some of my favorite work at the *Century* was to introduce that audience to evangelical luminaries who are influencing their congregations without them knowing it. Many are doing so because they're saying good things, not simply despite themselves. I have often found evangelicals more "inclusive" than mainline liberals. *Christianity Today* has always understood that much of its audience is the evangelical population within mainline churches. Billy Graham long asked for help on his crusades from Methodists and

Part 2: Searching for Jesus in Popular Evangelicalism

Presbyterians as eagerly as from Baptists and Churches of Christ. And *CT* often does a better job than more liberal publications of getting past obsession with American politics and religion, precisely because of its emphasis on missions. Readers of *CT* often find detailed accounts of politics in, say, Nigeria or Pakistan precisely because of their interest in missionaries' work in those places and the conditions for evangelism there. So a "conservative" interest (missions) drives a "liberal" outcome—awareness beyond America's borders (can we simply drop these tiresome labels, please?! But then, what would I write about . . .).

A little-known secret is that the staffs of *Christian Century* and *Christianity Today* often cavort far more than their readerships would appreciate. I was once at a party hosted by a friend who works for *CT*. In line for the drinks, I asked a relative of his what he did for a living. "I study at Southern Baptist Seminary," he said. "Where my professors call the magazine *Christianity Astray*." He laughed at the cleverness. Then he reciprocated: "What do you do?" If *CT* was unacceptably liberal, how would he find *me*?!

This is precisely why I loved writing for *CT*. It's not only that their publication *Books & Culture* is among the best reading available out there (go ahead: find something smarter about politics, books, religion, Jesus, the Bible, and everything else that matters). It's that the rules are simple. Show an evangelical that Jesus, understood biblically, is in favor of something, and they have to at least listen to you. They may disagree, and often do with zeal (witness the hundreds of negative comments online on my Jeremiah Wright piece in this section), but they have to respect it. Evangelicalism then makes for a meeting ground of genuine debate over things that matter. Within the bounds of Jesus and scripture, anything is fair game.

My hope in this section is that I haven't mocked anyone intellectually. I tease the founders of the creationist museum in Kentucky a little, but hope to make clear also that I admire their consistency and zeal. Theirs is a particularly interesting, if spectacular, failure. They point up our problem as mainline Christians: we're ambivalent. At least you can figure out what these creationists think. What do mainline Christians think about creation, history, and God's purposes in the world? No clue. Can't tell. We're entirely too muddled over it. And in an age of eco-catastrophe, the mainline churches' inability to tell a true word about God's delight in creation is a remarkable abdication of our responsibility. We are, however, paid up on the scorn we heap on fundamentalists.

These are some of the pieces dearest to my heart. The one on *Left Behind* was among the first I ever published and allowed me to get to know Amy Frykholm, who subsequently became a friend and then fellow editor at *Christian Century*. She got in touch to thank me for writing a review that suggested

Part 2: Searching for Jesus in Popular Evangelicalism

I understood her work. Who knew that friendship could spring from such sources? Further seeds of friendship were watered in doing research for the piece on new monasticism. If the West's economy ever collapses fully, I know where my family is washing up: on the front porch of one of these new monastic houses. They know how to garden, cook, clean, and put people to work amidst worship of Jesus. What else is there to life? After the housing collapse began in 2008, I told Jonathan Wilson-Hartgrove that I knew Jesus loved new monastic types more, but I didn't know not owning a house was also a good financial investment! The pieces in this section also show me the danger of publishing. Sharon Huey of Grace Fellowship told me her friends at church teased her as the "amiable Asian woman" for years after this piece appeared. Barbara Rossing was grateful to me for the positive review of *The Rapture Exposed*, but she remembered with precision one phrase I used about her: "Anger drives this Lutheran minister." Once you write something, it's out there and can be put to whatever use others want—the words are beyond your control. The profile of Jeremiah Wright in the last section is a case in point. After I draped praise on Trinity UCC and Wright for thousands of words, my one critical paragraph toward the end is what right-wing bloggers and pundits picked up upon and republished eagerly.

I hope the words in this section offered some grace and wisdom to mainliners about evangelicals' gifts, and some words of challenge to evangelicals from the mainline. For the lines between the categories are blurry at best and contradictory at worst. We Methodists, at our best, are evangelicals: we love Jesus, love scripture, and want the whole world to know about both and to change their lives. Our best ecclesial moments, then, are ones that smudge that line—or to mix metaphors, ones where we dance across it. For Jesus can be found in both places, and if anything holds us together it'd better be him.

The New Monastics

Alternative Christian Communities[1]

AT A TIME WHEN the church had grown too cozy with the ruling authorities, when faith had become a means to power and influence, some Christians who sought to live out an authentically biblical faith headed for desolate places. They pooled their resources and dedicated themselves to a life of asceticism and prayer. Most outsiders thought they were crazy. They saw themselves as being on the narrow and difficult path of salvation, with a call to prick the conscience of the wider church about its compromises with the "world."

I'm describing not fourth-century monks, but present-day communities of Christians who think the church in the United States has too easily accommodated itself to the consumerist and imperialist values of the culture. Living in the corners of the American empire, they hope to be a harbinger of a new and radically different form of Christian practice.

These "new monastics" pursue the ancient triumvirate of poverty, chastity, and obedience, but with a twist. Their communities include married people whose pledge to chastity is understood as a commitment to marital fidelity. Poverty means eschewing typical middle-class economic climbing but not total indigence—some economic resources are necessary for building this desert kingdom. Obedience means accountability not to an abbot but to Jesus and to the community.

The description *new monasticism* comes from the theologian Jonathan Wilson. In *Living Faithfully in a Fragmented World: Lessons for the Church from MacIntyre's "After Virtue"*,[2] Wilson responds to moral phi-

---

[1]. Copyright © 2005 by *The Christian Century*. "The New Monastics: Alternative Christian Communities" by Jason Byassee is reprinted by permission from the October 18, 2005 issue of *The Christian Century*.

[2]. *Living Faithfully in a Fragmented World: Lessons for the Church from MacIntyre's "After Virtue"* (Harrisburg, PA: Trinity, 1997).

Part 2: Searching for Jesus in Popular Evangelicalism

losopher Alasdair MacIntyre, who concludes his celebrated 1991 critique of modernity by calling for "the construction of local forms of community within which civility and the intellectual and moral life can be sustained through the new dark ages which are already upon us. . . . We are waiting for another—doubtless very different—St. Benedict." Wilson agrees, and as an Anabaptist theologian he recognizes the resources in his church to create precisely the sort of new monasticism for which MacIntyre calls.

Be careful what you write. Wilson's daughter is now a founding member of one such new community, the Rutba House in Durham, North Carolina. Rutba got its start and its name from the experience of a Christian Peacemaker Team that was in Iraq at the start of the war. Leah Wilson-Hartgrove and her husband, Jonathan, were trained in CPT's tactics of non-violent conflict resolution and of "getting in the way" of those who would do violence. Their group had a car accident in which a member was seriously hurt. They took him to Rutba, the nearest town with a hospital. The Iraqi doctor treated the injured American for no fee, but asked the group to promise to tell others what had happened to them in Rutba—that while their country was dropping bombs on his, he offered healing and peace. (Jonathan Wilson-Hartgrove tells this story in *To Baghdad and Beyond: How I Got Born Again in Babylon*.[3])

The Wilson-Hartgroves returned to the United States and started the Christian community in Durham, where Jonathan began study at Duke Divinity School. It's based in a sprawling old house with creaky hardwood floors in a largely black section of the city called Walltown; drug problems and civic neglect give the neighborhood a reputation as a dangerous place. Jonathan Wilson-Hartgrove describes Rutba's mission there as one of "hospitality, peace-making and discipleship." He contrasts the community's vision with that of the rural Southern Baptists among whom he grew up: "Jesus doesn't just forgive my sins, he gives a whole new way of life—the best way to live."

The community shares meals and daily prayers from the Book of Common Prayer. Its members do not have a common treasury in the strict sense. They tend their own finances, but they do keep a common purse that members are encouraged to give to or take from as they have ability or need.

Their theological commitments are visible in the pictures on the living room walls: one is of Martin Luther King Jr., the other of Dorothy Day, cofounder of the Catholic Worker movement. Rutba's members are committed to being in Walltown. When other Duke students travel home for

---

3. *To Baghdad and Beyond: How I Got Born Again in Babylon* (Eugene, OR: Cascade Books, 2005).

holidays, Rutba *is* their home. A bit worried that the Rutba members may be perceived as white do-gooders who intend to "save" the housing projects, Jonathan can only counter that they are committed to being a presence in Walltown—"unless the area gentrifies completely."

Wilson-Hartgrove heard a call to this sort of life while at Eastern College outside Philadelphia, where he studied with Tony Campolo. "A lot of Tony's students took his ideas more seriously than even he was ready for," he said. A number of Christian communities that include Campolo's students have cropped up in blighted neighborhoods in and around Philadelphia.

The Rutba community has only five members. In addition to the Wilson-Hartgroves, it includes another divinity school student, a forty-year-old man, and a high school student whom the community has taken in as a foster child. When I asked whether the neighbors think Rutba is weird, Jonathan said, "You should hear [the high school student] tell his friends where he lives. 'Well, I live in this house, they're Christians, white and black, who aren't really kin to me, but as Christians sort of are . . .'"

Despite its small size, Rutba House has a prominent place in the network of intentional Christian communities. In 2004 Rutba hosted a conference that led to the publication of a book, *School(s) for Conversion: 12 Marks of a New Monasticism*,[4] which includes essays on such topics as "Relocation to Abandoned Places of Empire," "Sharing Economic Resources," and "Peacemaking in the Midst of Violence and Conflict Resolution." Jonathan also tends a Web site that seeks to connect and support like-minded communities across the country (newmonasticism.org).

He is wary of having such a leading role in the young movement. "The Internet is the 'yeast' of the Pharisees about which Jesus warned," he jokes. Indeed, the Wilson-Hartgroves and Rutba could be accused of a sort of naive idealism, both in Iraq and Walltown, as they try to change a violent and racist world as twentysomethings. They are aware of that charge and reply that their steadfastness over time will refute it. (The rate of failure for these sorts of communities is quite high.) These communities' eager use of the Internet reveals some of what is new in the new monasticism. They do not reject technology as such. They embrace the Internet, as it serves their purposes of linking similar Christian communities to one another and sharing resources.

Newness is also evident in their embrace of Catholic and Orthodox sources of inspiration, which other Anabaptist or Amish communities who live in similar ways once eschewed. Wilson-Hartgrove often uses a

---

4. *School(s) for Conversion: 12 Marks of a New Monasticism* (Eugene, OR: Cascade Books, 2005).

Dostoevsky quote that Dorothy Day employed in her ministry: "Love in action is a harsh and dreadful thing compared to love in dreams."

In contrast to Rutba, Reba Place Fellowship in Evanston, Illinois, is a long-established intentional community. It was founded in the 1950s by a Mennonite professor from Goshen College who wanted a church more strictly modeled on the New Testament. Reba's membership peaked in the 1970s at about 150. Now it has thirty-three adult members, sixteen children and teens, five "interns" who are considering membership, and a half dozen or so people who simply "knocked on the door" to express interest, according to Reba leader Allan Howe. Some seminary students in the area have been steered to Reba by their professors. Those who want to know where they can find the way of life described in the New Testament actually lived out are directed to Reba Place Fellowship.

Reba members pool their money, and the community draws from the common treasury to cover members' housing, transportation, and health care. Over the years Reba has acquired considerable resources, including dozens of houses and apartment buildings in racially diverse South Evanston. The fellowship rents many of these apartments at below-market rates as a service to the community. In contrast to Rutba's young idealism, in fifty-plus years Reba's membership has grayed considerably. The community's decision to foreswear health insurance, trusting Providence for expensive medical care, may eventually tax even its deep pockets and those of its generous givers.

Reba is hesitant to refer to itself by using the ancient Christian terminology of monasticism. Mennonites have always rejected what they see as a two-tier church in which monks and priests are regarded as especially holy. Reba's David Janzen says the community has no interest in MacIntyre's ultimate purpose of "saving Western civilization." Rather, its members hope to show the world what following Jesus' way of justice and peace might look like.

A Chicago television station recently profiled Reba Place Fellowship by focusing on the Selph family. Doug Selph is a computer programmer who puts his $100,000 salary into Reba's common pot. Doug and his wife, Lisa, and her two children receive $762 a month from the community to cover the family's expenses. The WTTW program focused on one event that revealed how the community works. Lisa Selph's daughter Hannah was being encouraged by her violin teacher to buy a professional-quality instrument at a price of $10,000. The Selphs took the proposal to their "house group," with whom they pray regularly. The next step would have been to take the proposal to the entire fellowship.

Reba's leaders said they would be inclined to regard such a purchase as good for the whole community—like paying for a college education. But the question never got that far. The Selphs' house group suggested that Hannah earn the money to help pay for a new instrument and in the meantime continue to rent an instrument and develop her musical gifts. For the Selphs, Reba's practice of communal discernment kept the family from making an idol out of their child's talents.

Janzen, who contributed an essay to the *New Monasticism* volume, says that how the community's life works is not as important or interesting as why it works. "We keep returning to Jesus' teaching, [his] commands to love one another, to see to one another's welfare. There is a Spirit that grows up among us in doing that that is heaven on earth."

Even a casual visitor to the fellowship gets a sense of what he means. Their prayers crackle with evangelical piety and concern for peace, both global and local. The presence of a visitor from Christian Peacemaker Teams talking about her work in war-torn Colombia shows this is not merely private piety. The members of the fellowship want to make an impact, however small, on the world.

Something of a different animal from Reba is the Church of the Servant King in Eugene, Oregon. Many of its members are evangelicals who originally joined a parent congregation of the same name in 1978 in Gardena, California. The Eugene congregation was planted in 1987. Most of its key leaders have been living together in intentional community since the '78 founding.

Servant King started as an evangelical effort to live out scripture's vision of the church. A commitment to nonviolence evolved slowly, partly as members read the works of Stanley Hauerwas, partly as they decided who would clean the bathrooms. Peace is not merely about a position on the war in Iraq; it is about how one relates to one's neighbor, one's spouse, and one's adversary in the community. Community leader Jon Stock points out that most intentional Christian communities that are not committed to nonviolence don't survive, because when arguments erupt, someone has to win—and the community loses. The Gardena congregation that planted Servant King has had such a rupture and is now on strained terms with its ecclesial offspring in Eugene.

Servant King's members say that a key to its survival is its "overcoming of pietism." They are not rigid about drinking, smoking, or cursing; the atmosphere there can seem a bit like the early hours of a fraternity party. This is intentional. Members have worked hard to avoid any sense of competition over righteousness, both as individuals and in comparing Servant King to the wider church. Such pride can splinter a community, as in the Gardena congregation's case.

When I asked Stock whether he considers his community a model for the rest of the church, he almost visibly shuddered: "I'm much more comfortable talking about the mistakes we've made." Though smoking and drinking are permitted, the group is traditional in other moral matters. "We're quite conservative in what we do with our genitals. You have to get money, sex, and power straight or they'll ruin you."

Pietism can create artificial boundaries between a community and the wider church. Communities like these are born precisely out of impatience with the mainstream church, which they regard as compromised by or indistinguishable from the world. Servant King has, with some difficulty, reembraced the wider church. It follows the lectionary in its preaching and celebrates the Lord's Supper weekly. It invites prominent theologians to visit and teach in its midst.

On the Sunday I visited, the community added a new member to the group, which Stock says is made up of twenty-three adults, eight teenagers, and "I can't remember how many" children. The group gathers in the largest living room of its several houses in Eugene to sing "Down to the River to Pray" and to accompany the new member to her baptism—in a large tub in the backyard. She makes a public confession of sin, saying she has "idolized relationships above all." Stock almost whispers, "The Lord forgives." His fellow pastor, Brian Logan, shouts St. Paul's words as he dips her under the water: "If anyone is in Christ, there is a new creation!"

In a liberal university town on the West Coast, Servant King seems strange not because it's a commune of sorts, but because it's Christian. The community works to be known as such among its neighbors. It runs Windows Booksellers, a used bookstore with mostly theology texts on its rough-hewn shelves. Ten years ago the bookstore birthed Wipf and Stock Publishers, which employs many of Servant King's members. The community also runs a coffee shop. All these activities take place in a city block-sized building that includes a pizza parlor and a stage for performances, which draw others in. Eugene's small number of Christians (it has the fewest churches for a city its size in America) know the church, as do the colorful assortment of folks who stop by for pizza, coffee, books, or conversation.

By comparison with Servant King's members, Reba's Mennonites seem a bit more pious and plain. Reba's participation in a network of similar Anabaptist fellowships in the Shalom Mission Communities also stands in contrast to Servant King's independent status. But the two groups have some things in common. The life of the mind is important to both (one makes its living by selling books; the other has bookshelves filled to overflowing). Both communities are also quite wealthy. Reba's real estate is worth a fortune in the overheated Chicagoland housing market, and Servant King's property has tripled in value during the recent housing boom.

The New Monastics

Yet these communities are not investors. Their property is important to them only as a way of allowing members to live near one another and share life together, as Stock writes in the *New Monasticism* book, or of enabling them to offer low-cost housing to their neighbors. When I asked Stock and Logan what they plan to do when their members retire, they looked befuddled. Christians don't retire, in their view. "Florida is not on the Christian map," Stock says. They plan to work until they cannot, at which point they will trust others to take care of them.

If their care for one another now is any indication, others will be there for caregiving. Stock and Logan kiss each other on the cheek when they part for a journey of a few days, suggesting that three decades in intentional community has led to a deep friendship. "What we're after is a place that tastes and smells like the kingdom of God," Stock says. One gets a sense of such a place at the party after the baptism. The new member has requested a traditional backyard barbecue, but I'm told she could have chosen any food she liked. Really? Even lobster? Sushi? Caviar? "Sure, she's a new member of Jesus' body—when else do you celebrate?" Servant King is not opposed to extravagance as such, but wants to see it in the service of building the kingdom of God rather than in private consumption.

Another branch on the new monastic family tree is the Church of the Sojourners in San Francisco. Eighteen years ago some evangelicals who wished to wed a personal gospel with the social gospel helped begin a church and intentional community in the city's Mission District.

Tim Otto, part of a leadership team for Sojourners, speaks of rethinking vocation along Christian lines. The new monastic communities swim against the pull of the American dream—to be financially secure, to move across the country for a better job, to plan for retirement. Sojourners encourages members to resist the allure of relocating or borrowing for career opportunities, but to be eager to move or take out a loan for the sake of the church. When asked what he does for a living, Otto says, "I'm trying to become a saint." Only subsequently does he reveal that he is a part-time nurse. The flexibility of part-time work is important to him, as he devotes the rest of his time to the church.

Sojourners traces its founding to its members' realization that they were better at being Americans than at being Christians. Disparagement of America is not controversial in San Francisco, but the claim to be Christian is. The contrast is evident in Sojourners' concocted "Celebration of Yahweh's Kingship," held annually on the Fourth of July. Its goal is to "colonize" the holiday for Christianity the same way Hallmark and Madison Avenue have colonized Easter and Christmas for their purposes. Member Debbie Gish says the Sojourners' barbecue and fireworks are part of a "declaration of allegiance" not to the United States but to "Christ the King," by citizens "of a monarchy, not a democracy." That won't play in either red state or blue state America.

Another church that bears a family resemblance to the new monastic communities, though with some key differences, is Grace Fellowship Community Church. The largely Asian congregation, part of a small denomination, the Cumberland Presbyterians, began as an offspring of a one-hundred-year-old congregation in San Francisco's Mission District.

Grace looks like a "normal church," according to pastor Bob Appleby. Its members do not all live together as in the self-described intentional communities. But to join, one must submit to an intensive, nine-month catechetical program. The church takes Stanley Hauerwas and William Willimon's *Resident Aliens* as a sort of manifesto. Catechumens are asked, among other things, to take the church's trash out and make the coffee. Such tasks are seen as a sort of truth in advertising—the church is about service, not about having one's "felt needs" met.

Grace Fellowship's primary relationship to the new monastic communities is its effort to give the church prominence in its theology, rather than the state. Pastor Sharon Huey talks of Grace's catechumenate as preparation for taking something like a "vow of insignificance." Putting off prestige is hard, especially for "overeducated" and upwardly mobile Californians, and even more so for Asians, she says. But it is scriptural.

Huey and Grace Fellowship share with other evangelicals a love of scripture. But they have put it to use in reading Hosea as carefully as the rest of the Bible. The prophet taught Huey that the common reduction of Christianity to psychological help for the privileged is a sort of "whoredom." Reading the prophets is training in how "not to be nice," the amiable Asian woman says, for her community is "better at harmony than truth." In a time of empire when the church should tell a "more persuasive story" than one of exultation of the nation, Bible study is radical stuff. Community members say they were "ready" on 9/11, for the prophets had taught them to mistrust claims that saving power comes from anything other than God.

The communities I visited have important differences in organization, style, finances, and even theology. Some *are* churches, like Church of the Servant King and Church of the Sojourners. Some are *related* to churches. Reba sponsors two ecclesial gatherings nearby, so that one can worship with a Reba congregation without participating in Reba's common-purse arrangement. Rutba looks for support and wisdom from nearby St. John's Missionary Baptist Church, but members do not have to attend. Grace Fellowship is simply a mainline church committed to more radical living. Reba folks have a common treasury and give a stipend to members; Sojourners members maintain an agreed-upon standard of living and give the rest of their income to the church. Servant King members tithe 15 percent and open their books to one another to account for the rest. Servant King's rough speech and petty vices would make some people at Reba uneasy.

These communities can seem a bit inbred. Jonathan Wilson, coiner of the phrase *new monasticism*, is father and father-in-law of the key members of Rutba, which hosted the conference, edited the book, and sponsors the Web site by the same name. The woman I saw baptized at Servant King is Jon Stock's niece. Stock runs Wipf and Stock Publishers, which prints Jonathan Wilson-Hartgrove's work. Members of Sojourners and Grace Fellowship spoke at a conference organized by the Chicago-area seminary professors who send students to Reba.

Another problem the communities face is the challenge of transcending divisions along the lines of race and class. While those who do join are drawn to the scriptural norm of communities that transcend racial and financial barriers, they tend to be white, college-educated folks, despite great effort to reach out. For example, one of the Sojourners' original goals was to serve some of the tens of thousands of refugees displaced to San Francisco as a result of civil war in El Salvador. Three Salvadoran families joined the church and benefited from its legal clinic and job preparation aid. As soon as they acquired the resources, the families promptly bought minivans, left the church, and moved to the suburbs. Perhaps those who have had less of a chance at pursuing the American dream are not yet ready to be disenchanted with it.

Even with these difficulties, the new monastic communities say they are adding new members, and various new communities are sprouting up around the country. Camden House in New Jersey has planted a garden in an area of postindustrial blight, where homeless people can get fresh vegetables. The Open Door in Atlanta is billed as a sort of "Protestant Catholic Worker" house, where members staff a soup kitchen for the homeless and agitate for justice in the city. Others communities have arisen in such unlikely places as Shreveport, Louisiana; Omaha, Nebraska; Waco, Texas; Springfield, Massachusetts; and Lexington, Kentucky, now linked as part of the informal new monasticism network. Each has its own gifts, idealism, quirkiness, and commitment to local community. And each claims to be an alternative to the now-regnant empire and a foretaste of a coming kingdom.

Each of the communities I visited seeks also to serve the wider church—and even to convert it. Monastic communities have always had greater influence than their numbers. For one thing, they enable preachers and other Christians to point and say, "See, someone does try to live out the costly demands of Jesus with regard to possessions, family, nonviolence, and love." Their presence also encourages more traditional churches to alter their life in small but significant ways.

Part 2: Searching for Jesus in Popular Evangelicalism

Even if the effort doesn't have that effect, its adherents view it as worthwhile. As Jonathan Wilson-Hartgrove says, "Whether these communities proliferate or not, this life is good enough in itself."

Be Happy

The Health and Wealth Gospel of Joel Osteen[1]

When she came to church it was a big event. She wore her nicest dress and a grand Sunday hat. But then she wouldn't appear again for months. Every time I visited her she would assure me that she wasn't backsliding. "Don't worry—when I'm not at church on Sunday I'm watching Joel Osteen on TV."

Then, to curb my disappointment, she said, "You remind me of him. I bet you'll have a church like his one day."

That would have been quite a change from our eighty-member rural congregation. With some thirty thousand attending, Osteen's Lakewood Community Church in Houston has recently purchased the sixteen-thousand-seat Compaq Center, formerly used by the NBA's Houston Rockets, for its new home. Osteen appears before millions more on television. "The smiling preacher," as he is referred to, has also charmed his way into a longtime presence on the *New York Times* best-seller list with *Your Best Life Now: Seven Steps to Living at Your Full Potential*.[2]

Osteen has reason to smile. He has taken the congregation started by his father and turned it into what is reportedly the largest church in the United States. And he has (as he is quick to tell us) an elegant home, well-adjusted kids, and an adoring "partner in ministry." A dozen celebrities from the realms of politics, sports, and entertainment praise him on the book jacket.

Like most religious-television and -publishing moguls, Osteen has received scant attention in the mainline church world. And even evangelical

---

1. Copyright © 2005 by *The Christian Century*. "Be Happy: The Health and Wealth Gospel" by Jason Byassee is reprinted by permission from the July 12, 2005 issue of *The Christian Century*.

2. *Your Best Life Now: Seven Steps to Living at Your Full Potential* (New York: Warner, 2004).

Part 2: Searching for Jesus in Popular Evangelicalism

commentators have not been complimentary. One has referred to Osteen's "cotton-candy theology."

Indeed, there's not much substance here. *Your Best Life Now* is another entry in the long list of American contributions to the prosperity gospel: just improve your attitude, keep your chin up, and God's blessings will rain down on you. Russell Conwell said it a century ago, Norman Vincent Peale said it fifty years ago, and Bruce Wilkinson said it with *The Prayer of Jabez* a few years back.

Still, one has to acknowledge that something is working for Osteen, and that it isn't all quackery. A quick glance at his television audience shows his church to be a model of multiethnic ministry. Osteen doesn't talk about race much, but his church is full of people of different races. He's a good storyteller, helped by a caramel drawl and an aw-shucks Texas manner. He's not only affable but genuinely funny, with humor not infrequently directed at himself. Whereas many televangelists spew judgment and hate, Osteen seems like someone you'd like to meet, and who'd make you want to go to church and bring a friend.

In some ways Osteen echoes an ancient and venerable Christian tradition that borrows from Aristotle in calling itself "eudaemonistic." That is, Christianity offers the happiest life possible. The church fathers and medieval thinkers who picked up this philosophical tradition did have ample biblical material with which to integrate it. "Delight yourself in the Lord, and he will give you the desires of your heart," the psalmist promises. "Seek ye first the kingdom of God, and his righteousness; and all these things shall be added unto you," Jesus says. What Christian could fail to agree that our faith claims to offer the fullest life of joy and abundance possible?

Osteen certainly thinks so. He takes aim at all those who are content with "mediocre" lives and who think such negative thoughts as: My marriage never will get better. My finances never will improve. I never will get promoted or be respected at work. I'd better get used to not having friends. My health will never be fully restored. Pain will always be the final word on our lives. That family member never will get right with God.

To such people, Osteen says, "Friend"—few lines go by without him calling the reader this—"you have to start believing that good things are coming your way, and they will!"

The secret is to enlarge your vision. Are you satisfied with that little house you're in? You shouldn't be. You should want the sort of mansion the Osteens live in (his example). You should expect people to go out of their way to help you—then they will.

You must also "discover the power of your thoughts and words." If you beat yourself up all the time, if you don't think yourself worthy of divine abundance, God won't give it. God helps us, to be sure, but we must help ourselves first. You must "let go of the past." Rather than being consumed with bitterness, you have to forgive and move on.

Finally, you must "choose to be happy." You can't put it off till tomorrow or till that next financial milestone is reached. You should smile a lot, and good things will come your way. You also must work hard, for God won't bless someone who's slothful. You have to be a person of excellence. Arrive at work early, leave late, respect your boss, don't waste time on the job—then you'll be promoted and then you'll be happier.

Osteen imagines an objection: "You may be thinking, 'this sounds too good to be true, Joel.'" To which he replies: "I know it's true! I saw the power of our thoughts and words turn an impossible situation in my own family into a modern-day medical miracle." His mother was diagnosed with cancer and given only weeks to live. She overcame the disease by claiming victory over it, firing scripture verses at adversity and thumbing her nose at death. She is still living, decades later.

Osteen describes one occasion of a fairly direct encounter with God. It happened when he was about to run an errand while still wearing his ratty work clothes: "God spoke to me. I mean, if God has ever spoken to me, He spoke to me right there! . . . He said, 'Don't you dare go in there representing me like that! Don't you know that I'm the King of kings?'" Osteen went home, cleaned up, and represented God in a more princely fashion.

As these examples indicate, Osteen's illustrations are often less than compelling. Naturally, we cannot rule out God's speaking to us dramatically, but the claim that God took an active interest in Osteen's weekend attire seems to overreach a bit. Other examples seem even more dubious.

Osteen speaks of remaining positive as a teenager when police would pull him over for speeding around Houston. In several cases they recognized his father's name and let him off with a warning. Whether his attitude or the privilege of a famous father's name did the trick, the chief lesson he should have learned was to *slow down*. He frequently mentions a legal dispute that arose when Lakewood originally moved to purchase the Compaq Center. A lawsuit was brought by an opponent with deep pockets and fancy lawyers that could have prevented the church's move. But Osteen stayed positive, prayed, and won. Never mind that his church had its own deep pockets and fancy lawyers.

Nevertheless, Osteen has winning moments throughout his book. He speaks tenderly of his relationship with his dad, of his hesitation to enter the ministry and step into his father's large shoes, and of overcoming observers' assumptions that Lakewood would die with its founder. He suggests that we respond to a bad day or discouragement by helping others—for in giving

Part 2: Searching for Jesus in Popular Evangelicalism

we receive. One way of developing the sort of attitude God blesses with abundance is by giving money away, for it shows our trust. We have to plant seeds abundantly if we want anything to grow. Addressing a scandal close to Houston's heart, Osteen notes that the executives at Enron didn't wake up one morning and decide to bilk investors out of millions of dollars. Small lies accumulated until big ones became acceptable. Christian virtue ethicists would agree and so would their medieval forebears.

Similar examples of good advice appear frequently in the book. One doesn't doubt that his counsel helps people to have better marriages, careers, families, and lives. Salespeople, whom Osteen often addresses, will indeed perform better with more upbeat, self-confident attitudes. These claims are true, as far as they go. But that doesn't make them Christian.

It's striking how unnecessary God is to Osteen's project. People can "enlarge their vision" and "choose to be happy" with nary a thought of God. "Understand this: God will help you, but you cast the deciding vote." We have to be positive—only then will God bless us. Of course, since being positive itself gives those rewards, it's unclear what God has to do in the scenario. Even when Osteen speaks of the seemingly most supernatural of events—the healing of his mother's cancer—the accent is on her attitude rather than on divine activity.

Osteen's version of the gospel is full of "ifs." *If* we enlarge our vision, *if* we choose to be happy, *if* we think thoughts and speak words of victory and blessing, *if* we give of ourselves abundantly—then God will bless us with everything we want. The conditional nature of these sentences is telling. This is not a gospel of grace, in which God acts in spite of our lack of faithfulness to redirect our wants. Instead this is a gospel of reward in which God does nothing until we get our act together. In traditional Christian theology, Protestant and Catholic alike, we can do nothing in and of ourselves to merit God's favor. Rather, God comes to us in Christ when we are without merit, without ability to please God and without reason to think we can be saved or helped. Such a view of grace is surely part of the grumpy theology Osteen seeks to upend—but it is central to Christianity.

It's also striking how closely Osteen identifies wealth with divine blessing, to the point where he risks placing a Christian overlay on a pagan gospel of acquisition. In scripture, wealth is a much more mixed blessing, to say the least. It is a source of "peril and obligation," to quote biblical scholar Sondra Wheeler. For the prophets and for Jesus, especially in his Beatitudes, it is the poor who are truly blessed by God. The rich will be measured by standards of justice that demand care for the widowed and orphaned rather than for the ballooning of their own bank accounts. Not a few saints in the history of the church have heard Jesus' words as an invitation to divest themselves entirely of their wealth.

Osteen's book abounds with examples of trivial everyday concerns. Can't get a green light? Pray with faith, and that light will change. Can't find a parking place? Claim God's victory, and see divine favor as someone pulls out and leaves you a space in the front row. Worried that you haven't found the perfect date, someone like Osteen's wife (who is, by the way, praying for us as we read her husband's book, as Osteen promises in an epilogue)? You've guessed the answer by now: pray, stay positive, and God will build up the remarkable list of coincidences to have you meet that special person. Osteen knows enough to say this doesn't always happen. We can't treat God "like an ATM machine." But the qualification doesn't mean much in view of Osteen's repeated references to claiming God's promises for your parking and dating needs.

This theology is politically quiescent, accommodating itself perfectly to an imperial age. That is, it matters not what the government is doing, or what your company does as you work for promotion within it, or where you are driving while praying for green lights. The nature of our desires, and our potential self-deception about them, gets very little attention from Osteen. He assumes the standard set of American middle-class desires for a house, career, spouse, kids, etc. But what if I want a mistress? Or the cruel death of my enemies? What if it's the nature of my desires, or my vision of the abundant life, that is the problem?

If God matters little for this worldview, Jesus matters even less. "If you're always thinking positive, happy, joyful thoughts, you're going to be a positive, happy, joyful person, and will attract other happy, upbeat, positive people." If only Jesus could have heard Osteen's message—things might have turned out much better! His preaching could have been brightened up considerably. And his friends wouldn't have been the sorry bunch of losers he consistently attracted.

Osteen is an easy theological target. He merits attention mostly as an unreflective exemplar of temptations all ministers face—to translate the charged political and theological language of the scriptures into a vague religiosity, or into more easily digestible categories of self-help and self-improvement. His unending smile also reminds us of the ministerial temptation of relying on personal charisma, an upbeat attitude, or an eagerness to please rather than the more difficult claims of scripture.

Osteen is absolutely right in saying the gospel promises our "best life now." He's just mistaken on what the form of that life is. Jesus, God's best life lived among us, is the shape of our best life. That shape includes a cross and a totally unexpected triumph in the form of the resurrection. It offers hope

Part 2: Searching for Jesus in Popular Evangelicalism

rather than mere optimism, and a church gathered in worship to remind each other that God's promises will come true. In the meantime, those who weep now are truly blessed, for they see the incongruity between the promised kingdom and things as they stand.

This version of the gospel shows the most ironic failure of Osteen's promises of prosperity—they can't really lift the luggage psychologically. They may work to make midlevel managers mildly more successful, but in the face of genuine desolation—say, cancer that doesn't respond to prayer and a positive attitude—they fall to dust.

I wonder, then, what my parishioner saw in Osteen, and what help he gave her. Her husband had died decades earlier following an accident. He was severely burned and lost both arms, and he died before they could have children. She works in a fairly menial service job, and when not working mostly grumbles about coworkers and the manners of kids these days. Perhaps the dreariness of her life is alleviated somewhat by the smiling preacher, without the difficulty of encountering people in pews around her who would give her more to grumble about. The promises of unabated wealth and illustrations of lawsuits over sports stadiums are so disconnected from her life that they don't spoil the show. A light shines in her small house for that short hour, and Osteen's affability makes it possible.

Osteen is fine as one to "rejoice with those who rejoice," but not as one to "weep with those who weep" (Rom 12:15). He sounds like the writer of Proverbs in some of his more chipper moments, but not at all like the somber writers of Ecclesiastes or Job, or the psalmists who hit both notes. Without both heights and depths, the gospel offered by the smiling preacher on the screen is simply the same platitude over and over. What the church can offer instead is friendship with others in Christ, the chance to offer service to others, broken bread and wine poured out around a table, the grace to see in Jesus the promise of restored relationship and a healed creation. Something more like that would be my parishioner's "best life now."

En-raptured

Will We Be "Left Behind"?[1]

"I HEARD THAT WHEN THE tribulation comes, China will be one of the few countries with a big enough army to take over the United States." My parishioner looked at me earnestly, awaiting confirmation of her theological and political observation. This woman, the spiritual rock of the church, doesn't fit the media profile of those who believe in the "rapture." She is well educated, deeply involved in the community, and a successful businesswoman and civic leader—hardly a Neanderthal or escapist.

I decided to respond with what I took to be a fairly plain-vanilla, non-controversial geopolitical observation: "Actually, North Korea's army is bigger than China's." She nodded, satisfied, and headed off to her third church meeting of the week.

What a failure on my part. But I wasn't equipped to respond adequately. I had seen the glossy displays of the Left Behind series in bookstores, had heard claims that the novels (the twelfth and final installment is due out this spring) had sold more than sixty million copies, but had never met anyone who actually believed in the rapture, neither in my college evangelical fellowship groups nor in seminary. Then I received my first rural church assignment and quickly discovered that out here I was the only person who *didn't* believe in the rapture. My parishioners simply assume that this is what the Bible teaches. And why shouldn't they? They've never heard otherwise from their preachers.

That I didn't even know enough about dispensationalism to disagree with it intelligently is no accident. Mainline seminaries have ignored this phenomenon in inverse proportion to its growing social and political influence. Meanwhile, the rapture's proponents have not only established a

---

1. Copyright © 2004 by *The Christian Century*. "En-raptured" by Jason Byassee is reprinted by permission from the April 20, 2004 issue of *The Christian Century*.

Part 2: Searching for Jesus in Popular Evangelicalism

publishing juggernaut; they have also been influencing members of Congress and presidents.

This is deeply ironic. For generations mainline Protestants have tried to "demythologize" the contents of scriptures and creeds in an effort to gain social and political influence, while dispensationalists have avidly "mythologized" the Bible into ever more incredible systems of belief about the "end times." Mainline churches' influence has sagged as we have carried out this bargain, while the dispensationalists' has grown immensely. The rising tide of end-times fiction and politics urges us to take a long, hard look in the mirror.

For befuddled pastors, help is on the way. Two new and quite different books offer a glimpse into the thought world of those who believe in the rapture. Amy Johnson Frykholm analyzes the literature from a broad range of perspectives—literary, critical, historical, sociological, feminist, and theological. (The theological focus is impressive in a scholar who professes to be a recovering former fundamentalist and mostly nonreligious.) While Frykholm has no sympathy with the Left Behind series theologically, politically, or literarily, she has a great deal of sympathy with its readers and explores why people with interesting lives are drawn to such schlock in their religious reading. Her book is a good place to start if you're wondering what these novels are about and why they appeal to people.

Barbara R. Rossing's book is more polemical. Anger drives this Lutheran minister and seminary professor. She hates what Left Behind has done to popular Christian eschatology, to the Bible, to public policy, and especially to Christians' attitudes toward the environment. (Why save trees when the world is soon going to burn up anyway?) She seeks to rebut the dispensationalists' views and offer a more deeply biblical vision of Jesus' eschatological kingdom.

The basic storyline of premillennial dispensationalism—the system of thought that informs "rapture fiction"—originated in the mid-nineteenth century in the teachings of John Nelson Darby, a disaffected former Anglican priest. This version of eschatology holds that the Bible, read aright, contains a schedule for the final events that will precede the end of history. Darby believed that God deals with the world differently in each of seven "dispensations," or eras. We are now in the sixth era of world history, soon to be followed by the seventh—the end times.

The first event in the chain of dominoes that will lead to the end is the "rapture"—the secret return of Jesus to transport all true believers (i.e., not mainline liberal Protestants) to heaven. Cars, trains, and planes will fly into one another as believers are suddenly taken heavenward, leaving their clothes, personal effects, and vehicles behind (hence the bumper sticker: "Warning: in case of rapture this vehicle will be unmanned"). Those "left behind" will endure seven years of tribulation, mostly inflicted on the world by the Antichrist, disguised as the leader of a one-world government (read: the United Nations). Some of those shocked by the sudden disappearance of their loved ones will become true "Bible-believing" Christians who will band together to resist the wiles of the Antichrist and conduct secret evangelism campaigns meant to grow the power and numbers of their "tribulation force."

The plot of the Left Behind novels follows several characters who make up the heart of this force: Rayford Steele, an airline pilot; Buck Williams, a journalist; and their enemy, Nicolae Carpathia, the Antichrist. Our heroes will be quite busy. According to the "biblical prophecies" on which the novels are based, the Antichrist will support a Russian invasion of Israel, rebuild the Jerusalem temple, and lead nation into war against nation. This global warfare, coupled with a series of horrible natural disasters, will make the world a truly nasty place.

Finally, after seven years of death-dealing by the Antichrist and growing resistance by the tribulation force, Christ will return a second time to defeat the forces of evil at Armageddon, a large plain in Israel. He will then reign, before the world finally ends, for one thousand years, over a politically reconstituted kingdom of Israel, full of Jews who have converted to Christianity.

This system is subject to endless variations. For example, the enemies can change. In Hal Lindsey's 1970s rapture fiction, all the bad guys are Soviets. The villains can also morph into Muslims, as they often have in the post-9/11 world.

Frykholm's book helpfully situates the Left Behind series in relationship to previous generations of rapture fiction, which stretch back to the early twentieth century. These books have traditionally begun with the rapture of a significant woman character. In *Left Behind*, the first book of the series, Steele's wife, Irene, leaves only her nightgown and her open Bible behind in a rapture that occurs while he is away on the job, flirting with another woman. Faithful, long-suffering women should be extolled for their virtue but should not expect any this-worldly justice, the books imply. In this regard, the Left Behind series is no different from its many predecessors.

Historians note that dispensationalism and its fiction arose just as American culture was undergoing seismic social shifts in the late nineteenth and early twentieth centuries. It offered reassurance that conservative social values some day would be vindicated. The Left Behind series stands in a long line of books reacting against change—not only against independent and strong women, but also now against gays and lesbians.

Yet the series leaves its predecessors far behind in its embrace of technology. Steele and Williams use ultra-high-tech computers, satellite phones, the Internet, covert underground bunkers, superfuturistic weapons, and massive range rovers driven in ways that conflict with local traffic laws. They rely on their elite educations, political connections at the highest levels, and limitless reserves of cash.

In other words, this is not your grandma's Scofield Bible-inspired tribulation force. The first line of the first book makes that clear: "Rayford Steele's mind was on a woman he had never touched. With his fully loaded 747 on autopilot above the Atlantic en route to a 6 a.m. landing at Heathrow, Rayford had pushed from his mind thoughts of his family." Frykholm calls this description "an image not so subtly connected with sexuality and worldly power." The series' combination of social reactionism, an embrace of technology, and an engagement with a prognosticated global geopolitical clash is a heady cocktail, and the source of the books' widespread appeal.

Frykholm suggests that dispensationalist categories have so affected not only evangelical and fundamentalist believers but also nonbelievers, mainline believers, and politicians that they have blurred the distinction between "mainline" and "fringe," "religious" and "political." Yet the books retain the rhetoric of presumed social isolation. Their authors, Tim LaHaye and Jerry B. Jenkins, and their adherents expect to be criticized or snubbed by mainline ecclesial institutions and academic elites. Critiques like this one will undoubtedly serve to fortify their view of themselves and the world.

Frykholm also offers the beginnings of a theological critique. She notes how the books assume that the mass global conversions expected to take place during the tribulation will be of the Protestant fundamentalist sort, engineered by giant "Promise Keeper-like rallies in sports stadiums" that, the authors presume, "the entire world finds as captivating as Americans do." All of the books' Christian characters, "whether they are Middle Eastern, Greek, or from the American Midwest, speak in the idiom of American evangelicalism," a sort of "protestantese."

Frykholm asks what, precisely, these people mean by conversion, by the "accepting" of Christ at altar calls. She suggests it reflects a willingness to take on the worldview and speech of evangelicals. She wonders about Tyndale Press's claim that millions of people have been converted through these books. In conducting dozens of interviews, she has failed to find a single convert who traces her or his conversion to the books. When she asked the publisher for proof of its claim, she received copies of seven letters by writers who said they knew of someone else converted through reading. Frykholm concludes that the books are captivating only to those who already share their theological worldview, and are often repulsive to those who do not.

Frykholm's criticism of the novels is balanced by a positive portrait of the Left Behind readers. Though some might view these readers as mindless droids in a pro-apocalypse army, they actually are diverse and thoughtful people. They argue with the books, they read them for reasons at cross-purposes to those for which they were written, and they put them to interesting uses. Readers insist that the books are appealing because they make the difficult and disparate writings of scripture "come to life." Rapture fiction also connects the dots between chaotic and frightening world events, and it points toward an ultimate coherence in things.

The idea of a secret band fighting an underground war for good appeals not only to our apocalyptic instincts—as demonstrated by the popularity of *Star Wars* and *The Lord of the Rings*—but also suggests a more exciting life than most of us lead, a life full of mystery, intrigue, and moral certainty. The description of believers who physically vanish and others who, left behind, receive a special mark identifying their allegiance to good, suggests that the now invisible divide between the righteous and the wicked will be revealed. Finally, these books create community. The volumes are read, discussed, lent, and borrowed.

Rossing issues a salvo with her opening line: "The rapture is a racket." Her first paragraph is a full-blown jeremiad: "In place of healing, the rapture proclaims escape. In place of Jesus' blessing of peacemakers, the rapture voyeuristically glorifies violence and war. In place of Revelation's vision of the Lamb's vulnerable self-giving love, the rapture celebrates the lion-like wrath of the Lamb. This theology is not biblical."

The rest of her short book is devoted to demolishing the dispensationalists' reading of the Bible, and to offering a counterstory of the incarnate love of God that refuses to leave his church or his world behind. Rossing describes her opponents' view with a twist on John 3:16: "God so loved the world that he gave it World War III." Not that the true believers will be around for all the bloodshed. Those raptured away will watch the desolation of the earth from a front-row seat in heaven, enjoying the tribulation poured out on those left behind, says proponent John Hagee, founder and senior pastor of Cornerstone Church, a nondenominational charismatic megachurch in San Antonio.

Rossing sees all this as a frighteningly stark contrast to the actual message of the Bible, in which God comes to be incarnate in God's world and promises not to leave God's church. She speaks of the message of the gospel as a sort of "rapture in reverse," in which God refuses distance and comes to be present, as opposed to a world left bereft of God and church, abandoned to punishment.

Unlike Frykholm, Rossing makes no attempt to find sympathetic points of contact with the fiction or its readers. She has no problem imputing malicious motives to the Left Behind writers ("Slaughter sells books").

Most compellingly, she presents a frightening list of political statements by powerful people, demonstrating that their belief in the rapture leads them to support ugly public policies. Dick Armey, the retired House majority leader, promoted the removal of all Palestinians from their ancestral land to an unpopulated desert. Ronald Reagan's secretary of the interior, James Watt, discouraged pro-environmental legislation because of what he saw as the likelihood of the Lord's imminent return. Conservative pundit Anne Coulter recently paraphrased God's giving over of creation to human sovereignty by saying, "God said, 'Earth is yours. Take it. Rape it. It's yours.'" Oklahoma Senator James Inhofe supported the expansion of Israeli settlements in the West Bank by citing Genesis and calling the debate on the issue "not a political battle at all. It is a contest over whether or not the word of God is true."

Finally, Rossing cites a number of religious broadcasters who insist on the impossibility of avoiding Armageddon. The end is near. Resistance is futile. Why should anyone support peace in the Middle East, or anywhere else? Or environmental conservation? Rossing accuses the rapture's supporters of a kind of "sickness," a Caligula-like lust for war that rivals anything promoted by the imperial cult of Rome. "It's blood," notes Steele of the red-stained snow and burning hail falling all around him in *Soul Harvest* (number four in the Left Behind series), "and a sense of peace flooded his soul."

Rossing also dissects dispensationalists' reading of scripture and advocates a more faithful eschatology. She describes the dispensationalist interpretation of Daniel 9's "seventy weeks of years" as a schedule for the end that was interrupted by the Jews' refusal of Jesus as king. The "prophetic stopwatch" is now stuck at sixty-nine. The final week of years—the tribulation—will come when the rapture begins. Simply laying out these sorts of arguments has the effect of making their facile nature plain. An appendix to the book gives a detailed critique of the dispensationalist reading of crucial biblical passages.

Rossing praises the line often attributed to Martin Luther that if he knew the world was to end tomorrow, he would plant a tree. True eschatological insight ought to press Christians into deeper, more loving, even more mundane dealings with God's world, she argues. Rossing attempts to present a counterstory about God and his world to that told by dispensationalists, one that focuses on "Lamb power" rather than phantasmagoric fantasy, one marked by Jesus' eschatological proclamation of a kingdom of nonviolence, charity, and peace.

The strength of both books lies in their authors' lively engagement with the subject. Both Frykholm and Rossing raise a key question: To what degree can we call dispensationalism "heresy"? Frykholm suggests parallels to Gnosticism, Rossing to the Manichees. Do mainline Protestants even have heresy anymore? What would such a pronouncement from ecclesial bodies accomplish? It might just reinforce the dispensationalists' rhetoric and view of themselves as culturally isolated, even as they sell millions of books and elect powerful legislators.

Or it might force mainline pastors like me patiently to explain precisely why this view of the world conflicts with scripture and orthodox teaching in ways that lead to contorted lives and twisted church practice. It might lead us to offer a contrasting vision of a politics informed by a slain lamb whom we claim rules the cosmos, whose rule encourages us to participate in God's peacemaking between Americans and Chinese (or North Koreans), between Israelis and Palestinians, between pastors and parishioners, between liberals and conservatives, between humanity and the rest of God's creation.

Dinosaurs in the Garden

A Visit to the Creation Museum[1]

FUNDAMENTALISTS ARE OFTEN JUSTLY lampooned for being uncritical about matters of history and science. I have heard young-earth creationists haplessly respond to questions about dinosaur bones by suggesting that they were planted by the devil to test believers' faith or fabricated by scientists with an axe to grind against God. Sooner or later creationists' kids are likely to take a science class or sneak off to a natural history museum to see those reassembled dinosaur bones—and begin to wonder.

To provide "biblical" answers to the children's questions, a group called Answers in Genesis (AiG) constructed the $27 million Creation Museum in Petersburg, Kentucky (just west of the Cincinnati airport), to present its version of the unfolding of creation. Creationists can now bring their kids to their own state-of-the-art museum—with computer-generated effects and life-size displays—where they can gawk at dinosaur bones and hear about how the Tyrannosaurus fits into a literalistic biblical worldview.

These are some serious fundamentalists—"young earth" creationists who insist that creation took place in six twenty-four-hour days about six thousand years ago. To them, "old earth" creationists, who likewise reject Darwin but who argue that a "day" in Genesis could be a symbol for millions of years, are theological wimps. As for advocates of "intelligent design"—the media-savvy group that has brought its ideas to school boards and courtrooms—they aren't even worth a mention by AiG, which makes abundant references to Darwin himself at the museum in the course of doling out ammunition with which to attack him.

The first exhibit that one sees at the Creation Museum takes on Darwin on his home field: the Galapagos Islands. The variety of species of

---

1. Copyright © 2008 by *The Christian Century*. "Dinosaurs in the Garden: A Visit to the Creation Museum" by Jason Byassee is reprinted by permission from the February 12, 2008 issue of *The Christian Century*.

finches Darwin discovered in the islands was a key piece in his argument for natural selection. "Scientists are puzzled that there is such a variety of finches," the exhibit notes, and "the Bible provides an explanation." God (in Genesis) commands creatures to "multiply upon the earth." An exquisite collection of colorful birds flits and chirps about the exhibit, confirming the truth of God's word. Fossils of dragonflies, wasps, and mushrooms are also displayed to show that they haven't changed at all over the years—they look like what's in your backyard. The display on the chameleon takes a page (unattributed) from the advocates of ID, arguing that the animal's eyes are irreducibly complex and couldn't have evolved, since multiple parts would have to be fully functioning for them to work at all.

The makers of the Creation Museum have cleverly integrated staples of evolutionary theory into their own narrative. Dinosaurs are not only acknowledged but shown frolicking with Adam and Eve and the other animals in the Garden of Eden. One dinosaur is shown in remarkably lifelike form eating a pineapple (according to this narrative, there was no carnivorism until the Fall). You may have heard that dinosaurs died out some sixty-five million years ago, but really they were created with the rest of the animals in 4004 BC. Where did they go? The answer (in Genesis, of course) is: they died in the Flood.

Not all of them died, however. Noah took two of "each kind" of animal into the ark, so there were dinosaurs aboard. But the enormous geographical change brought on by the Flood destroyed most of their habitat, so most died off soon afterward.

The museum is liberally peppered with signs challenging skeptics' views of the Bible. If Cain and Abel were Adam and Eve's only sons, whom did they marry? Their sisters, we are told—and that was okay, because genetic mutations had not had time to emerge. Occasionally the museum takes an impressive midrashic approach to the text, as when Adam and Eve's slaying of animals to make skins to cover themselves is seen as a hint of the sacrifices to come to repair their sin. That could preach.

AiG cites the Flood to try to refute multiple elements of evolutionary theory. The Ice Age, for example, happened because of the enormous evaporation after the Flood. The movement of the continents likewise took place because the geological tumult of the Flood allowed landmasses to move with relative ease. The evidence? Check out the terrain around Mount St. Helens. That volcano's eruption moved seven cubic miles of sand within minutes, and cut canyons in soft rock within years. Couldn't a worldwide flood do that and more—such as move continents and cut the Grand Canyon? The Flood also explains geographical oddities—why there is sand from the Appalachian Mountains in the Grand Canyon, for example.

But how did all those animals fit inside the ark? The museum answers this question with an enormous display of a ship built to biblical specifications (the display is purported to be a fraction of the size of the actual ship). It's still not clear how a Tyrannosaurus would fit inside and leave room for the rhinos, but never mind. A computer re-creation shows the ark bobbing about above mountains. The exhibit is agnostic, however, about where the ark landed—it may or may not have been on Mount Ararat in what today is Turkey.

The Creation Museum does not merely offer grand-scale models. There is also a nod to astronomy in the form of the Stargazer's Planetarium, outside of which is displayed the planetarium projector that reportedly was used to train the Mercury astronauts in 1956. A crackly, mission-control voice reads the opening lines of Genesis, and the dome above flashes with simulated starlight.

The geocentric universe against which Galileo fought has been replaced with a gloriously vast one with no center. Our own solar system is some six billion cubic miles in size, with space for four thousand more such cubes between us and the nearest star system, Alpha Centauri. There are billions of these in our galaxy, and billions more galaxies. The presentation acknowledges that it has some explaining to do here: how could light from these faraway stars travel to us if the universe is only six thousand years old? The answer has something to do with gravitational fields.

On to the Special Effects Theater, where a film titled *Men in White* features two angels speaking to a forlorn girl gazing at the stars. She fears she'll be thought stupid if she disagrees with the theory of evolution. One problem for her is evidence for the age of the earth. "But radio isotope dating comes with a host of unproven assumptions!" the angels tell her. The girl's other problem? Dinosaurs. The Flood is again invoked, and seats rumble and water sprays as the ark bobs on the screen up front (I took two or three squirts to the face before I was able to block the spray nozzle in front of me).

The angels are shown sitting in a public school classroom presided over by a nerdy, arrogant teacher who mindlessly chants phrases like "separation of church and state." The angels respond with wisecracks and not-so-innocent questions such as, "Well, if all agree the sea is getting somewhat saltier every year, why, after billions of years, isn't the sea all salt?" The teacher is flummoxed, and returns to her formulae. "There is no God in the universe!" she exclaims. Creationists are presented as open-minded questioners and public school teachers as doctrinaire fools.

The school being mocked in this scene is named Enlightenment High School—which is ironic, since the museum manifests great trust in the Enlightenment. It is, after all, creation *science* that is presented as superior to Darwinian theory. The scientists in the videos bandy their academic credentials: "PhD in astrophysics," or "PhD in molecular biology." (Sometimes the credentials are a bit loose, as in "former trainer for Microsoft" or "former air traffic controller.") An astronomy expert explains that he draws on the same data as his secular colleagues, but arrives at different conclusions because "I start from the assumption of biblical truth and they do not."

One video, running alongside the display of a particular animal, intones, "The origin of such complexity is a mystery to scientists. But it makes perfect sense in a biblical worldview." Note that the word *mystery* is a bad word—something a foolish Darwinian would fall for—whereas the mystery is readily solved in this biblio-scientific world.

The entire enterprise is very American, calling to mind other "scientific" revolts against elitist views—on global warming, say, or the dangers of tobacco. The battle is presented as a case of free inquiry against tyrannical opponents.

As interesting as the exhibits are, its visitors are almost more so. I arrive late in the morning on a weekday expecting the museum to be relatively empty. But it's packed. A bumper sticker on an enormous passenger van in the parking lot gives me a clue: "Warning: Unsocialized Homeschoolers Aboard."

These homeschooling families tend to be large: eight children here, nine there, a dozen over there, each set of siblings accompanied by their parents. A few curious visitors walk in unawares. One asks the ticket-seller whether the museum "integrates the Bible and Darwin." The clerk replies, "It's more like the Bible *versus* Darwin" and then leads the visitor inside.

This museum must have the world's nicest volunteers. They all beam at you, eager to be helpful, trained for the occasional visitor who wants to argue about paleontology. Apparently there are church ladies by the boatload who are eager to work at the museum.

Every section of the museum ends with a presentation of the gospel and an invitation to pray the "sinner's prayer" and commit oneself to the faith. The planetarium concludes its exposition with a description of God's coming to earth and dying for us. Ditto the special-effects theater. A video midway through the tour consists only of a reading of biblical verses, set to a starry background that swooshes from the screen into the viewer's face like the opening credits of *Superman*.

The final stop is the Last Adam Theater, which tells the story of Jesus' sacrifice and concludes with another altar call. The theater is adjacent to a small chapel, where more volunteers are eager to pray with you. You may have thought you were going to get more anti-Darwinist propaganda, but actually you're getting the opportunity to be saved.

One has to admire the consistent logic of the AiG worldview. The museum takes the visitor from the dawn of time, past the pineapple-eating

Part 2: Searching for Jesus in Popular Evangelicalism

Velociraptor and a tastefully concealed Eve to a truly terrifying serpent. The next room comes at you with images of genocide, pain in childbearing, African children with swollen bellies, a mushroom cloud, a cemetery, and a black slave with a scarred back. "This room is very depressing," one woman whispered behind me. "And very honest," her friend replied. The Fall changed everything, and it explains why there is such suffering in the world.

The Tower of Babel explains the world's many religions and even explains Darwin: "All religions have followed their example, inventing myths to replace God's account of creation and Noah's flood."

The lily pads of history on which this narrative leaps are far apart. It moves from Genesis 1–11 to Jesus and then to the Reformers. Israel's calling and the first fifteen centuries of the church are hardly mentioned.

Liberal Christians turn out to play an important role in the creationists' worldview. A timeline describes the declension from the biblicism of Martin Luther and John Calvin to the thought of Descartes, Francis Bacon, Galileo, Darwin, and Charles Hodge (he may be an archconservative to most Presbyterians, but his acceptance of Darwinism lands him in the hall of shame here) to a certain Charles Templeton, who once traveled with Billy Graham but unfortunately accepted evolution and ended up writing the atheist tract *Farewell to God*.

Later we see the exterior of a church with shattered stained glass and a wrecking ball out front. The preacher inside is spouting liberal platitudes: "We know more than the Bible did about science," "We can't make an idol of scripture," and "We have to see beyond the letter to the meaning!" The parishioners squirm with boredom. A sign beside the wrecking ball quotes an official of the Church of England as saying that at current rates of membership loss, the church in the United Kingdom will be dead and buried within a generation. The message could not be clearer: if you accept anything less than the young-earth creationist view, sooner or later your church will die and you will no doubt become an atheist.

On the other hand, if you accept the biblical worldview, things might improve. Insistence on biblical science is just a first step toward renewing the church generally: "This will have a ripple effect as the church wakes up to biblical authority on any number of other issues."

Like any good museum, the Creation Museum has a gift shop near the exit. One item for sale was an enormous sculpture of St. George and the dragon. Why, I wondered, is a fundamentalist museum paying homage to a medieval Catholic legend?

I decided to head back to a part of the museum I'd skipped: the Dragon Theater. It tackles—again—the question of dinosaurs. (Someone at AiG must have listened to the pedagogues who say that no one learns except through repetition.) Why doesn't the Bible mention dinosaurs if they coexisted with humans in the time of Genesis? Well, it does. Read Job 40. The behemoth mentioned there is not an elephant or a hippo; verse 17 says, "his tail sways like a cedar." Obviously, Job is describing dinosaurs here. And though their habitat was damaged by the Flood, the sauropods that made it onto the ark managed to live, and they show up in medieval tales of battles with dragons (Job 41:21 says of the Leviathan that "flames dart from his mouth"). One expert opines that the few dinosaurs remaining after the Flood were hunted by knights seeking to prove their valor and save their damsels. Once again, the biblical worldview is confirmed, human reasoning is dethroned, and the altar call is repeated.

Clearly, the museum's creationists are not unintelligent people. They take knowledge that their fundy forebears mocked—about dinosaurs, the Ice Age, and so on—and weave it into their biblical worldview. Their intellectual gymnastics are impressive to watch. And these are fundies with funds: $27 million buys some nice limestone, pyrotechnics, and a botanical garden with a Loch Ness Monster look-alike protruding from the lake.

How does young-earth creationism make sense to intelligent, well-meaning people? Well, much of any religion appears counterfactual. After all, preachers in liberal churches proclaim that a Jewish peasant executed by an empire is the God who rules the cosmos, and that we should love our enemies and that the poor are blessed. If you can believe that stuff, you can believe a lot.

But AiG's worldview is impossible to sustain. The *Men in White* angels lampoon the science class's view of evolution, calling it the "goo to you" approach because they want to speak of humans as souls made in the image of God. They ignore the fact that—as the process of human reproduction suggests—humans do begin as goo and in a sense remain goo. That is, they remain part of the animal world even as they reflect the image of God. In its horror at the evolutionists' claim that humans are animals, AiG forgets that for much of Christian history, theologians heartily agreed that humans are animals—"dependent rational animals" is how Aquinas described us.

A further theological problem for AiG is that it seems to think that the move away from its "biblical worldview" explains all wars and suffering—as if the Fall has to do with the loss of a worldview, not the human condition of sin.

Reconciling Christian claims about God, creation, and humanity with the findings of Darwin and his successors is an important and daunting task, one that mainline theology has still not satisfactorily accomplished. AiG can hardly be faulted for attempting the task, though its effort is a spectacular failure.

Jeremiah Wright, Evangelicals' Brother in Christ[1]

Go ahead and disagree with Obama's pastor. But remember: He's family.

REPORTER: "HOW OFTEN DOES Obama go to church?"
Wright: "About as often as you do."

There was truth in Wright's outing of Obama as a less-than-regular churchgoer. This is no surprise: Ask the other two candidates for proof of their Sunday attendance and you'll see what I mean. Celebrities in general and politicians in particular might have a better (if still theologically poor) excuse than many of us for not worshiping corporately.

When I visited Trinity to cover the then-young controversy over Africentric theology in early 2007, I was craning my neck, looking for Obama, who I'd read was in town. The man beside me asked what I was doing. "I kind of thought he'd be here," I said. He answered, "To tell you the truth, he isn't here much." I was probably part of the reason celebrityism and church attendance don't go well together: we were looking around for the famous guy when we should have been looking for Jesus.

Jeremiah Wright goes to church looking for Jesus. And that's why evangelicals should pay attention to him. This is not to say they should agree with him. But Jeremiah Wright is a serious Christian. He didn't have to be—many gifted black intellectuals have gotten off the bus with the church for having been, as it inarguably has, a slave religion. (Wright has argued with Muslim friends that Islam's track record is no better on slavery.) Even within the young tradition of Africentric theology, birthed by James Cone at Union Seminary

---

1. Copyright © 2008 by *Christianity Today*. "Jeremiah Wright, Evangelicals' Brother in Christ" by Jason Byassee is reprinted by permission from the May 2008 (Web-only) issue of *Christianity Today*.

Jeremiah Wright, Evangelicals' Brother in Christ

in the late 1960s, former theologians have left Jesus behind in their effort to embrace the wider black diaspora worldwide. Cone himself worries that exclusive attention to Jesus yields something he calls "Christofascism," by which he seems to mean exclusivity. His brilliant student Dwight Hopkins, a leader at Trinity, also seems to think the Christian church too narrow an allegiance, and wants black folks generally to ally over race rather than religion. (Wright has repeatedly endorsed Cone and Hopkins, yet he doesn't use language like "Christofascism"—this is one of the things you should ask him about). In conversation with his teacher, Cone, and the most distinguished theologian at his church in Dwight Hopkins, Wright is staking his claim solely on Jesus—respectfully, of course, in dialogue with Islam and black nationalist thought, but he's standing on the promises of *this* God. (It's worth noting that the rest of the black church is not so enamored with Cone's theology.)

Therefore charity requires that evangelicals do business with Wright. He, like them, is part of the body of Christ. Not less than John Hagee or Rod Parsley—extremist ministers aligned with John McCain—Wright's churchmanship means he is more brother than enemy. One of the rhetorical missteps Wright has made is to say an attack on him is an attack on the black church, and to imply that a rejection of his theology makes one *ipso facto* a racist. This is simply untrue. If you disagree, go ahead—part of the reason we're so bad at talking about race in this country is we're all afraid to offend, so we leave it to the screamers on cable. Let Wright know what you think.

But expect him to give as good as he gets. He's been at this a while. He has scratched and clawed for stronger schools, better support from the city, and, above all, church growth on the far South Side of Chicago. He has taught that blacks should be proud of their heritage and never ashamed—and that they should do theology as subjects rather than objects. He's summoned altar calls and prayed for healing (there is a subterranean charismatic ministry at Trinity) and led the people's praise of Jesus for more then three decades. He has things to teach us. And, as ever in the church, he has points that could stand rebutting. But let's keep those points in perspective. Wright's break with America is no unforgivable sin—only blasphemy of the Holy Spirit cannot be forgiven.

Wright's recent media tour was so unfortunate. It would have caused him no harm to wait to travel and speak until January 21, 2009. But of course, on that day, the audience would not have been near as large or as attentive. He got the cameras and front pages because of his parishioner running for president. He knew full well that appearing in public would hurt Obama—he'd been warned, begged, pleaded with not to do it. (The week before, a friend in the campaign told me, "They're freaking out up at HQ—Wright's going on tour, and they can't do a thing to stop it.") Wright was throwing Obama, a parishioner and former friend, under the bus—and he knew it.

But coming from a community that's been told for so long what they're allowed to say and not say has an impact on you. Precisely when you're told to shut up, you preach. At the top of your lungs. For you've got a fire locked up in your bones.

Evangelicals, I think, know something about that.

The Almost Formerly Important

Lessons of the Old Mainline for the New Mainline[1]

ON HIS *DAILY SHOW* one evening, Jon Stewart compared the importance of his home region in presidential elections with that of his guest, Newt Gingrich. "I'm from the Northeast," he said. "We used to be important."

Let me play Stewart to *Christianity Today*'s Gingrich: "I'm a mainline Protestant. We used to be important." Though we Methodists boasted allegiance from three of the four members of the ballot in 2004's presidential election, this seems to have been more a cultural accretion than anything else. The one whose faith mattered—President Bush—has made a career out of his fluency in speaking evangelicals' language. The Republican Party has courted evangelicals long enough and well enough to have almost an insurmountable majority in Congress and, soon, in the Supreme Court as well. Congratulations, evangelicals: You're in charge.

We mainliners had our day in the sun. Remember Prohibition? It was more than an opportunity for cool gangster outfits and Kevin Costner's best movie. The national banning of alcohol by constitutional amendment was a result of Methodist efforts to "spread scriptural holiness over the land." Oddly familiar, isn't it? Groups like the Woman's Christian Temperance Union, led by the great Methodist social prophet Frances Willard, prayed, raised money, and badgered politicians to get their way. The Temperance Union was the forerunner of the cute old ladies of the United Methodist Women (UMW) who, in a church I pastored, often gathered to bake and gossip and pray.

We did then what you do now: We imposed our way on a divided populace by sheer force of electoral muscle and religious rhetoric. Our effort to take America for Christ is now a peculiar cultural artifact, a curiosity

---

1. Copyright © 2006 by *Christianity Today*. "The Almost Formerly Important: Lessons of the Old Mainline for the New Mainline" by Jason Byassee is reprinted by permission from the March 2006 issue of *Christianity Today*.

gathering dust on the shelf of early twentieth-century history. We built triumphant monuments to our importance. At the Metropolitan Memorial United Methodist Church in Washington, DC, a prime, front-pew seat features a plaque marking where the president of the United States should sit when he attends—not unlike churches in Constantinople that once featured imperial boxes for the emperor to ride his chariot into without having to dismount. But Caesar's seat goes empty these days, even with a Methodist President.

This is not to denigrate monuments from a more triumphant age of mainline Protestantism—many such places still do fine ministry. But church influence on politics is fickle. "Give to Caesar what is Caesar's, and to God what is God's," our Lord says. The last people in the world who want to be caught dead pledging allegiance to the wrong Lord ought to be evangelicals.

I expect you'll amen this general warning, but let the preacher step on a few toes. I understand why you support the war on terror, for instance—to defeat evildoers, to spread democracy. But remember that a just war in the Christian tradition, according to many theologians, requires penance by its wagers—not celebration. Christians ought to be the most eager repenters around.

I know you are used to being a persecuted minority, but isn't it time to drop the inferiority complex, rule graciously, and love your enemies, even if they are liberal? I know politics makes strange bedfellows, but do you really want to be allied with foulmouthed know-it-alls on AM radio or with politicians who don't care a lick about Jesus?

C. S. Lewis's Screwtape advised his nephew Wormwood, "Once you have made the world an end and faith a means, you have almost won your man, and it makes very little difference what kind of worldly end he is pursuing. Provided that meetings, pamphlets, policies, movements, causes, and crusades matter more to him than prayers and sacraments and charity, he is ours." We mainliners were once offered the deal you have now—social action in exchange for faithfulness—and we bit hard. We're so far out of political power now that we're remembering the first task of the church is to be the church, not to play chaplain to a political party or nation. It's tempting to trade fidelity for influence, but it's hard to get fidelity back, and influence doesn't satisfy.

These dire warnings aside, enjoy your time at the top. "The grass withers and the flowers fall, but the word of our God stands forever," Scripture says. Political power is a good deal more transient than the things we both hold most dear. When the powers that be are done with you, we mainline liberals will have a rocking chair for you at the retirement home of the formerly religiously important. Maybe then we can finally see each other as sisters and brothers.

Part 3

Searching for Jesus in the Church in Africa

ONE GIFT OF GETTING to work at Duke Divinity School from 2008 to 2011 was a chance to travel and see some of the church's work in East Africa. Duke has partnerships in Uganda and Sudan and was interested in developing new ones in Kenya, where I also traveled. I'd long been interested in testing the theses of Philip Jenkins, Dana Roberts, Andrew Walls, and others that the future for Christianity will take place in the Southern Hemisphere, especially Africa. These pieces are snapshots of what I saw there.

I'm glad these trips coincided with my work at Leadership Education at Duke Divinity on transformational leadership and vibrant institutions. I learned from Duke's now former Dean Greg Jones what I later saw with my own eyes: African Christians have astonishingly faithful and creative people in leadership. What they lack are vibrant, trustworthy institutions. Here in the West we have the luxury of lampooning and dismissing and attacking institutions. In Africa, where they lack reliable hospitals, universities, governments, denominations, etc., they have no such luxury. Individuals, however faithful and creative, can only do so much. Institutions—that is, the efforts of communities toward a goal over time—can do so much more.

Upon visiting in person, I found some of the cheerleading about a future for Christianity in Africa to be excessive. Not that the church wasn't breathtakingly impressive. It's just much less triumphalistic about itself than Westerners tend to be on its behalf. One priest in Uganda told me that if

Part 3: Searching for Jesus in the Church in Africa

Westerners wanted their aid money to reach the villages and not just the palaces of the capital, they should give it to the church. He said this making clear that he was *not* saying the church was without corruption. It has plenty. It just has less than the government! Clearly, standard church/state divisions to which we're accustomed in the West don't quite apply in East Africa. Nor do theological fault lines. As Stanley Hauerwas told me upon my return from Uganda, if he lived in Africa he'd be a Constantinian.

There is a similarity in these portraits of leaders in the church in Africa. They're scrappy, inventive, funny. They're also often poor, dependent on Western help, which their personal connections and interpersonal skills help them procure. At the church in Uganda where they hang the banner that reads, "Welcome to our American visitors" (notice the lack of specificity), one American told me the Ugandans call the summer "the American visiting season." "It's like a bird migration," she said. Sure enough—and are such short-term mission trips doing more harm than good?

Yet meeting people like Joseph Taban Lasuba (who appears in every Sudan piece—he was a student at Duke and then principal of New Bishop Gwynne Theological College until his death, terribly young, in 2013—makes me wonder: are we really so "privileged" in the Northern Hemisphere and the Western world? Or is our wealth in fact an albatross around our neck, something that keeps us from becoming who God wishes us to be? Is the poorer church in Africa truly blessed right now, not in some eschatological future?

I also traveled to Africa interested in hearing about stories of the miraculous that take place there more often than in North America. What do we make of stories of healings, of exorcisms, of miraculous deliverance from violence, and of the growth of the church? I found that the more I heard such stories, the more I believed them. Not because I saw any miracle personally. Or, better said, maybe I did: in a place where the church has been squeezed by tyrants—African and Arab and English—it has grown numerically and in wisdom and as a servant to its people. Perhaps there *is* a future for Christianity, perhaps it's African, and while that's only an ambiguous good (what good is *not* in this time of sighing?), it is a good indeed.

Perilous Presence

Christians in Uganda[1]

"You can't understand Africa without understanding religion," said Emmanuel Katongole, a Catholic priest from Uganda. As he led a tour of Kampala, Uganda's capital, it was soon clear what he meant. Slogans such as "Jesus cares" and "Try Jesus" adorn taxicabs. Ads for a Catholic bank named Centenary print the letter *t* as a cross. Businesses have such names as "Holy Light Clinic," "Born Again Bankers," and "Holy Hair Care." "There is no Western-style division between secular and sacred or public and private here," Katongole said.

But the infusion of religion into everyday life has not made Uganda a peaceful land. "We have a culture in Uganda of taking power by the point of a gun," said Archbishop John Baptist Odama. The archbishop's see, based in the town of Gulu in the north of the country, has been the scene of a vicious civil war for the past twenty-two years. The Lord's Resistance Army (LRA), led by Joseph Kony, has waged an antigovernment insurgency, savagely attacking rural villages and abducting children, who are turned into soldiers or sex slaves. An estimated twenty-five to thirty thousand children have been kidnapped over the years.

Uganda's president, Yoweri Museveni, himself took power at the point of a gun in 1986 after leading an uprising in the west of the country. The battle between Museveni's National Resistance Movement and the then-government army, made up largely of Acholi people from the north, left some three hundred thousand dead. After Museveni came to power, northerners were left with no jobs but plenty of military training, resentment, and time on their hands. They were ripe to be recruited for Kony's army.

---

1. Copyright © 2009 by *The Christianity Century*. "Perilous Presence: Christians in Uganda" by Jason Byassee is reprinted by permission from the February 10, 2009 issue of *The Christian Century*.

Part 3: Searching for Jesus in the Church in Africa

Museveni has run a relatively stable government in the southern region he controls. He is a wily politician who switched the focus of the nation's fight against AIDS from condoms to abstinence when Bush took power, and who made Uganda part of the "coalition of the willing" in the U.S. war in Iraq.

Katongole, who now teaches at Notre Dame after a tenure at Duke, stressed that the failure of political and economic systems to serve the country's people has left a vacuum that the church tries to fill. "What works is the church—not only for religion but for water, education, health care," he said. Father Sebastian, a priest in Kampala, put it more forthrightly: "Only money from the church gets to the people. Westerners should really give to the church, not to our government."

A stunning case of the church stepping in to fill the void occurred in the north, where for years tens of thousands of Acholi children would leave their villages in the evening to walk to the town of Gulu to avoid being kidnapped by Kony's forces. Townspeople in relatively wealthy Gulu called the children "ants," since they were constantly underfoot. (These children came to the world's attention through the 2005 documentary film *Invisible Children*.) Archbishop Odama helped organize a walk of solidarity with the night-walking children. He gathered the Orthodox and Anglican bishops and the Muslim imam in Gulu to walk with him and to sleep on the street with the children. One parishioner brought a mattress for the cassocked archbishop. "Give it to the children," he said. When another worried about his safety, he said, "My security is linked with that of my people." Gulu Walk (guluwalk.com) has organized solidarity walks around the world.

Archbishop Odama helped broker a fragile peace between Kony's LRA and the Ugandan government, an act that opened him to charges of disloyalty from both sides. When an indignant government official questioned whether he was too close to the rebels, Odama replied, "For the sake of peace I will go into the bush." When the rebels accused him of being a government agent, he said, "I am also your bishop." Then he delivered the same message to both government and insurgent leaders: "Like two elephants you are walking on us."

Religious defiance of government authority has a venerable history in Uganda. People treasure the story of how in 1886, forty-five Ugandan Christians—twenty-three Anglicans and twenty-two Catholics—were martyred at the hands of the king, Kabaka Mwanga. The Christians were pages in the king's court. After they resisted the king's sexual advances, the furious Mwanga, who already believed that Christians were a threat to his kingdom, demanded that the pages pledge their allegiance to him, not to Christ. Those who defied their earthly sovereign were speared, and some were dismembered while still alive. Most were burned slowly, feet first, to give them a chance to recant. They sang hymns until they died.

On the marytrs' feast day, June 3, a million or more pilgrims travel to the Martyrs' Shrine at Namugongo. Many of the dozens of Catholics I met were named for martyrs, as are many of the country's institutions. In the chapel of a Catholic retreat center I saw a stained-glass window portraying martyr Charles Lwanga. The archbishop of Kampala is named Lwanga. Part of the martyred Lwanga's story is that he died just after baptizing a teenage boy named Kizito—and many schools today are named St. Kizito's.

Among the Christians working with the destitute are the Good Samaritan Sisters, an order founded in the wake of Idi Amin's brutal regime. One of the leaders recruited by the order is Sister Mathias Murumba, who heads the Santa Maria Goretti school for girls in Mukono. "You train one girl, you train the nation. Even these men here came from women," she said, her boundless energy and ease of laughter drawing laughter in response.

The students come from harsh backgrounds, and many of them have been abused. Many are AIDS orphans, and some have AIDS themselves. Sister Mathias boasts that all of her graduates get jobs. She investigates the workplaces to be sure that the girls will not be further mistreated. They are trained in sewing, secretarial work, agriculture, hospitality, English, catering, manicure and pedicure, and computer work. More important, they are helped to grow in confidence. "We can start our own business after this," one girl said.

The seventy-six girls at Santa Maria Goretti are the lucky ones. Scholarships pay their $200-per-trimester fee. When asked how she pays her teachers and maintains the building, Sister Mathias said, "I beg." When asked whether the archdiocese supports her, she turned and punched a priest beside her on the arm—which I took to be her way of saying no.

The group I traveled with to Uganda had started a small organization called Share the Blessings, which supports the installation of wells in rural villages in Uganda at a cost of $1,500 apiece. It has also paid to rehabilitate the crumbling village school that Katongole once attended. Everywhere we went, Ugandans were very welcoming—they raised banners, brought out drums and dancers, gave speeches and banquets. But I noticed one such banner that said simply, "Welcome to our American friends"—nothing specific about our group. "They raise it during the American visiting season," one veteran U.S. traveler explained.

When we went to christen a new well that Share the Blessings had built in one rural village, children with distended bellies, bulging eyes, and torn clothes appeared to pump their first clean water. The parents of these malnourished kids presented us with sugarcane, eggs, corn, and a live chicken—generous gifts in gratitude for something that cost a North American church rather little.

At St. Kizito's school outside Luwero were hundreds of bright-eyed, hopeful students. Yet the school's computer lab had no Internet connection and only one terminal. Its library had no books for borrowing, only ones for sale—at a price no student could afford. As the principal addressed the children, he pointed to Katongole and visitors from North America and insisted, "If you work hard and trust God, you can be successful." He repeatedly mentioned the one graduate who the year before was admitted to Makerere University to study to be a veterinarian—leaving unsaid that dozens of others have no such opportunity. Government scholarships are available in Uganda, but most are procured through bribes. An intern in Luwero, Meghan Good, told me of a graduate named Gonzaga with immense intellectual talent who is doing manual labor around the school while supporting a sibling's family. "He has no way to pay for more school," she said. She added, "The prosperity gospel isn't heresy here. It's more like trust."

The influence of charismatic Christianity is obvious in Ugandan Catholicism. Every Catholic church we visited offered "healing masses," in which parishioners can come forward not only for the Eucharist but also for the laying on of hands. Many claim dramatic healings. This is not surprising in a country where public health services hardly exist and hospitals serve only the paying customer.

"The biggest problem in Ugandan Catholicism is that we're losing people to the Pentecostals," Sister Mathias told me. "And if we have healing masses they come back." Healing masses can last four or five hours or more. Worshipers play drums and wave their hands during mass; they clap at the elevation of the host—the point in the mass at which bells once rang in European masses. "That's all from the charismatics," one priest told me. "They've influenced all of us."

A group of hyper-Catholic laypeople called the Marians presses both for greater piety and for charismatic expression: they kneel to receive the host, publish a monthly magazine promoting their goals, and worry the hierarchy. "The bishops try to resist their excesses," Father Sebastian told me. Any hint that one mass is better than another, that one priest has more gifts to offer, is contrary to ancient Catholic thought, yet it persists. "Since I'm not charismatic I'm looked down on," Sebastian explained.

When I expressed skepticism about the effectiveness of charismatic healing, I was told to go see Father Gabriel Mpamibwe. "So how did you come to have the gift of healing?" I asked the white-cassocked priest, whom I'd just seen dancing with the students as part of the welcoming event for our group. "Well, I was dead for seven hours," he said. How does a skeptical Westerner respond to that?

Father Gabriel told me the story of how a hole in his liver had led to his experience with death. He was wrapped in a shroud and about to be put in a casket when he sat up, spit the cotton out of his nose and mouth and asked to be untied. There was no Jesus to order someone to unbind him: the witnesses all ran away. "Since then I've had the gift of healing," he said. He has traveled to Britain and India to practice his trade. He is the chief evangelist for the diocese—with a clear charge to win back Pentecostals. He is also the diocese's chief exorcist. "Demons hate the name of Jesus," he said.

When I asked Father Gabriel how he differs from the Pentecostals, he said he doesn't ask for money up front as a condition for healing. If you do that, he said, it's "a business, not a ministry." If someone wants to give a gift afterward, that's fine with him. He finds that those with doubts are those he most often helps—which contradicts the usual Pentecostal claim that one must believe to be healed. "It can't be hard work. If you have to strain, it's your work, not God's." He tries to avoid talk of offering a special ministry: "The church is always charismatic, she can't do without the Spirit. But the church is renewing herself now."

Father Gabriel has a calm, joyful manner. The gleam in his eye makes you want to believe him. But Father Sebastian expressed his incredulity. "These people are our fanatics," he said. And, he contends, money is changing hands in these services: "Father knows what to say to suggest a gift, even if he doesn't demand it first."

A more undeniable personal charism is that of peacemaking. Todd Whitmore, a Christian ethicist at Notre Dame, is on the hunt for it in the north of Uganda. "Christian ethicists in North America talk a lot about war, but most have never seen one. And they talk a lot about social location, but they do so from the library." Whitmore was influenced by what he learned at the Kroc Institute for International Peace Studies, and it inspired him to live in the IDP (internally displaced people) camps in the north of Uganda, where he learned the Acholi language, gathered people's stories and, as he put it, "saw what real Christianity looks like." "The church never left northern Uganda" even when Ugandans of means and NGOs did. Seventy-eight Catholic catechists have lost their lives in the twenty-two years of fighting.

Whitmore found the most practically helpful people in the IDP camps to be the most apocalyptically oriented. "I call them reasonable apocalypticists," he said, and wondered if their outlook would shift with the coming of peace. In a war zone, they believe, no human effort could be relied upon for help—only God could intervene. In the United States people who talk that way are often accused of being mentally unstable. But

Part 3: Searching for Jesus in the Church in Africa

in the IDP camps, "They were among the most rational. They'd ask, 'How do we cooperate with the NGOs?' Or 'We want to help with orphans.'" The Bible was written to people in crisis with promises of an intervening God; perhaps it is best read there.

This combination of a providential God and personal piety can be seen in the work of one extraordinary Ugandan woman. In 1996, Mama Angelina Atyan's daughter Charlotte was kidnapped by the LRA from a Catholic boarding school, along with 138 other students. A determined nun followed the LRA into the bush and browbeat their commander, forcing him to return all but thirty of the students. But Charlotte was not among those who returned. "We cried for weeks," Angelina said of the abduction of her daughter, then fourteen years old. "Then we asked ourselves, 'Will we only cry?'"

Mama Angelina and mothers of other abducted children began the Concerned Parents' Association (CPA) to advocate for their loved ones and badger policymakers to resolve the conflict. Mama Angelina eventually spoke to the United Nations about her cause, which was championed by Hillary Clinton, among others.

President Museveni launched military ventures that promised to crush the rebels, but Mama Angelina, with a daughter in that rebel army, hardly wanted to see Charlotte crushed. CPA members would fast on Saturdays for the return of their children, and while praying during such a fast, Mama Angelina focused on the words, "Forgive us our trespasses." She realized that she hadn't forgiven the ones who had so grievously trespassed against her.

"God wants us to be practical Christians," she said. She sought to forgive her child's abductors. She visited Joseph Kony's mother and offered her forgiveness to a woman whose child was surely as lost as her own. "The magnitude of one another's pain binds us together," she explained. She claims to have unconditionally forgiven an unrepentant Kony himself.

One night during Charlotte's seventh year of captivity, Angelina prayed and reminded God that in scripture the seventh year is the year of liberation. "Have you forgotten or changed? My daughter is not one but a great multitude."

That same night, Charlotte, now the mother of two children by an LRA commander, had a dream in which she was set free. "Today you will see your people," she heard a voice say. The next day, when the column of abducted child soldiers and wives was marching, Charlotte heard a voice tell her, "Go left"—when the LRA went right. Obeying, she walked away, unnoticed by her captors. She was reunited with her mother, and her children are now with her. For Charlotte, however, the joy is incomplete: part of her is with the people who are still captives in the bush with Kony.

Amid the violence of Uganda, Christians are practicing forgiveness, reaching out to abused children, caring for the sick, and seeking miraculous healings. Christianity is only one hundred years old in Uganda, but perhaps, Katongole muses, the Ugandan church is now "at the height of our fervor. We may be at our peak."

Holy Space in Uganda[1]

THE MOST INTERESTING CHAPTER in Dana Robert's beautiful new book *Christian Mission: How Christianity Became a World Religion*[2] describes the relatively recent cult around the feast day of Bernard Mizeki, a Mozambican missionary and martyr who evangelized the Shona people of southern Africa in the nineteenth century. For some time, white Anglicans observed his June 18th feast day with English reserve. And then, amidst the rejection of colonialism, the observance became Africanized, Bernard a symbol of indigenous African Christianity. Gatherings of hundreds at the place where he died became gatherings of hundreds of thousands, where "the mountainside is alive with worship to God." Some aspects of this long weekend celebration are alarming, as with any (humanly) unplanned new movement of the Spirit. For example, some pilgrims seeking healing, already being frail, will likely die during the feast. When this happens it is said that Bernard's spirit takes one person with him in revenge for his martyrdom! Such excess enthusiasm is to be expected alongside vast multilingual communion services, healings, exorcisms, theatrical reenactments of his life, and more.

One might take this enthusiasm to be typical of "African religion"—with the sort of sneer Westerners once reserved for animists and Muslims. But with Africa as Christianity's future (as Robert and others prophesy), and such respectful treatments of its layered sophistication as hers, what more faithful thing can we say about such observances of the faith as the cult of Mizeki?

On a recent trip to Uganda I discovered a dramatically different Anglican way of observing revered founding missionaries: in almost total silence. And I saw a very different Roman Catholic way of remembering the same missionary founders. Could Africa's greatest gift to the church catholic

---

1. Copyright © 2009 by *Books & Culture*. "Holy Space in Uganda" by Jason Byassee is reprinted by permission from the July/August 2009 issue of *Books & Culture*.

2. Dana Lee Robert, *Christian Mission: How Christianity Became a World Religion* (Malden, MA: Wiley-Blackwell, 2009).

through time and space be the blurring of such lines as these ("Catholic" and "Protestant") in a new conflagration of the Spirit?

We all know why Catholics and Protestants have different conceptions of holy space. The Reformers rightly worried that if an object or material space could hold holiness like a ziplock holds water, then people would revere bones, statues, and cathedrals instead of Jesus. Catholics have always responded that material things are blessed since God became matter in Christ and that it is not inappropriate to reverence the church, the Eucharist, and the saints in continuity with this fleshy God. Both sides have strong cases.

Last summer I asked (the obviously Catholic) Cardinal Emmanuel Wamala, archbishop emeritus of Kampala, whether the Methodists were growing in his country. He said, "If it is a religion, it is growing in Uganda." Around 80 percent of Uganda's thirty million people are Christian, with about one-third each belonging to Rome and the Anglican Communion.

The foundational story in Ugandan Catholicism is that of the Uganda martyrs. In the mid-1880s, Catholic and Anglican missionaries from France and England were finding some success among the pages who served at the court of the Kabaka, the king of Buganda (that kingdom is still the most powerful of several kingdoms that make up the modern republic of Uganda). A previous Kabaka had been open to Christianity, if a bit confused as to why the English mission agency and the French White Fathers couldn't get along. But his son, Mwanga I, listened to traditionalist religious leaders and Muslims who warned that the Christians just wanted his throne. Did not his pages pray that some *other* kingdom would come? The Kabaka expected his pages, like sycophants (politics is always politics), to cheer him when he returned from a hunt. Once when they failed to do so, he was enraged to learn they were at the missions. The pages who converted also began resisting the king's sexual advances. Finally Mwanga was alerted that a new mission was approaching from the east. Unfortunately for the Anglican missionary and bishop James Hannington, Bugandan legend said a usurper would come from that direction. Once Bishop Hannington was dispatched, the Kabaka's Catholic prime minister, Joseph Mukasa, defiantly told the king he was wrong to kill the bishop. At last the Kabaka demanded that the Christians in his court choose him or Jesus. Forty-five of them, about evenly divided between Catholic and Anglican, chose the King of kings over the King of Buganda, and paid with their lives: by torture and then slow burning—feet first, to give them a chance to recant. They sang praises to God instead.

The story is important in both Anglican and Catholic communions in Uganda. But Catholics do a bit more to show it. Actually a lot more. Most of the Catholics we met were named for a Ugandan martyr (Ugandans choose their children's surnames in addition to their first names, so they have more

Part 3: Searching for Jesus in the Church in Africa

names to dole out). Countless institutions like schools, shops, and of course churches are named for Saints Kizito, Mukasa, Lwanga, Mathias Murumba, and more. The story appears in Catholic stained glass and painting from the greatest to the most humble churches. And the Feast of the Uganda Martyrs is celebrated every year on June 3, with some one million people from all over Africa attending. Dozens of bishops attend and co-preside. These gather near Buganda's Calvary, Namugongo—once Buganda's place of execution. An outdoor pavilion has been built for the throng around the pond where the executioners used to wash after their gruesome work. Pilgrims now bottle that water, once mixed with the blood of martyrs, to drink and bathe in.

The Catholics have built a magnificent shrine at Namugongo. It is shaped like a traditional Bugandan hut, with twenty-two pillars reaching to the heavens, symbolizing the twenty-two Catholic martyrs. If from the outside it looks unfortunately like an enormous lunar module, on the inside it looks like heaven, with oceans of dark mahogany. The altar is built over the spot where one Charles Lwanga died, and his bones and ashes are visible if you kneel down low enough (not a bad posture for any Christian). A photo on the wall shows Pope Paul VI kneeling to kiss the spot, as millions have since his visit. "Two hundred and thirty popes came and went before one visited Africa," a tour guide told us, explaining the continent's love for the pope who canonized the Uganda martyrs. A number of nuns seem to spend all their time at the shrine, like Simeon and Anna in the temple, awaiting their savior.

To say the Anglican shrine was a letdown would be a vast understatement. The Anglicans had *no* commemorative structure until the announcement of Paul VI's upcoming visit in the late 1960s. So they built a historic reconstruction of the event. Statues of martyrs bound in reeds lie in a hut, as though about to be burned. In another corner of the yard sits a re-creation of the executioner's hut. A plaque says a certain tree grows in the spot where a previous tree stood that had been a site of torture before the martyrdoms. Another commemorates Paul's visit. Other plaques teach of famous conversions: the executioner of the Uganda martyrs and eventually the kings of Buganda who succeeded Mwanga.

The church in the place was in pitiful shape. The cross above the steeple was crooked. Windows in plastic, not stained glass, were shattered. Pews were arranged haphazardly. Chickens and dogs wandered the yard. No tour guide was even present when we arrived, so we showed ourselves in. Even if one wanted to kneel or pray, there is no place to do so. This is Protestantism to the nth degree: historical re-creation, stories of famous conversions, and no provision to hallow ground or bones.

Things were little better at the magnificent Anglican cathedral of Namirembe, one of the grandest ecclesial structures in East Africa. I went in and asked to see the tombs of Bishop Hannington and of his successor and fellow martyr-bishop Janani Luwum, killed for standing up to the dictator Idi Amin. In a beautiful gesture, he was originally buried beside Hannington—one Episcopal opponent to tyrants at rest by another.

The receptionist at the cathedral glared in response to my question. "Luwum has been moved. Hannington is out back." I went looking for the cemetery and found it in disarray. Vines grew over stones. The grass was not cut. There was far more mud to traverse than sidewalk. I couldn't find the man whose last words were, "Tell the king I die for Uganda." I almost gave up, till I saw his stone off to the side, out of view, with nothing to distinguish it from any of the other graves. At least his last words were etched there. Perhaps the dying words explain the lack of reverence: they can be interpreted a bit too messianically for Protestant taste.

Anglicans have long claimed that their church occupies a middle ground between Protestant and Catholic, with elements of each. To my mind, why be Anglican at all if not to worship with smells and bells—and, among some Anglo-Catholics, with Latin and bones? But the Church Mission Society that evangelized East Africa was as low church as one can be, and that heritage persists in Ugandan Anglicanism.

Ugandan Anglicans are right to be wary of pagan elements in drinking holy water and kissing bones. Catholics themselves have pastoral admonitions they'll make against moments of excess, even if they don't heed them as often as we might like. It would be hard to argue against money going to evangelism or feeding Uganda's legions in poverty. But I felt deprived of a place to pray at Hannington's grave, a kneeler at the Anglican Uganda martyrs shrine, maybe even a place to touch reminding me of the quite physical death of the martyrs in imitation of Christ.

The glory of the story of the Uganda martyrs is that it is so deeply ecumenical. It is as important in Ugandan culture as the Virgin of Guadalupe is in Mexican culture, yet it is so much more approachable than La Virgen for Protestant sensibilities. We might be able to understand or sympathize with Guadalupe, at best. But I actually fell in love with the story of the Uganda martyrs. I can see why one would name a child, a church, a school after them.

If you have a story like that of the Uganda martyrs, why not make *some* space, both literally and figuratively, for others to love the story and ask for the grace to imitate it? Zimbabwean Anglicans have done so in spades—setting aside an entire mountain with which to remember what God has done in Bernard Mizeki. Perhaps we in today's West, for not the last time, have something to learn here from African Christians.

How the Church Grew in South Sudan[1]

"They shall all be left to the birds of prey of the mountains and to the animals of the earth. . . . At that time gifts will be brought to the Lord of hosts from a people tall and smooth . . . whose land the rivers divide, to Mount Zion."

(ISAIAH 18:6–7)

ON MY RECENT SOJOURN in southern Sudan, I learned that in the view of the Christians of the Episcopal Church of Sudan (ECS), Isaiah 18's description of the sufferings of a people "tall and smooth" refer to them. (Manute Bol, the late Sudanese professional basketball player, was seven feet, seven inches tall.) Suffering came to the people of southern Sudan when President Omar al-Bashir in the predominantly Arab-Muslim north sought to impose Islamic Shari'a law—an effort that sparked a southern uprising and years of civil war. Isaiah's reference to the "gifts brought to the Lord" is taken by the Sudanese churchpeople to mean the mass Christianization of the south; in the midst of civil war the ECS grew from a fledgling missionary enterprise to a church of five million (that's twice as many Episcopalians as there are in the United States).

From one vantage point this interpretation of Isaiah can seem arbitrary. Fundamentalists in the United States, for example, sometimes argue that the "land of whirring wings" in Isaiah 18 refers to Apache helicopters and therefore to coming events in the United States. But looked at another way, the Sudanese Christians' explanation of the passage may be true historically; Ellen Davis of Duke Divinity School says that the Dinka (or Jieng) people of southern Sudan likely were the southernmost Africans known to the Israelites. The

---

1. Copyright © 2010 by *The Christian Century*. "How the Church Grew in South Sudan" by Jason Byassee is reprinted by permission from the December 3, 2010 issue of *The Christian Century*.

Sudanese interpretation also places the south's Christians in the midst of a biblical drama with a cruciform shape of suffering and redemption.

Philip Jenkins has argued that Christianity's future is an African one. If so, what does the area that is poised to become Africa's newest independent nation tell us about Christianity's future?

The people of Sudan have lived with war virtually from the time of independence from Egypt and Britain in 1956 until the signing of a Comprehensive Peace Agreement in 2005. (There was a period of relative peace from the early 1970s to the early 1980s.) President al-Bashir and his predecessors in Khartoum have pursued a policy of Arabization—including the imposition of Shari'a—in an effort to unify their massive and unruly country. Revolting against these policies, the south sparked a civil war that has left some two million southerners dead since 1983. The growth of the Sudanese church amid the conflict is remarkable indeed. (The International Criminal Court has charged al-Bashir with war crimes, crimes against humanity, and genocide.)

When foreign missionaries were expelled from Sudan in 1964, they left feeling that their efforts had been wasted. They had made few inroads into the cattle-based culture with its polygamous households and indigenous animist religions. Missionaries had tried to draw converts away from a practice of cattle sacrifice to the jak (local gods) and introduce them to Western-style education, literacy, and worship. Their approach eventually worked—but only by accident, as it turned out.

During the decades of civil war, many southerners sought refuge in Khartoum, Cairo, Beirut, and other Arab metropolises. They found themselves isolated from their traditional land and their herds. Western-style institutions for education and worship strengthened ties among southern Sudanese during this time of exile, and embracing Christianity became a way to reject both enforced Arabization and English colonialism. When these exiles returned to their land, they swelled the ranks of the churches. The diocese of Bor, for example, had only four parishes and four priests in the early 1980s; a decade later it numbered 230 parishes and 120 priests. The charismatic bishop Nathaniel Garang of the Bor diocese is reported to have confirmed ten thousand people in a single day.

So unlike the situation of churches in the West, Sudan has the problem of catching up with church growth that has spun out of control. ECS bishop Ezekiel Diing of the diocese of Twic East compared church growth in Sudan to the parable of the sower. "The seed," he said to me, "was thrown and reached everybody. Now we have to prepare ministers after the fact, and work more carefully to sustain the church from generation to generation."

Part 3: Searching for Jesus in the Church in Africa

The church hopes that New Bishop Gwynne College (NBGC) in Juba—the leading Anglican college of the five in Sudan—will be a foundation for a future university in Juba, the south's regional capital. There are signs of strength: the college is building a new and improved campus, it has dedicated students and a stable faculty, and enrollment is up this semester. But to call its facilities humble would be generous. The electrical power works only occasionally, as does the plumbing. The bathing stalls are outdoors. Students live in rooms designed to be faculty offices. Interim administrator Trevor Stubbs told me that the school loses money on every student enrolled. Students pay 750 Sudanese pounds (about $500) per term, yet in return they expect room, board, health care, and spending money—the result being a net loss for NBGC. And squatters are an impediment to the progress being made with building construction.

Other Episcopal colleges in Sudan are in worse shape. One of them relies on donors for more than 90 percent of its income. Another holds classes near a trash dump that reeks and poses health hazards. When a wealthy American donor was late with her contribution, one school had to borrow money from its own diocese just to function. In the mid-nineteenth century, missionaries talked about the need for an indigenous church independent of foreign donors. Such a church is still pretty much a pipe dream.

Despite its financial woes, the church is primed to play a key role in what the people of the south hope will soon be the new country of Southern Sudan. A referendum on independence is scheduled for January, and the anticipation of the birth of a new nation is palpable. But many fear that mutual hatred of the north is all that's holding the tribes of the south together and that once their mutual enemy is out of the picture, ancient tribal enmity may take over among the Dinka, the Nuer, and other ethnic groups. And although the situation in southern Sudan is relatively calm now, whether the referendum is actually held may depend in part on whether the conflict in western Sudan's Darfur region is resolved. Fierce fighting continues there despite the 2005 peace agreement, with more than three hundred thousand killed and almost three million driven from their homes.

The church could be the glue that holds a newly independent south together. Indeed, church and state seem as fused in southern Sudan as they were under Emperor Constantine. I heard priests and bishops extol the south's liberation from northern tyranny with biblical references, from "Let my people go" to the star of Bethlehem—which is on the flag of "New Sudan," as some southerners call their gestating country. When I complimented one church leader on his vehicle, I was told it came courtesy of the south's government. Political leaders occupied the front row of both church services I attended, and at the service at Juba's Emmanuel Parish, one of them was given worship time to deliver an impassioned political speech. NBGC professor Simon Lual Bang, preaching at Juba's All Saints' Cathedral one day, argued that the country would be better off if the politicians were less corrupt. Some politicians were sitting in the front row there too, but they only laughed and nodded.

More worrying is the widespread uncritical praise of the government of southern Sudan and of the Sudan People's Liberation Army, which fought for southern independence. SPLA leader John Garang is spoken of as a martyr, as are the two million war dead. "The SPLA soldiers are the greatest rebels in the world," one priest cheerily told me as we watched the army on parade. But Garang was hardly a holy man; the SPLA's human rights record is far from pristine; and much of the killing was the result of intertribal violence and internecine warfare within the SPLA.

I heard stories about pastors on the take from the government in Khartoum as secret agents, about others causing schism or enriching themselves from church coffers, and about a bishop who is not even living in his own diocese and so is failing to carry out what he was consecrated to do.

Despite the economic and political challenges facing the ECS, the level of theological discussion I observed was remarkably high for church leaders who have little formal training. In one such discussion, someone asked why God would allow Christian Sudanese to suffer so. A young man who was eager to attend seminary suggested that it was because the Sudanese didn't listen to the missionaries who first preached to them. But others disagreed. Simon Lual argued that tribes like the Dinka have often trusted in the power of war. "God doesn't curse people" but rather gives humans freedom and lets sin be its own punishment.

Bishop Diing weighed in, citing Jeremiah as an argument that God punishes like a parent who rebukes her children. A priest named Joseph Taban Lasuba objected to the notion that God is punishing Sudan for anything at all. "The Bible says all fall short and sin. Looking around, there are more wicked nations than ours that go unpunished. Aren't we rather victims and not only sinners?" Others pointed out that in a time of peace and greater prosperity, the churches aren't as full as they were during the war. They wondered whether adversity might be a strange sort of gift.

The ability of the Sudanese to see their own lives in light of the Bible often makes for breathtaking exegesis, such as their reading of Isaiah's reference to a people "tall and smooth." The Sudanese also sometimes see their leaders in the shadow of biblical history. Bishop Elinana Ngalamu, the first indigenous ECS archbishop, was buried behind the cathedral in Juba—but only after being exhumed from his first burial site in Khartoum. "It's like

Joseph in the Bible," Joseph Taban told me. "We won't even leave our leaders' bones behind in the north" (Josh 24:32).

Several church leaders insisted that when they and their people were on the run from government soldiers, they were miraculously spared injury from snakes and wild animals—just as the psalmist and Mark 16 promised that believers would be. Bishop Hilary Adebe of Yei comes from a diocese that experienced its own exodus. In the mid-1990s, when SPLA leaders forced Yei's people to leave, the Episcopal bishop and his Catholic counterpart gathered thousands of people and walked with them into temporary exile. Not surprisingly, there was much suffering from disease and anguish as a consequence of the displacement. But church leaders insisted, "Don't worry, God is in control, and the war is going to end."

"This enabled growth in miraculous terms," says Bishop Hilary (as Adebe is called), "and when people came back, the church was already there," waiting for them (unlike the foreign-based NGOs who left and didn't return).

Archbishop Daniel Deng Bul Yak, the primate of the ECS, told me that his favorite book of the Bible is Leviticus. In fact, Leviticus has had such appeal for people in southern Sudan that European missionaries often refused to translate it. What need would there be for people to convert to Jesus if they felt they had found all they needed in the Old Testament?

Ellen Davis says she once mentioned on a visit to Sudan the common taboo against eating a cow that has been dishonorably killed—for example, by being gored—and her Sudanese listeners shuddered with disgust. They understand and appreciate the letter of Leviticus law much more than Westerners do.

"It's a lively book to us," the archbishop said, "because it shows the movement of God with our people. God was leading and teaching us. We were practicing without a book." In other words, in many ways the Sudanese were living biblically before the missionaries came; they just didn't know it.

Archbishop Daniel weaves his traditional culture and his people's newer, Christian culture together in a remarkably seamless whole. Writers Marc Nikkel and Andrew Wheeler have pointed out that Sudanese ancestral faiths always entailed a most high god, Nyaleech, to whom people turned only in their greatest need and to whom access was limited. They dealt more often with lower, more accessible gods (the jak). Christian leaders called these lower gods demons and named Nyaleech the Father of Jesus Christ. The faith of the Dinka people in particular took off once indigenous church leaders began to take up biblical themes relating to the exorcism of demons.

Andrew Walls, a historian of missions, discusses how non-Westerners have adopted Christianity in their own way, bringing to the rest of the church their culturally specific stories even as they make the stories of the

Bible and Western Christianity their own. I saw an example of this process when Bishop Hilary Deng of Malakal explained that he decided to stay in Sudan during the civil war after reading Dietrich Bonhoeffer. "I discovered Bonhoeffer, who remained during the persecution of the Nazis. Whenever we hear of Bonhoeffer now, God uses him to speak to people." The bishop returned from study in Germany to Sudan to be with his people, despite multiple arrests and threats on his and his family's life.

The longer I was in Sudan the more the miraculous nature of the people's tales of resistance to imperialism and of the advance of the Christian faith seemed plausible. In 2009, for example, the Ugandan rebels in the Lord's Resistance Army were operating in southern Sudan. Ten thousand refugees suddenly flooded into the town of Mundri, doubling its population. Townspeople and refugees alike gathered at the cathedral, and the church agreed to take the refugees in, with each Mundri family making room for a refugee family under its roof. Tribe did not matter: all were fed and housed for seven days, until United Nations relief began arriving. "Why are you doing this?" the guests asked. Because God wants us to, was the reply. "How will we all survive?" The Lord will provide.

When Bishop Daniel arrived in the Diocese of Renk, he saw that the town had a Muslim school on almost every corner and feared that his mission was doomed. "My church is trying to kill me," he said. He was arrested on his first day at his new post. Later, government soldiers commandeered the town's Catholic school to turn it into a barracks. But the Christian townspeople wouldn't stand for the closing of the school. They surrounded the soldiers, then pushed their way into the school and staged a sit-in, singing hymns and daring the soldiers to shoot. One commander was ready to open fire. But some southern Sudanese soldiers in his unit who had been drafted into the national army refused to fire on civilians.

After hearing these and other stories of courage in the name of the faith of the southern Sudanese, I thought of Tertullian's dictum, "The blood of the martyrs is the seed of the church." In some cases Tertullian's teaching is simply wrong. Persecution can choke off the church's life. The designation of martyrdom can be slippery. In southern Sudan some of the killing involved southerner fighting southerner. And some deaths didn't lead to growth, only to death.

Yet Tertullian's claim cannot be ignored where Sudan is concerned. And if the hospitality and faithfulness that I witnessed can continue throughout southern Sudan, then something even bigger than independence will be happening there.

Surprises in Sudan
Reading the Bible with Southern Sudanese Christians[1]

EARLIER THIS WEEK, PRESIDENT Barack Obama announced that the United States would renew economic sanctions against Sudan for another year. In part, the decision stems from Sudan's support for Islamist terrorists, but it also reflects the crisis in Darfur, wracked by genocide. In the perception of most Americans, wherever they are located on the political spectrum, the situation in Sudan is nothing but an ongoing disaster. But this is not the perception of Southern Sudanese Christians, as I discovered when I visited their country this summer. We Americans are rarely accused of modesty in our claims about God's action in our affairs of state. Yet after my visit to Southern Sudan, American civil religion now seems to me almost reticent. Consider this praise chorus:

> For I'm building a people of power
> and I'm making a people of praise,
> that will move through Sudan by my Spirit,
> and will glorify my precious name.

I've sung many similar songs here in the United States, but not one has mentioned America by name.

Southern Sudanese might be forgiven for thinking God is up to something new in their midst. The semi-autonomous country of some eight and a half million souls emerged from a savage half-century on-again, off-again civil war having experienced remarkable growth in the church. Western missionaries were expelled in 1964 and left disappointed. They should have waited for a few more decades. The most recent bout of war, from 1983 to 2005, left some

---

1. Copyright © 2010 by *Books & Culture*. "Surprises in Sudan: Reading the Bible with Southern Sudanese Christians" by Jason Byassee is reprinted by permission from the November/December 2010 issue of *Books & Culture*.

Surprises in Sudan

two million dead, and five million in membership of the Episcopal Church of Sudan (ECS). Package that in your next "how to grow your church" bestseller: 1) resist the imperial claims of your own Shari'a-imposing government, 2) endure genocidal bombings of villages, 3) have millions of refugees suffer thousand-mile walks (including the famous lost boys), and 4) emerge with a church twice the size of the Episcopal Church in the United States. That's not even counting millions of Catholics. "Khartoum tried to swallow the South," Bishop Hilary Garang Deng of the ECS told me. "But Christianity was like a bone, stuck in the throat, causing it to vomit."

I came to Sudan for a leadership and bible conference of bishops and heads of theological colleges, led by Old Testament scholar Ellen Davis of Duke Divinity School. I had never been in a country that was trying to get born. The air was electric. And I could hardly escape a conversation without the January 9, 2011 referendum coming up. Right now, this expectant country feels like a giant delivery room. Bright-eyed people speak in hushed, eager voices, anticipating their freedom. Southerners are not naïve to the fact that the child could be stillborn. They knew Omar al-Bashir was a genocidaire long before the International Criminal Court indicted the president for crimes in Darfur. They know he covets the oil under the south's sand as much as they do. Yet the southerners I spoke with have a "bring it on" bravado about them, exemplified in Bishop Hilary's comment. They know there could be war again, but they beat Bashir before without tanks and missiles, and without international attention and personnel.

The area around the South's capital of Juba, where I was this summer, didn't feel like a place preparing for war. Busy backhoes and road-paving equipment suggested that this is a time of relative peace, funded by the oil revenue coming in from the Comprehensive Peace Agreement signed in 2005. Southern Sudan is a place preparing for freedom. I heard an entire sermon in All Saints' Cathedral on the theological significance of the upcoming referendum. "On January 9, we will be like the Israelites marching to freedom," the preacher promised, perhaps innocently enough. What oppressed people informed by the Bible have *not* drawn on the exodus? Even the banners flying near the grave of the martyred (by their definition) leader of Southern Sudan, John Garang, proclaim, "Let my people go!" It's inspiring in one way; in another, it's pretty thin theology. All anyone would have to do to draw on this theme is rent a certain Disney movie. When I mentioned this exodus theme to friends in Kenya later, they sighed in memory of a simpler time. Kenyans used similar rhetoric during their fight for independence from Britain in the 1960s.

But the preacher went on: "God put into motion his plan to free Southern Sudan from the North. . . . [A]s we walk into freedom in January

Part 3: Searching for Jesus in the Church in Africa

2011, we recall that the plan for freedom is God's; yours is to be obedient." A visiting bishop provided the benediction: "Lord, as we look forward to that great day" (you know where he's headed by now: *not* toward Jesus' return and the eschaton), "bless us all as we prepare to vote." I lost count of the ingenious acts of biblical interpretation that found this upcoming vote in the Scriptures: Abraham and Lot wisely separated after their conflict. Moses grew up in Pharaoh's house and then departed with his people. An ECS priest named Joseph Taban Lasuba pointed out to me how often in Scripture Israel's enemies appear from one direction. You guessed it: the North.

This may all seem pretty extraneous to the Scriptures themselves, on par with American fundamentalists reading Isaiah 18 as prophecy of the United States suffering and returning to God (those whirring locusts *must* be helicopters). The Sudanese I met, in fact, interpret Isaiah 18 to be about themselves. Who else are the people "tall and smooth," who live "in the land the rivers divide" (that is, the two branches of the Nile), of whom Isaiah speaks? Ellen Davis, with whom I traveled, agrees that this passage is probably a reference to the Dinka people of Southern Sudan, likely the most distant tribe of whom the Israelites knew. Even the people at the edge of the earth would suffer and bring their gifts to Zion's God. And the raised "signal" referred to in verse 3? What could it be but the flag of independence the South will raise sometime after (you guessed it) January 9, 2011. What could be clearer? "That's an impressive piece of Sudanese political exegesis!" Davis said, with an enthusiasm that belies the scholarly, objective distance of her actual words. The Sudanese see themselves in the Scriptures, and unlike, say, Americans who see Apache helicopters there, they have a shot at actually telling the truth.

Sudanese Christians taught me to be more pugilistic in my faith. It took what was for me a harrowing experience to see this. There was a parade celebrating "Martyrs' Day" while I was there, commemorating the mysterious plane crash that killed Garang and his companions a month after the signing of the CPA. The Sudanese People's Liberation Army (SPLA), once a freedom-fighting bush militia and now more a state army, marched in the streets, interrupting our worship. So we went to watch, and I, being the tourist, pulled out my camera to snap pictures. A tall (they don't have short people) commander marched over to me, stuck his hand through the iron bars of the cathedral compound, and barked at me, demanding my camera. I slunk behind my tall (what else?) friends of the ECS in their collars and purple shirts and watched with some astonishment as they barked right back at the soldier, waving their arms exaggeratedly, commanding the commander to be gone. I learned later that in Arab militaries, in which some SPLA trained, those who take photos are assumed to be spies—and are dealt with accordingly. What amazed me was the chest-thumping insolence with which the pastors treated the soldiers, as though to say, "Can't you see he's with us? Now buzz off!"

Later, I participated in an interview with the archbishop of Sudan, with the impossibly wonderful title of the Most Reverend Doctor Archbishop Daniel Deng Bul Yak. He told us of his response to ethnic fighting in Jonglei state earlier this year. He and his entourage loaded themselves into three vehicles and headed toward the conflict. In Jonglei they came upon a bush fighter waiting in ambush, who saw only the first and third car and readied to shoot. Then the second car jumped over the hill and startled him, leaving him dazed—a semi-miraculous deliverance. The archbishop later learned that those soldiers meant to kill anyone who came down that road. So Archbishop Daniel arrived and met the Dinka and Nuer, "And I cursed them. If you don't leave this fighting God will curse you, you will die, your selves and your clan and your family." As I said, pugilistic. And perhaps the perfect tonic not only for Southern Sudanese intertribal fighting, but for the sickly sweet versions of faith we drink so deeply here in North America.

Yet the ECS leaders whom I met are against their people only in order to be for them. Their church has a certain statesmanlike posture about it. When the Reverend Joseph Taban Lasuba, who teaches at New Bishop Gwynne Theological College, got over his incredulity that I *had* indeed photographed the parading soldiers ("You did *what*?" he asked, with a look that said, "Silly American"), he used it as a teaching opportunity on the future of what southerners often call "the New Sudan." "It will take education. These same guys are in church Sundays. But the church hasn't really shaped their imagination yet," he said. Then he paused. "They can do their thing for now. But we'll get them on Sundays." Archbishop Daniel's pugnacity against the warring tribes comes from awareness that intertribal violence could scuttle an independent Southern Sudan before it's weaned. Not a few of those two million "martyrs" died from such internecine warfare; Bashir could use chaos as a pretext for invasion. The ECS is as much a state church as there can still be in the world anymore, and that has both strengths and weaknesses. Taban told me that when his bishop heard that Garang died, "He collapsed, and could not speak for four hours." Taban himself, then dean of the cathedral in Khartoum, took to the pulpit and read the book of Joshua. The cathedral in Juba erected a marble stand on its grounds for Garang to lie in state. When the fledgling government of Southern Sudan recently decided not to pray before its parliamentary meetings, the church erupted. The archbishop's arguments led the way, reported to me by Taban: "We advocated for you in war, raised awareness internationally, now there's peace and you don't need the church?"

Part 3: Searching for Jesus in the Church in Africa

The danger of such a posture, of course, is that it can tip into fawning over the government. As soon as the church has access to the plush carpets and whispering huddles of power, it tends to do whatever it takes to stay there and to forget about a certain crucified Jew who is its reason for existence. One hedge against this danger in the ECS is its vision of reconciliation. "Everyone else here in Southern Sudan is peddling revenge," according to Robin Denney, a missionary from the Episcopal Church (USA) teaching sustainable agriculture in the country. "Only the church can tie people together after independence."

This posture of conciliation is clearest in the church's talk about Islam. There is every reason to disdain the sons of Ishmael in a place where the imposition of Shari'a law was the ostensible purpose for Khartoum's violent hand. Bishop Hilary Garang Deng of Malakal said from the pulpit of Juba's cathedral that he was often tempted to hate Muslims. After all, he'd been chased with his family to a refugee camp where the brackish water they drank to survive gave little relief from the heat or thirst. "Yet I learned that Muslims and Christians are like Jacob and Esau, descended from the same family." "It's not all Muslims that are the problem," another priest told me. "Just their politicians." Again, imagine the competing rhetorics about Islam in a place where the dead number seven figures. Perhaps the best comment on religious reconciliation came, again, from Taban. "I feel I am a missionary of peace among Muslims," he said. "Both Muslims and Christians suffered under the North's brutality. But only Christians have a mandate to forgive. All Muslims can do is get angry." Taban sees his role now as one of evangelism, and perhaps even beyond Sudan. For he speaks Arabic, as do many educated southerners. What would it mean if God were preparing to use Southern Sudanese to evangelize the very people whose faith once brutalized them?[2]

Finally, Sudanese Christians taught me how to *see* politics anew. I've already mentioned the theological readings of the upcoming election. If the vote is held as scheduled and conducted fairly (big if's: no one should trust an indicted genocidaire like Bashir—and no one in Sudan does), the vote will go overwhelmingly for independence. But is this a good thing? Bishop Hilary is not so sure. "Perhaps God will unite Sudan in a miraculous way we can't imagine. The gospel is moving now in the Nuba Mountains, the Blue Nile, Darfur, and even among extremists where it wasn't before." What will happen to the two to three million southern refugees now living in the North if the South is independent? (The ECS itself plans to stay united,

---

2. I cannot think of Joseph Taban Lasuba's death without weeping. He led New Bishop Gwynne College with brilliance for years after my visit and then died of cancer in a Kenyan hospital in 2013, leaving behind his wife Esperanza and their children. Blessed in the sight of the Lord is the death of his holy ones.

Part 3: Searching for Jesus in the Church in Africa

whatever happens politically.) Bishop Hilary speaks in the eschatological tones—and with the impish and mischievous smile—of a man who has seen miracles before. Who would have thought there would be peace after fifty years of war? (Or, from an American vantage, that it would have been the administration of George W. Bush that brought it about? Or that the administration of an African-descended president might be letting it slip away?) Could God unite Sudan finally under evangelical rule where Shari'a failed before? Whether the bishop is right or not, shouldn't a bishop's job be that of reminding Christians that God could work in a way that both astounds and, upon reflection, matches the mightiest ways God has worked in the past?

A future of miraculous evangelism can't be brought about by human force, of course. The church in Sudan knows that in its bones. Pugilism does not mean violence. It does mean statesmanship, and acting on behalf of all the people, not just one tribe or religion. And it means offering a vision of reconciliation, and a reading of history and current events as part of the unfolding of God's intentionality.

All that said, who's to say the bishop's wrong?

The Muse of Church Revival in Sudan[1]

I THINK I MET the Charles Wesley of the church of Sudan.

Just as Charles' hymns powered the Methodist movement across the British Isles, the Americas, and now the Global South, so too did Mary Alueel Garang's songs power a revival in the Episcopal Church of Sudan (ECS), helping bring in millions of members during that country's brutal two-decades-long civil war. "I just found myself singing," she explained when asked how she wrote so much and so movingly. If songs come to her, she writes them down, "if they are meaningful." She herself describes their themes this way: "During the war there was suffering, we ran from place to place, but we encouraged people not to give up and to come to church. You can't save your life on your own."

One can hear her songs' power even in translation from Jieng (often called Dinka by outsiders) to English:

> Let us give thanks.
> Let us give thanks to the Lord in the day of devastation,
> and in the day of contentment.
> Jesus has bound the world round with the pure light of the
> word of his Father.
> When we beseech the Lord and unite our hearts and have hope,
> then the demons have no power.
> God has not forgotten us.
> Evil is departing and holiness is advancing;
> these are the things that shake the earth.

I went to Sudan with one question at the forefront of my mind: How did a church battered and on the run "in the bush," as they say, hiding from government soldiers and bombers, grow like the ECS did? When I asked

---

1. This essay was first published on September 22, 2010, as post to *Call & Response*, a blog on the Web site of *Faith & Leadership*, the online magazine of Leadership Education at Duke University.

The Muse of Church Revival in Sudan

the Sudanese, they gave me some answers I expected: Tertullian was right ("the blood of the martyrs is the seed of the church"), there are no atheists in the bush, indigenous Christianity was a way to resist Arab and European colonialism. But they also gave me an answer I did not expect: the singing.

I caught a glimpse of the impact of song on the ECS at a Jieng parish called Emmanuel in Juba. This service, in a former movie theater, had easily one thousand people inside and as many people out. And most of the worship was singing, without hymnbooks, songs that went on for ten, fifteen, twenty minutes (a people until recently without literacy still have long memories). They were Mary Alueel's songs mostly, telling of God's faithfulness as people were on the run and of hope for a new and glorious day in Sudan. They are the people's songs, intersected with God's song, and as they sang from memory and swayed, I gave thanks for the songs and their composer.

Mary herself is an unassuming woman, quiet, hard to coax into talking about herself. She talks more easily about her new work as director of a church and development office in charge of gender equity. She tries to convince parents to send their daughters to school, and—not surprisingly, for those who've met her—she has been successful: "I tell them educated girls can still get married, they can bring a bigger dowry, they can help with in-laws and build houses for their old age." She reported that the girls in Bor, a key diocese in the ECS, are all in school now.

Mary has been in school as well, studying theology in Kenya for five years, as much as any leader I met in the ECS. This is a great advance, for while the ECS has not been opposed to ordaining women in principle, there simply aren't many who are ordained (I met none). In that setting Mary stands out as a sort of mother of the church, one whose songs joined with the Spirit's power to lure a people to freedom in Christ.

Mary says she hasn't written songs for years. She sounds like she misses it though: "When I write them I feel free." The songwriting was a gift from God: she had studied no theology at the time, and she herself had only recently converted. Yet God gave her a song.

"I don't know why a song works. But when I have a problem, or a happiness, I continue singing. All days are the same to God."

Why Haven't They Left?

Stability in the Church of Sudan[1]

BEFORE VISITING SUDAN, I was surprised that I had never heard that the Anglican Church in that country had been tempted to join its sister provinces in Nigeria and Rwanda in absenting themselves from the Anglican Communion over Western churches' perceived openness toward gays and lesbians. The members and leaders of the Episcopal Church of Sudan (ECS) whom I met, sure enough, seemed unhappy, even angry, that the Episcopal Church in the USA would consecrate gay and lesbian bishops, and that Archbishop of Canterbury Rowan Williams wouldn't do more to sanction the American church.

So to paraphrase the title of Marc Nikkel's great book on the church in Sudan, why haven't they left?

For one, the ECS is not in a position to shed friends. While they've been blessed with almost miraculous growth in church membership, they now have concomitant "big church" problems. How do they raise up and train enough leadership for a church twice the size of that in the United States? None of the priests I met is paid a salary; the bishops in the ECS are only paid because of support from Western churches. Yet young people still line up out the door to enroll in seminary (which they can't afford either) to enter a profession where they'll make no pay. Now, how exactly could the ECS afford to put off its various partnerships with Western churches, however "liberal"?

The ECS leaders I met are incredibly savvy about money. They want to accept Western help without having to accept everything their Western brethren believe. They also accept money from their own Southern

---

1. This essay was first published on October 13, 2010, as post to *Call & Response*, a blog on the Web site of *Faith & Leadership*, the online magazine of Leadership Education at Duke University.

Sudanese government—some bishops have cars, some leaders have traveled abroad courtesy of the government of Southern Sudan. Archbishop Daniel Deng Bul Yak mentioned this in passing in a recent sermon. "If someone wants to give you a car, let them give you a car," he reportedly said, "but don't let them buy your vote." The church of the poor in Sudan has no choice but to be as wise as serpents and innocent as doves.

The last paragraph may sound like partnerships with Western churches are only about money. They are about money, but they are bigger than that. Christians I spoke to remember with immense gratitude the visits paid to Sudan by Pope John Paul II and by Williams' predecessor, Archbishop George Carey. Both helped bring attention to the plight of Southern Sudanese persecuted by their northern government. Anglicans also remember Bishop David Stancliffe of Salisbury who visited the South at the height of the civil war. Such partnerships helped mobilize world opinion in favor of the South and brought pressure to bear on Khartoum, resulting in the 2005 peace agreement.

Sudanese are a people who remember. Missionaries who first carried Christian faith to Africa are not always remembered fondly in the West, to put it mildly. This puts African Christians in an odd position. Dana Robert writes of a speech to the faculty of Boston University by Ambassador Gertrude Ibengwe Mongella. Then the highest female political officeholder in Africa, Mongella praised the missionaries who founded the school that educated her in Tanzania. "Why are Americans not focusing on founding schools and hospitals like they used to?" she asked a presumably squirming audience. Likewise, we would never have heard of Nelson Mandela were it not for the Methodists in his village who educated him.

So too in Sudan. Among the most animated prayers I heard there was that of a professor at New Bishop Gwynne Theological College named David Kamandala, who gave thanks to God for a missionary named Kenneth Fraser: "He went thirty-five years without the comforts of children, and gave his life for the salvation of Sudan. And now his children are the bishops and priests who remember his name." The people of Scotland may not now be proud of the missionary doctor who once left their shores for Southern Sudan, but the Sudanese remember and give thanks.

This brings us back to the Sudanese and their unwillingness to leave the Anglican Communion. By temperament these are not people inclined to leave behind the ties that bind them. The Shar'ia law–imposing government in Khartoum tried to get Southerners to leave their faith for the better part of half a century—by bombing villages, denying food to non-Muslims, killing leaders, and destroying institutions—and Southern Sudanese Christians did not leave their church then.

Why would they leave now?

University Presidents in the Congo
How to Stop a War[1]

"When there is war, business and governments rush in. Why should the church rush out?"

DAVID KASALI IS PRESIDENT of the Bilingual University of the Congo (more commonly known by its French initials UCBC), located in Beni, North Kivu province in the Democratic Republic of the Congo. We spoke during Duke's Center for Reconciliation's Summer Institute, where he was a faculty member. UCBC is only two years old and already has hundreds of students working away not just for professional accreditation, but to be Christ-shaped leaders in a country that's seen too few of them.

I'd asked Kasali not only about his vision for the fledgling university, but also why he'd left his previous post to start it. He'd spent nine years as president of Nairobi Evangelical Graduate School of Theology (NEGST), one of the strongest postgraduate schools in all of Africa. On one hand, it made sense that as a native Congolese, he'd want to contribute to rebuilding his country after its decades-long civil war in which five million died. But on the other, wasn't this a very risky project? Couldn't he give everything to start a new university and then watch it vanish overnight in a new outbreak of fighting? His response was the quote that opened this essay.

Notice our differing instincts. Mine: Institutions need a stable social order to survive. His: Unstable social orders can be made more stable with the presence of institutions. I wouldn't bet against UCBC or its energetic

---

1. This essay was first published on August 10, 2010, as post to *Call & Response*, a blog on the Web site of *Faith & Leadership*, the online magazine of Leadership Education at Duke University.

and charismatic president. By the end of our conversation he was trying to convince me to spend some time guest teaching in the school's journalism program.

Another university president who was also at the summer institute, Katho Bungishabaku, talked about the founding of his recently renamed school, Shalom University. At one time it was Bunia Theological Seminary, located in a town that had been decimated by the war. About fifty thousand residents died in the fighting and 98 percent of the remaining population had fled. Among those who stayed were children from both warring tribes, many of whom sought shelter in the seminary. As one tribe grew stronger, the school would take in the children of the other.

It just so happened that the two rebel armies were arrayed against one another with the school in between. And one rebel commander said, "I will not fight. We would destroy that school, which has saved our children." The other commander also said, "I will not fight. We would destroy that school, which has saved our children." Over thirteen hundred children were saved as a result of the seminary's willingness to offer them shelter, and the school changed its name to reflect Jesus' gift of peace in which it was privileged to participate.

Bungishabaku has an impish grin that suggests a willingness to bring about holy mischief. Looking around at Duke Divinity School's beautiful Westbrook building, where the summer institute was being held, he said Duke and similar schools don't really need new buildings. But schools like Shalom do. As if sensing he should shift the venue in order to needle us further, he mentioned a school in the United States he had recently visited where a $250 million fund-raising campaign had just been successfully completed. "Just give us 1 percent of that," he said. "That's all I'll say."

I'm struck that in the West, the one thing all Christians—whether evangelical, liberal, Catholic or whatever else—seem to agree on is that institutions are bad. That works because we've all had experiences in which we've seen individuals ground down. But it also works because we have strong institutions in this country. It's easy for us to take them for granted, so we run them down habitually and fail to thank God for the gifts they bear to us.

In the DRC they have no such luxury. This is a country the size of Western Europe with all of fifty miles of paved roads. Neither Bilingual University nor Shalom University is far from rebel armies still in the field. Neither is safe from further violence. Yet both offer hope for peace in the claim that a new generation of Congolese leaders is going to train as hard to build up society as others are to tear it down.

And whatever else Christians in the DRC might disdain, I'm betting strong, life-giving institutions are not among them.

Leadership as Dancing the Dance of All Your People[1]

SOMETIMES IN THE CHRISTIAN journey you meet someone who makes you think the whole thing might be true: the Father, the Son, the Holy Spirit, the world God loves and the church through which he is saving it.

I met such a person recently: Paride Taban, a retired Catholic bishop from Torit in the south of Sudan.[2] Taban was at Duke Divinity School's Center for Reconciliation, speaking at the center's Teaching Communities Week event. Since Taban's "retirement" as a bishop, he has founded the Holy Trinity Peace Village in Kuron, in a remote area near the border with Ethiopia. The goal was to have a village without tribalism. Not that all tribes are bad: Taban speaks of his own tribe disliking having a gun in a hut. The presence of a gun brings the rebuke, "You have brought death in the house." He speaks of another tribe, the Ik, in which members hold their nose if a quarrel breaks out. The Ik deal in honey rather than cattle, since no tribe raids another for bees.

The primary problem with tribalism in Sudan is conflict between the Muslim and Arab and often Sharia-imposing north, and the Christian and animist south, which, unfortunately, has oil under its sand. The north is unlikely ever to let that rich resource go. Hopes for peace on geo-political terms look absurd. But Holy Trinity Peace Village is a sign that the church and the world may have reason to hope.

The peace village was inspired partly by the sawmill village in which Taban grew up. It was a new village, founded by British colonizers, with

---

1. This essay was first published on January 20, 2010, as a post to *Call & Response*, a blog on the Web site of *Faith & Leadership*, the online magazine of Leadership Education at Duke University.

2. For more about Taban's life and ministry, see "Paride Taban: Voice of the Voiceless," a 2009 interview with him in *Faith & Leadership*. Online: http://www.faithandleadership.com/multimedia/paride-taban-voice-the-voiceless.

Leadership as Dancing the Dance of All Your People

workers brought in from all tribes. So the place knew no tribalism (colonialism brought other problems, to be sure). It had a chapel, not a church or a mosque, and the children prayed with whoever led services: "Catholic, Anglican, Muslim, didn't matter," Taban said. This is remarkable, especially in a country in which the Muslim north has launched a civil war, resisted by the Southern People's Liberation Army's (SPLA) state-like army in the south, that has left two million largely Christian southerners dead.

The most moving story for me from the Teaching Communities Week was told by a seminary student named Joseph Taban (no relation). He attended the bishop's enthronement even though he is Anglican. He watched as the bishop danced the tribal dance of each of the tribes in his parish. A new tribe would rise to dance in welcome and celebration and the bishop would dance with them. "I saw you," Joseph said. "Even though I was Anglican, I didn't care, I went. And I still have the pictures."

What an image for leadership. Dancing the dance of your people—all of them. Going to them even if it means putting your own life at risk. Building a village to model a life of abundance and peace, even in the middle of nowhere. And being able, through it all, to poke fun at yourself.

That's not just an inspiration to lead. It's an inspiration to believe, not just in God, but in the human beings with whom God is so unendingly patient.

Part 4

Searching for Jesus among Roman Catholics

I FIRST GOT INTERESTED in Roman Catholic thought and practice by reading a collection of meditations by then-pope John Paul II. I was surprised how much I loved the book, until he quoted a priest friend of his on his deathbed, prognosticating, "If the victory comes, it will be through the Virgin." I closed the book and almost threw it away, and then I was mad at myself for being mad. What else did I expect from a pope?

The biggest change in Christianity in the last half-century, bar none, is the shift in attitudes between Catholics and Protestants. We haven't even begun to catch up with the significance of this shift. We evangelicals used to speak of the Roman Catholic Church as the whore of Babylon, the antichrist, or at best, just one more form of paganism from which millions of unfortunates need immediate rescuing. I don't even pretend to know what Catholics used to say about Protestants, but it couldn't have been much nicer (see the end of my piece on the Latin Mass for a glimpse). Then Vatican II happened. The dean of Duke Divinity School participated as an observer and came back with the earth-shaking (and curriculum-changing) observation that Catholics are, indeed, Christians. George Lindbeck of Yale was at the Council as well, and postliberal theology ever since has been marked by a love for the church catholic (small c—across denominations) and Catholic, headed at Rome, in love with the saints and the Mother of God and the bonds of community across the bonds of death. For more conservative

Part 4: Searching for Jesus among Roman Catholics

Protestants this rapprochement came because of John Paul II himself. Many figured that someone that courageous in the face of the culture of death, with all its various faces, couldn't be all bad. Nowadays it's hard to drum up much enthusiasm for denouncing the people on the other side of the Tiber. And that's a great reason to rejoice over the body of Christ.

Not that it doesn't dredge up new problems. With the cultural accrual of thoughtless anti-Catholicism gone from much of the church (though still very much present in the press organs of our bourgeoisie), we have few arguments left for why someone should *not* be Catholic. If they're not the antichrist, if in fact they're exemplary Christians, well, why not sign up? Duke's appreciation for the Catholic Church creates problems too. One outsider friend, commenting on Duke Divinity School, joked, "That's the place where evangelicals go to become Catholic." There's something to that. A Methodist theologian friend who teaches elsewhere said this: "Methodists are the only people who were fooled by the ecumenical movement." United Methodist schools hired Catholics and many others. Others' schools stuck to their Lutherans or Presbyterians or whatever the case may be. Their schools retain more of a doctrinal coherence. In our schools tolerance alone seems to rule. The alternative would be to hire theologians who long for a church catholic that has not yet quite come to be. That demands a kind of patience that's hard to summon up.

Aside from this relatively narrow issue of whom schools should hire, the point of evangelical catholicity is to recognize Jesus on the other side of the Protestant/Catholic divide. Finding more of Jesus to adore is always a good thing. Even for those tempted to switch sides, it's a good catholic argument to stay in the church that raised you, baptized you, gave you space to worship and to become yourself, growing up into the full stature of the disciple God calls you to be in the world. Individuals will convert, sure enough. But that shouldn't be encouraged. One remaining problem with the Roman Catholic Church is this—it's not catholic enough. I, we, recognize its genuine identity as the church of Jesus Christ. But often enough it doesn't recognize ours. I recognize its catholicity through time in the teaching and lives of the saints, but our teachers and lives are usually omitted from their canons, from Luther and Calvin to Barth and Bonhoeffer (as one friend of mine summarized Hans Urs von Balthasar's book on Karl Barth: "This is nice. Now let's go to Mass"). For many Catholics, Protestants remain defective ecclesial communities, in need of conversion, raiding, convincing. Even here I maintain some sympathy—liberal Protestants can be minimally Christian at best, especially when we embrace some form of Tillich's ridiculous "Protestant principal," in which no created thing can be God (really? Jesus? God incarnate? The Eucharist?

Part 4: Searching for Jesus among Roman Catholics

God's flesh to save us?). That said, Catholic maximalism in recognizing the diverse forms of God's presence in the saints, icons, miracles, and all the rest, could at least extend also to us Protestants.

Stanley Hauerwas differentiates between Catholics and Protestants this way: Protestants ask, "What's the least I can believe and still be Christian? Can we cut out x, y, z, or the other thing?" Whereas Catholics say, "Wow, look at all this great stuff I get to believe!" If this is the distinction, the latter wins every time hands down (as it has often done in Duke's students). But of course the word *Catholic* doesn't simply mean "Roman Catholic." We still have more reforming and ecumenizing to do on the way to adoring Jesus together.

John Paul II was right. If the victory comes, it *will* be through the Virgin. Because Jesus will eternally be the one born of a virgin, and he will reign.

What about Mary?
Protestants and Marian Devotion[1]

The name of the Theotokos expresses the whole mystery of God's saving dispensation.

—ST. JOHN OF DAMASCUS (655–750)

In the doctrine and worship of Mary there is disclosed the one heresy of the Roman Catholic Church which explains all the rest.

—KARL BARTH (1886–1968)

There would not seem to be much chance of reconciling these two descriptions of Mary, the mother of Jesus. For John Damascene, a touchstone figure for Orthodox and Roman Catholic theologians, calling Mary the *theotokos*, "God-bearer," or more provocatively, "Mother of God," is a thumbnail description of the entire saving work of Christ. The Council of Ephesus in 431 codified *theotokos* as Christian dogma, insisting that anyone who fails to affirm Mary as the Mother of God commits a heresy—that of denying that the one who gestated in Mary's womb is God. Such descriptions of Mary vindicated and encouraged popular Christian devotion to Mary, including the invocation of her aid in prayer, the praise of her in liturgy, and the depiction of and devotion to her in icons and statuary.

---

[1]. Copyright © 2004 by *The Christian Century*. "What about Mary? Protestants and Marian Devotion" by Jason Byassee is reprinted by permission from the December 14, 2004 issue of *The Christian Century*.

Part 4: Searching for Jesus among Roman Catholics

It is precisely such practices that Karl Barth railed against. For him, as for most heirs of the Reformation, such attention to Mary is an extrabiblical intrusion into Christian faith that deflects attention from Jesus. Devotion to Mary may well land its practitioners in idolatry, leading them to worship one who is not God, and who called herself merely a humble "servant of the Lord" (Luke 1:38).

Much of what being Protestant has historically meant has involved a protest against the Catholic devotion to Mary. Nevertheless, the Second Vatican Council declared in *Lumen Gentium* that Mary is a potential ecumenical bridge, a source of the future unity of all Christians. That suggestion might seem either ridiculous or insulting to Protestants. But recently there has been a flurry of publications by Protestants on Mary, works that suggest she could be an ecumenical bridge—or at least that the Protestant aversion to Marian devotion is eroding.

Beverly Roberts Gaventa, a biblical scholar at Princeton Theological Seminary, has led the charge with *Mary: Glimpses of the Mother of Jesus*[2] and with a collection of essays she coedited called *Blessed One: Protestant Perspectives on Mary*.[3] Meanwhile, Robert Jenson's monumental two-volume *Systematic Theology*[4] and another collection of coedited essays, *Mary: Mother of God*,[5] has given a certain pride of place to the Mother of God.

Church historians of all stripes have long granted that Marian teaching and devotion dates from the earliest days of the church. And they grant that devotion to Mary was not discarded even by the leading Reformation figures Luther, Calvin, and Zwingli. The fruit of ecumenical labor on this topic can be seen in such balanced and helpful resources as *Mary in the Plan of God and in the Communion of the Saints*,[6] a product of years of dialogue between French Catholics and Protestants that calls for both Catholic and Protestant "conversions" on the subject.

The most interesting new book on the *theotokos* in terms of its form is *Mary: A Catholic-Evangelical Debate*,[7] by two graduates of the fundamen-

---

2. *Mary: Glimpses of the Mother of Jesus* (Columbia: University of South Carolina Press, 1995).

3. *Blessed One: Protestant Perspectives on Mary*, ed. Beverly Roberts Gaventa and Cynthia L. Rigby (Louisville: Westminster John Knox, 2002).

4. *Systematic Theology*, 2 vols. (New York: Oxford University Press, 1997-99).

5. *Mary: Mother of God*, ed. Carl E. Braaten and Robert W. Jenson (Grand Rapids: Eerdmans, 2004).

6. Alain Blancy et al., *Mary in the Plan of God and in the Communion of the Saints: Toward a Common Christian Understanding*, trans. Matthew J. O'Connell (Mahwah, NJ: Paulist, 2002).

7. Dwight Longenecker and David Gustafson, *Mary: A Catholic-Evangelical Debate* (Grand Rapids: Brazos, 2003).

talist Bob Jones University, one now an evangelical Episcopalian and the other a Catholic convert and professional apologist. Dwight Longenecker (the Catholic) and David Gustafson (a lawyer by trade) manage to defend their positions tenaciously while being gracious toward one another.

Many Protestants who have plunged into the thought and spiritual practice of the ancient church have found a Mary more appealing to them than she was to their forebears. Kathleen Norris, a Protestant participant in Benedictine monastic life, wrote the foreword to the most recent Gaventa book. She notes that she was not familiar enough with the Bible to know where the monks' nightly vespers prayer comes from, and only later learned that the stirring words of the Magnificat come straight from Mary's lips in the scriptures. It took Catholic monks to reintroduce Norris to one of the treasured practices of Protestant Christians—memorizing and singing scripture.

My own participation in such monastic worship has also sent me back to the scriptures to ponder Mary's place in them—more prominent than I had thought on the basis of her place in the churches that reared me. Yet those same monks whose chanting is so beautiful engage in a most un-Protestant practice: they turn and face a statue of the Virgin with her child on her lap. They sing, "Hail holy queen, mother all-merciful, our light, our sweetness, and our hope we hail you. To you we cry, poor banished children of Eve, to you we send our sighs, while mourning and weeping, in this lowly valley of tears. Turn then your eyes, most gracious advocate, oh turn your eyes, so full of love and tenderness, upon us sinners."

The description of Mary as "our light, our sweetness, and our hope" seems to offer her praises scripturally reserved for Jesus. The song concludes, "and Jesus, the most blessed fruit of your virgin womb, show us, when this earthly exile is ended. Oh clement, oh loving, oh most sweet, virgin Mary." Jesus seems an afterthought in the song, just as his place in the statuary seems secondary—the lesser god on the lap of the greater. The prayer is a beautiful way to end a day of contemplative prayer, with candles flickering on Mary's bronzed face. But is it true?

We might begin considering the place of Mary in devotion by noting some ways *not* to renew a discussion about her. We ought not speak as though all that matters about her is the virgin birth. This question, central in the fundamentalist-modernist controversy of the early twentieth century, treats Mary herself as a side issue, a mere conduit for the one she bore. A second way not to proceed is to use Mary to say anew that which Protestants already say. For example, when Luther treated Mary he tended to depict her as a model for justification by grace alone—that is, as further evidence for what he already believed. If we are to attend to Mary anew, the effort should yield something fresh, something neglected in our own churches and lives.

Part 4: Searching for Jesus among Roman Catholics

The most important contribution of these recent reflections is to give fresh attention to the incarnation. The Council of Ephesus insisted that what Christians hold true about God is that God is not unwilling to get involved in the flesh and blood of human life. The Christian God is enwombed. To say otherwise is to introduce some sort of split in the Son himself, to suggest that the man Jesus is born of Mary and the divinity is not (perhaps the divinity is added later or not at all). To call Mary *theotokos* is to safeguard the fleshiness of God, and so the entire saving work of God in Christ.

As the Catholic theologian Lawrence Cunningham puts it, there is an "almost outrageous particularity" about saying that God's presence in the world is localized in the womb of an unmarried teenage girl from Nazareth. Anyone can claim God as "almighty" or "omnipotent" or "omniscient" or whatever philosophical word we wish to append to him. To claim that God is enfleshed, that God has a birth and death date, that God is Jewish, is the scandal of particularity to which Christian faith is committed. Claims about Mary are ways to keep from smoothing out the scandal. As Luther said, "Mary suckled God, rocked God to sleep, prepared broth and soup for God." She also taught him the songs, stories, and practices of the Jewish people whose messiah he would later claim to be. Similarly, Charles Wesley (as Methodist theologian Geoffrey Wainwright points out) praised God as one "who gave all things to be / what a wonder to see / Him born of his creature and nursed on her knee." In Mary the church ties a string around its finger to remember the particularity of its claims about God. (John Henry Newman argued more than a century ago that the churches that had maintained strong doctrines on Mary are those that had not abandoned strong christological ones.)

Not surprisingly, this string has led Christians to focus intense scrutiny on Mary in her own right. The early church assumed that to bear a sinless child she had to be sinless as well, and Roman Catholics codified this as dogma in the nineteenth century in the doctrine of the Immaculate Conception—the claim that by a special work of God, Mary was spared any stain of original sin.

Protestants argue instead that it is Mary's ordinariness that keeps the incarnation scandalous, not her sinlessness. That God is born in the midst of a quite average life is the claim Mary safeguards.

A focus on Mary also gives us a fresh approach to scripture. A standard Protestant objection to Catholic Mariology is that she is not as important in scripture as she has become in ecclesial traditions. To a degree this is true. No one can argue for her immaculate conception, her assumption into heaven, or her coronation as heaven's queen directly from scripture. Yet argument over those points has clouded other scriptural claims about

What about Mary?

Mary. What she lacks in quantity of appearance in scripture she makes up for in quality. Luke's telling of the gospel begins with her, and her *fiat* ("let it be" in Latin) to Gabriel's announcement of God's incarnational intent opens the way for a new eruption of grace into the world. She is present at and indeed an instigator of Jesus' first miracle at Cana in Galilee (John 2:1–11). She and other women are present at the cross, when the male disciples flee. Depending on how one reads the resurrection narratives, she is present there too (Mark 15:40; 47).

It is striking that Mary is in the upper room at Pentecost—the only woman present there who is named—to receive the outpouring of God's Spirit at the birth of the church (Acts 1:14). When Paul makes his one oblique mention of Jesus' mother it is to point to her as a sign that he was indeed born, and so was genuinely human (Gal 4:4). To cite a more contested passage, her image in Revelation 12—as a woman clothed with the sun, with the moon under her feet and a crown of stars, in the agony of giving birth to a son who will rule the nations—is, at the very least, impressive. Mary's appearances in scripture are indeed limited, but they are tied to crucial moments in salvation history, without which there would be no church.

Scripture presents Mary as an important agent in her own right, not just as the mother of her son. If her Magnificat is any indication, she is an extraordinary reader of the Bible, lyrically weaving together Jewish scripture into a new song that is perhaps the most frequently sung canticle in church history. We are twice told that she "treasures" the words entrusted to her by angels and shepherds and that she "ponders these things" in her heart (Luke 2:19, 51). Aged Simeon promises her that her child's destiny to be for the "falling and rising of many in Israel" will cause a "sword to pierce" her own soul too—suggesting that Mary's importance continues in the saga of salvation long after her child's birth (Luke 2:34–35).

Mary's interaction with her son on the cross is striking, since one of his final acts is devoted to naming John as her new son, and her as John's mother. In this and other scenes she is depicted as an image of the church, the mother of believers, and one to whose care Jesus is devoted to his dying breath. Scripture presents a vision of Mary as one whose importance is not limited to the Annunciation and to Christmas, but extends into the life of the church.

At the same time, scripture also portrays Mary as misunderstanding her son on several occasions. A precocious Jesus seems exasperated with her failure to understand that he would rather be in his father's house than traveling home from Jerusalem with his parents (Luke 2:49). Jesus speaks to Mary harshly at Cana before granting her wish (John 2:4). Later, Mary and fellow family members come to collect Jesus when a crowd accuses him of being crazy in Mark 3:21 and 31–35. Jesus redirects a passerby's blessing on Mary to all those who do the will of God (Luke 11:27–28).

Nevertheless, Mary is far more than an eyewitness to key kerygmatic events and a crucial early theologian and church leader. She is "a space for the spaceless one," to quote an Orthodox prayer. Her womb was the physical site of the enfleshment of God. This leads Robert Jenson to a conclusion that may sting Protestant sensibilities—we ought to ask Mary to pray for us.

Jenson argues that death does not sever the bonds of the body of Christ—as even most Protestant eucharistic prayers make clear. To ask for a departed saint's prayer, then, is not in principle different from asking another Christian for her prayers. We hold that the saints are not simply gone but are ever alive to God, and so we ought also to consider them available to us as intercessors, and powerful ones at that.

This is precisely the point at which Protestant theologians get most nervous. Such a request of prayer from Mary smacks of an effort to gain divine favor by some route other than Christ—the height of idolatry. To prop the door open here even an inch threatens to bring back the medieval system of veneration of scores of saints in an effort to earn the favor of a distant and foreboding Jesus. Hence we slam the door shut. To honor Christ, the saints must be excluded.

Yet this needn't be so. Jenson insists that "the saints are not our way to Christ; he is our way to them." Each saint's particular graces can be seen as reflections of the grace of Christ, whose greatness grows in our eyes as we attend to the saints' individual stories. The strengthening of the bonds of the body of Christ, stretching as they do across the divide between earthly life and death, should bring tribute to Christ rather than discredit.

Attention to Mary has been embraced by some theologians as part of a feminist strategy of overcoming patriarchy. They point out that the Protestant rejection of Mary has meant losing the powerful woman who gave birth to Christianity in the beginning. As Reformed theologian Christopher Morse notes, at the "most important event of all history the mighty male is excluded!" Simeon the New Theologian argued in the eleventh century that God had already made a child from no parents (Adam) and had made one from a male with no female (Eve). God often makes children from two parents, male and female (the rest of us). One thing only remained for God to do—to make a child from a female alone. Hence it was fitting for God to work through a woman, Mary, without aid of a man. Perhaps God's enfleshment in human history via a woman alone should be seen as a resource for feminism, if used carefully.

On the other hand, some theologians regard an emphasis on Mary's submission, self-effacement, and purity as a potential step backward for

What about Mary?

women. And there is always the danger of treating Mary as a "blank screen, a perfect canvas for our projections," according to the historian Shari Thurer.

If there is a common theme that resonates in Protestant attempts to recoup something lost in the rejection of Mary, it is the description of her as the archetypical Christian, the mother of believers. "We too are 'virgins' who are incapable of bearing God," until God deigns to be born in our ordinariness as in Mary's, argues Presbyterian theologian Cynthia Rigby.

Sarah Coakley articulates a particular kind of mariological feminism by defending *kenosis*, self-emptying, against feminist objections. With mystical theologians throughout the history of the church, Coakley argues that self-emptying does not mean submission or loss of self; it means growing into the fullness of creation, becoming as radiantly full of the divine presence as was Mary at the ninth month of her pregnancy.

So what can we conclude? May a Protestant sing praise of Mary at compline, and "hail" her as a "holy queen"? Yes, we can participate in Marian liturgy that reflects her crucial role in scripture, that protects christological confession, and that directs our attention to Christ in new ways. Such a yes will necessarily entail a no to practices that ignore the rich texture of scripture's portrayal of her, that attend to her instead of her son, and that offer back doors for patriarchy's return. In this area, as in others, Protestants have often thrown out the baby with the bathwater.

A friend of mine, speaking of the Catholic move to prune excessive Marian doctrine and practice after Vatican II by moving her statue to the side, observed that Protestants moved her out the door altogether. We can return Mary to the pew beside us, in the communion of saints, in our highest dogmatic confessions—the apple of our eye as the first to believe in God's new work in Christ. Not to do so is to lose something at the heart of things. As Reformed theologian Willie Jennings says, "Salvation begins with Mary's yes."

If that's true, Protestants can talk about her at other times of the year in addition to Christmas and perhaps Mother's Day. Lutheran theologian David Yeago suggests observing the other mariological feasts of the ancient church, such as the Annunciation on March 25 (nine months before Christmas) and her saint day on August 15. He also suggests we sing the Magnificat as often as possible.

Perhaps we might even say a Hail Mary or two. Luther objected only to the second half of the Hail Mary, not to the first. To pray "Hail Mary, full of grace, blessed art thou among women and blessed is the fruit of thy womb, Jesus" is merely to cite scripture, he thought. To say "Holy Mary, mother of God, pray for us sinners, now and in the hour of our deaths" seemed to him to express an extrascriptural accretion. But perhaps asking Mary for her prayers is not in itself un-Protestant. To do so may even guard christological dogma and defend against patriarchy. Who knows? Mary might just be key to the future of ecumenism after all.

On the Grace-Filled Life[1]

"Hail Mary, full of grace, the Lord is with thee, blessed art thou among women, and blessed is the fruit of thy womb, Jesus."

Now, before our Protestant instincts cause us to flinch too hard at this first half of the Hail Mary, we should remember that Martin Luther himself posted no objection to it. How could he? It's all scripture, chapter and verse (see Luke 1:28, 42; 2:21). The extrascriptural second half, especially its request of prayers from the dead, is what troubled him. Luke describes the angel Gabriel's praise of Mary as "full of grace"—but she was about to get a good deal fuller, as her belly would miraculously swell with the enwombed God. When Jesus first fluttered within her, say, four to five months in, that was God fluttering; when jabbed by a sturdy elbow or knee in the rib, that was God's fledgling bone sticking it to her. And when she looked him in the face for the first time it was God's visage that beamed back at her and caught her breath.

That's all biblically explicit enough to satisfy the most Protestant doctrine of inspiration. Yet it was indeed the Catholics who helped teach me that Mary *is* the grace-filled life (it had to be—a Methodist minister friend says that if Vatican II saw Catholics move Mary from the front of the altar to the side, we Protestants have ushered her right on out of the building! She seems too . . . Catholic). At the monastery I visit I noticed a particularly beautiful chant comparing Mary to the burning bush of Exodus 3. I asked a church historian why this would be, and she smiled—the sort of teachable moment professors would kill for. "Simple. Like the bush that burned with the presence of God, Mary too was filled with the divine *but was not consumed.*" This seemed about right, biblically speaking. Creatures cannot see God's face and live (Exod 33:20). Poor Uzzah discovered that just touching the ark to steady it and keep it from falling can be a fatal error (2 Sam 6:6–7).

---

1. Copyright © 2007 by the *Covenant Companion*. "Hail Mary, Full of Grace: Living a Grace-Filled Life" by Jason Byassee is reprinted by permission from the December 2007 issue of the *Covenant Companion*.

Part 4: Searching for Jesus among Roman Catholics

The New Testament agrees that, ordinarily, the bush in the desert and the baffled girl to whom Gabriel appeared ought have had no prayer, for "Our God is a consuming fire" (Heb 12:29). But Mary too was filled with God's dangerous, fiery, consuming presence, and yet was not destroyed.

Too often our discussions of grace are really discussions of good luck or unexpected fortune. Master wordsmith Frederick Buechner speaks of grace this way: "There's no way to earn it or deserve it or bring it about any more than you can deserve the taste of raspberries and cream or earn good looks or bring about your own birth. A good sleep is grace and so are good dreams. Most tears are grace. The smell of rain is grace. Somebody loving you is grace."[2] Glorious.

And yet, where is Jesus in this description? Often Protestant discussions of grace offer it in contrast to "law," reducing it to some sort of antidote against God's demands or our obedience. Grace can be shrunk down to a vague warm feeling or get-out-of-jail-free card that ignores what is most difficult and most interesting about Christianity—its particularity. That is, the election of a specific people—Israel; the incarnation of the Son of God in an unmarried Jewish teenager from the sticks; the demand to forgive more times than we can count; the future coming of the Lord in glory and triumph—to name only a few. Perhaps when we hear the word *grace* we should discipline ourselves to think immediately of *Jesus*, since the one scripture names as "full of grace" was, most literally, filled with the Christ child.

My wife's delivery of our first son was not an easy one. She was hospitalized after what was intended as a final prenatal checkup revealed that his heart rate was too low. With plans to induce her the next day the doctors told her she could eat whatever she wanted. I was dispatched to IHOP where I explained the situation to a waitress who quickly shushed me: "Say no more." She came back with a heaping takeout order of chocolate chip pancakes with extra whipped cream and extra chocolate chips—a radical act of sisterly solidarity from a stranger. Even full of the grace of pancakes, delivery was difficult and led to an emergency C-section. As she held our baby she wept and shook uncontrollably—why didn't anyone tell me she would seem so frail, ghost-like, shivering like that? After reassuring me she was fine the doctors and nurses shook my hand in congratulations and fussed over my wife and boy. This is grace, I thought: communal, sustained by the kindness of others, creative, difficult, even deadly, life-giving, and raucously joyful.

But there I go again, speaking of grace without speaking of Jesus. It's easy to do. Catholic legend has it that Mary gave birth without pain. How

---

2. *Beyond Words: Daily Readings in the ABC's of Faith* (New York: HarperCollins, 2004) 139.

could the presence of God in this climax of salvation cause the normal agony of birth? I protest at this point—if Jesus was really human, surely his birth was more like my boy's than any painless arrival on the scene, as though born by some stork. In any event scripture is clear that Jesus' birth eventually brought her pain aplenty: "and a soul will pierce your own soul too," old Simeon promises her in the temple, and sure enough—her son tortured to death before her eyes (Luke 2:35; John 19:25). In his dying moments he provided for her a new family (John 19:26-27), and after his resurrection she was among the first to receive his Spirit (Acts 1:14). The church has always seen Mary as the mother of believers, and we can see the course of the Christian life in her—God's personal step into history, great joy initially, the sorrow of difficult discipleship over the long haul, and a final divine triumph celebrated in community and shared with the world. Rowan Williams has written of Mary's pregnancy and pregnancy in general as "conspiracies of hope," and so discipleship always is for Mary's sons and daughters—a gift, a peril, deadly, and then glorious.

An icon from an Episcopalian church in western North Carolina depicts Mary at full term, literally bursting with life. Around her the scene is dark as she points to an eclipsed sun above her. It is darkest in the deep midwinter; the Son bursts forth when hope is most deeply veiled. She is the life full of grace, dangerously expanded with faith and love, feet swollen and back sore because of God's crazy way of gaining his world back, on the threshold of agony and delight, filled with the divine presence and yet not consumed, but giving life to the world.

And maybe, just maybe, the taste of raspberries and the birth of a child, insofar as they are good, reflect the Good that is responsible for all that is and for all of our redemption. When we go looking for grace, and claim to have spotted the elusive creature, we'd best be sure it bears the shape of a womb—for if there is grace at all, it is a little incarnation in imitation of *the* incarnation that is grace for the world.

Sanctuary

Mary, Methodists, and Immigration[1]

HISPANIC METHODISTS IN NORTHERN Illinois do not often receive national press coverage. But since one of their number, Elvira Arellano, took refuge from U.S. immigration officials in her Methodist church on the West Side of Chicago, the media have sensed a drama unfolding: Would immigration officials, in their effort to deport Arellano, march into Adalberto Memorial United Methodist Church and drag Arellano and her seven-year-old son away? Is a new civil rights movement being launched, with Arellano playing the part of Rosa Parks?

When I asked the local caucus of Hispanic Methodist ministers, La Junta Hispanoamericana, about events at Adalberto Church, their first response wasn't about immigration. It was about the Virgin Mary. Adalberto's altar space—visible in the television coverage—is dominated by a statue of Mary, covered with rosary beads and surrounded by candles. "It's not Methodist," said Orlando Moller, pastor of El Buen Pastor Church and president of the caucus. "It's Catholic. We Methodists have our own traditions."

Oscar Carrasco, a Hispanic member of Northern Illinois Bishop Hee-Soo Jung's cabinet, counseled his colleagues to respect the work of the Spirit at Adalberto and leave the issue of Marian practice for another time. "It doesn't matter how [the people at Adalberto] worship, as long as they're working for the uplift of the Hispanic community," he insisted.

Walter Coleman, pastor at Adalberto, was not present at the caucus meeting. One could understand why: he's busy talking not only to the media but to lawyers who are working on behalf of Arellano, a lay leader in his congregation, in her fight against deportation for being in

---

1. Copyright © 2006 by *The Christian Century*. "Sanctuary: Mary, Methodists, and Immigration" by Jason Byassee is reprinted by permission from the October 31, 2006 issue of *The Christian Century*.

the country illegally. Coleman and Arellano have referred powerfully to their faith before the cameras, saying, "I fear God much more than I fear the Department of Homeland Security."

The Hispanic ministers eventually approved a nonbinding resolution (the caucus has no doctrinal or disciplinary authority) expressing opposition to Marian devotion and practice and rejecting any form of religious syncretism.

The Methodist hierarchy has eagerly lent its aid to Adalberto's cause. Bishop Jung and Bishop Minerva Carcaño of New Mexico met with the Arellanos and were photographed in prayer with them. But the Hispanic pastors with whom I spoke were not of one mind about the sanctuary case.

How does the place of Mary in Protestant worship become part of discussions about a church giving sanctuary to a Hispanic immigrant? Because conversion from Latin America's deep-seated Roman Catholicism to a Protestant group like the Methodists is such a major cultural and religious shift that any flirtation with Marian practice is seen by other converts as a betrayal. Hispanic pastors may have been trained at liberal institutions like Garrett-Evangelical Theological Seminary in Evanston or Perkins School of Theology in Dallas, but on this issue they act and sound very much like conservative evangelicals.

One pastor insisted, "If people want masses or images of the Virgin or to observe the Feast of Guadalupe, they should go to a Catholic Church." Another pastor complained that when her ex-Catholic parishioners see Adalberto on TV, with its images and rosaries, they're shocked. "That's a *Methodist* church?" they ask. Another declared that it wasn't until Arellano left Catholic things behind that her eyes were opened and she saw Jesus. When Carrasco commented that it's important to take people where they are and offer cultural symbols reminiscent of home, one pastor retorted: "So we should just tear pages out of the Bible?"

The pastors' concern isn't just that Adalberto Church is misrepresenting Methodist practice in the eyes of their churches' laypeople. It's that Adalberto is too focused on gaining publicity. Enrique Gonzalez, vice president of the Hispanic caucus, said Adalberto "has always wanted media attention and now they've got it."

Gonzalez claims that Adalberto is known for endorsing a far-left agenda, including independence for Puerto Rico, the cause of Zapatista rebels in Mexico, and Hugo Chavez's populist policies in Venezuela. Gonzalez says his parishioners at El Mesias Church in Elgin suspect that some other Latinos besides Arellano "have taken refuge" at the church "because they're not able to make as much noise in their home countries." He worries that Methodist bishops are unwittingly being used to bless such agendas.

Part 4: Searching for Jesus among Roman Catholics

When I visited Adalberto I saw no signs of extremist politics, but the church is unabashedly political. A banner proclaimed (in Spanish), "Yesterday we marched, now we vote, tomorrow we will bring transformation!" and announced a voter registration drive. Arellano, speaking through a translator at a press conference, declared that "our greatest hope is in new elections and a change toward legalization for twelve million undocumented workers. Those with the right to vote have to come out and change these unjust laws."

Coleman tells me explicitly, "We have to get control of the Congress." Coleman, a longtime activist in the city, was an adviser to the late Chicago mayor Harold Washington. He and his wife, pro-immigrant activist Emma Lozano, have taken to apocalyptic language in defense of Arellano. In a letter to the *Chicago Tribune*, Coleman thundered: "A nation that does not take responsibility for its actions is a doomed nation." Lozano shouted at a press conference that "this nation should be punished" for turning on the very migrant workers it once welcomed.

Concerning the debate in the U.S. Senate on immigration reform, Coleman said: "Not a senator would say we must take responsibility for what we've done—one hundred years of cheap and unprotected labor, ten of open borders. Elvira walked through a turnstile. And now we want to deport *her*?"

Coleman sees explicit racism at work and points to comments by Pat Buchanan (with whom Coleman appeared on Geraldo Rivera's TV show) to the effect that the United States is experiencing an immigrant "invasion"—a common claim on right-wing radio. Coleman also sees partisan politics at work on the anti-immigration side: "In 1996 Republicans saw that their red states were turning brown," so they launched a xenophobic preemptive strike. Arellano's allies think big. Carrasco told the Hispanic caucus that "the story of what this church is doing will be remembered by millions one day."

Gonzalez suggests that Luis Gutierrez, an Illinois representative in Congress, is behind much of the political theater going on at Adalberto—an effort to bolster Democratic support in advance of November's elections. (If that's the goal, it may be failing: the public is mostly opposed to Arellano's bid for asylum, according to polls taken by the *Chicago Tribune*.)

Gonzalez is also skeptical of Adalberto's claiming for itself the description of "sanctuary church"; every Hispanic church plays that role, he said. "Beyond the immigration debate, beyond the culture, the church is a place where real people express their identity and faith." Regarding Carrasco's defense of the Virgin as a cultural symbol that could help draw immigrants to the Methodist Church, Gonzalez caustically referred to the Virgin of Guadalupe's pre-Christian ancestry: "Could we mix in a little Aztec worship also?"

Whatever their skepticism about Marian practice, the Hispanic pastors all support Arellano's case and oppose any attempt to turn immigrants into criminals. They have differing views, however, on the details of immigration policy. Barb Greicar, a pastor on the city's West Side, thinks it makes sense for the government to conduct background checks on immigrants. "My parishioners don't want people here who are pedophiles," she explains. Gonzalez, however, says a crackdown on immigrants that would involve asking for Social Security numbers would cost him most of his volunteers at church. He vets volunteers personally; he accepts them only after they've participated in church life for several years.

When I asked Coleman about the images of Mary in his church, he argued that the Virgin of Guadalupe is a symbol of resistance to Eurocentric Christianity. "The Spanish hierarchy resisted devotion to her for years," he said.

When I asked Arellano about the church of her baptism, her eyes brightened, and for a moment she left the talking points to which she normally sticks. "I'm still Catholic. I have my rosary, I ask the saints for help. John Wesley was a Father too, with a rosary." I didn't tell her that Anglican priests like Wesley are not Catholic—and don't carry rosaries.

"If I'm in another country I can go to another church," Arellano insisted. "God didn't make churches, just like God didn't make borders."

Joseph

Stepfather to God[1]

It's hard to be a stepparent. There you are, probably later in life, you wish to marry someone and hopefully get it right this time and there are these... kids. They're not yours, they just come with the package of being with this person. What do you say to them? How should they address you? What do you do together? It's a recipe for long-term relational disaster. No wonder stepparents are so often vilified in everything from children's stories to Hollywood movies.

Now, imagine this scenario: you're a widower recently engaged to a younger woman. Your own kids are grown, and seem supportive, even though she's quite young. You're eager to marry again. Then, this: she's pregnant. Not by you. What she's saying is that the baby is from God, leading you to wonder that she's not only sleeping around, she's also hearing voices.

Then you start to hear voices too: "Joseph, son of David, do not be afraid to take Mary as your wife, for the child conceived in her is from the Holy Spirit" (Matt 1:20).

Right. No longer is this a marriage to a young trophy wife to take care of you in old age, but marriage to the mother of the savior of Israel, the mother of God, the Lord of the universe. Who'll need a little side trip to Egypt to avoid being killed too young by the authorities. Whose own hearing of voices will cause others in the family to question his sanity. Who, long after you're gone, will be tortured to death on a Roman cross. And rise again. That's all.

And *we* think stepparenting is hard?

---

1. Copyright © 2008 by the *Covenant Companion*. "Stepfather to God" by Jason Byassee is reprinted by permission from the December 2008 issue of the *Covenant Companion*.

Joseph

Joseph cuts an odd figure in the history of the church—one worthy of our attention for this approaching Advent. In early Christian iconography of the Nativity he is often portrayed as an old man (has to be clear he's not the daddy!), off in the corner, being whispered to by a figure with horns and hooves. The early church is not known for humanizing its saints. Holy ones come off as superheroes, easily besting any enemy. But this is an amazingly human portrayal of Joseph: unsure whether the story he's being told by the angel and his fiancée is true, open to the temptation to doubt, even to despair. Yet he goes: off to Egypt, no need even to implement his merciful plan of divorcing Mary quietly (when he could've stoned her). Then teaching young Jesus a craft: woodworking, or stonecutting, whatever a *teknon*, or builder, did in those days (probably some of both). Imagine the mundane scenes in their house and shop: eyeing a board to see that its angle is just right, smashing a thumb with a hammer, bragging about a bit of new construction on the way to synagogue. In the middle of the extraordinary life of Jesus, things are quite ordinary—Joseph is part of that—and we learn nothing of it in the scriptures.

For much of the history of the church Joseph was as forgotten as he is in the bulk of the gospels. Mary's glory was and is celebrated widely in the church, but Joseph—it's as if he listened when the devil tempted him to despair, and was ushered out of the picture as deliberately as Judas. This was all reversed with Vatican II, after which Joseph's statue became prominent in the side aisles of Catholic churches, parallel to Mary's in the opposite aisle, with a crucifix front and center. Both mother and stepfather were crucial for raising this child of God, and both deserve the church's emulation. Joseph is often portrayed as a worker, with a compass and other tools of his trade in hand. All work is holy, Joseph's statue says, including backbreaking manual labor, creative skilled building, diaper changing, and Son of God raising.

My own experience with stepparents has been a tumultuous gift. After my parents divorced, each married someone as unlike their previous spouse as possible. My dad left my impetuous, emotionally demanding mom and married someone as predictable as a librarian, who reads as much as one too. "I finally decided not to read while driving," she said. "It's just too dangerous." Her sigh suggested every minute away from an open volume was a minute wasted. My mom left my PhD psychologist dad and married a blue-collar manager content to drink beer, eat bratwurst, and watch baseball. "Dang, no sports on tonight," he said to me once. "Want to hit the dog races?" Their new marriages brought people into my life I'd not have had otherwise, of a kind quite different than our old household. Make no mistake: divorce is awful, but I can't check out a library book or down a Miller

Part 4: Searching for Jesus among Roman Catholics

Lite and watch the Cardinals without thinking of people I love, whom I'd not have known otherwise.

That's not to say these relationships were easy. What did my stepmom think to say to me, when I was ten and she was the lady dating my dad, with a kid of her own in tow? What was my stepfather to say to me when I was twenty and he was dating my mom, making space amid bowling tournaments and dairy plant management? They said something right or I wouldn't love them; but just think of the awkwardness of talking with a child of an age you're not used to, then quintuple it—since in this case the new grownup is sticking around after dinner.

It might in fact be better to imagine the church as a stepfamily than as a family—the much more common image. A family suggests, almost entirely inaccurately of course, domestic harmony, tranquility, bliss—as though we traipse through family life as carefree as we look in our photos. But a stepfamily immediately suggests something cobbled together, unplanned, doing the best we can and not necessarily delighted by it. The latter image is truer to the nature of the church, into which we're adopted not just as infants but when we join as adults, and in which we're lumped together with everyone from the homeless to the millionaire, none of whom we'd have chosen on our own.

Then add in voices, angels, a plan for salvation worthy of a God who would choose a people like Israel, and you got one heckuva stepfamily. Not only do you have an inspiration for carpenters and fathers, important as that is—you have an image of the church. People who didn't choose each other but who can't imagine life without one another. People who have to get over initial awkwardness, even irritation, because they're family, and will all be there the next time we get together. People who make you better than you are and who, if everyone's lucky, love each other in the process. God's assumption of all we are to make us all God is includes participation in a family as varied and messy as any of ours—and just so, as redemptive.

Mass Appeal?

Attending a Latin Liturgy[1]

THE SUNDAY AFTER POPE Benedict XVI authorized the wider use of Latin in the Catholic Mass, I went to St. John Cantius Church in Chicago, which has been celebrating Mass in Latin for years. In fact, Catholic priests could always use the Latin version of the 1970 Vatican II–inspired liturgy (which at St. John Cantius is called the *missa normativa*). What the pope did was authorize use of the pre-Vatican II Tridentine Mass—named for the sixteenth-century Council of Trent—by any priest in any parish without the special permission of the local bishop. The Tridentine Mass, or the "extraordinary form of the Roman Rite," as Pope Benedict called it, has also long been celebrated at St. John's, which has had special permission from the archbishop to worship as the church did for half a millennium before Vatican II.

I expected to find gray-haired ladies. But the enormous Baroque-style church was filled mostly with families and young professionals who seemed to follow the Latin easily enough, even joining in the Gregorian chant with the men's choir that sang from an unseen loft. There was one family of six, the father sweating profusely in a three-piece suit, the mother in a black dress. The parents genuflected each of the several times they exited the pew with a screaming child.

The Tridentine Mass was as crowded as the *missa normativa*, even though the priest faced away from the congregation and said many of the prayers inaudibly. Perhaps that aura of priestly distance is part of the appeal. At both masses the scripture lessons and homily were delivered in English, and at both Gregorian chant was part of the liturgy, as befits a church well known in Chicago as a guardian of ancient sacred music.

---

1. Copyright © 2007 by *The Christian Century*. "Mass Appeal? Attending a Latin Liturgy" by Jason Byassee is reprinted by permission from the August 21, 2007 issue of *The Christian Century*.

Part 4: Searching for Jesus among Roman Catholics

Benedict's pronouncement will likely mean little for traditionalists in the United States, who have had little trouble gaining permission to use the Tridentine Mass. Nor will it affect the vast majority of U.S. parishes, which are quite happy to worship in the post-Vatican II style: in English, with the priest facing the congregation. It will likely have more of an impact in Europe, where anti-Vatican II reactionaries in France may be drawn back into the church, since pro-Vatican II bishops can no longer outlaw Tridentine worship. According to Father Tom Reese, former editor of the Jesuit magazine *America*, writing on *Newsweek*'s blog, with this pronouncement the pope is saying that "he does not trust the pastoral judgment of the bishops."

What draws worshipers to St. John's? William See, an undergraduate at Northwestern, told me that young people like worship in which something is demanded of them. "To worship here you either have to show up a lot to learn the Latin or follow along in the missal. Either way you have to pay attention." (The church also offers classes in Latin and Greek.) See said many Catholics of his age feel like they were "robbed" of something by the liturgical changes of the 1960s and 1970s. They find it at St. John's.

The sermon at the *missa normativa* was on Jesus' sending of the seventy-two and his lament that "the harvest is plentiful, but the workers are few." Father Scott Haynes, a converted Southern Baptist, identified the laborers with priests and vowed religious. "Have you ever considered being a priest or a nun?" he asked. "A priest holds in his hand the living Christ just as Mary of Bethlehem did." Not a word about the ministry of the laity. The preacher quoted an authority on the glories of the priesthood: "If a priest knew the importance of what he did, he would die. Not from fear, but love."

The queue for those seeking to say confession before communing snaked around the apse, moving quite slowly, right up to the moment of consecration. A Polish (or Italian, Irish, or Mexican) immigrant could have arrived directly from the old country in 1893 and felt right at home at this service. Clearly, that's part of its attraction. St. John's literature boasts that though the neighborhood around the church has gentrified and trendy lofts have replaced immigrant tenements, the church's worship is "virtually untouched by the changes of recent times."

Pope Benedict has often lamented the near-complete extinction of the rich form of the Mass that first drew him to the priesthood in his native Bavaria. For those who follow the Tridentine Mass in the Latin-English missal, there are treasures to be found, like the note explaining that water is mixed with the communion wine as a sign of the blood and water that flowed from Jesus' side and also as a sign of Christ's two natures. That's rich theological teaching, or mystagogy, in the language of the ancient church. A prayer after communion asks that the Lord's body *adhaereat visceribus meis*—will "cleave to my inmost parts," or more literally, "will stick to my guts." Where else does one hear prayers like that?

Even so, the effort at "restoration of the sacred" with a form of worship frozen in time seems a bit quixotic. As Reese said to the *Chicago Tribune*, the mass is mysterious because of the presence of Christ in the Eucharist, not because the language is foreign. At St. John's, the priest presiding over the Tridentine Mass seemed positively proud that he was inaudible, actually turning off his lapel microphone. In the Middle Ages, worshipers wished for quiet so they could say their prayers by themselves, usually with rosary in hand, praying mostly for the souls of their departed loved ones. I heard no prayer beads clicking during the interminable quiet at St. John's, and only the briefest of (nonaudible) prayers in the missal mentioned the departed. In short, even with enormous effort, the Middle Ages can't be imitated exactly.

But so what? Whereas the post-Vatican II church has suffered from a shortage of priests, the order that runs St. John's has grown to twenty-seven brothers in less than a decade. Perhaps the renewal of Catholic priestly vocations depends on a two-tier form of Christianity, in which the religious life is clearly marked off as superior to lay Christianity. Commenting on Jesus' promise that those who give up possessions will gain back a hundredfold, Haynes pointed to his own experience: "I grew up with one sister, but here at St. John's, I have twenty-six brothers. What the Lord says is true." His enthusiasm for vowed religious life was palpable.

A Protestant visitor to the Tridentine Mass, even one who appreciates the history of the liturgy, will still wonder: Does it even matter that I'm sitting here?

The answer is clearly no. The priest would be doing the same thing if presiding alone, or in front of monks or nuns. The missal explains many of the gestures but not all.

Each time the priest kneeled, which was often, two fellow priests, one on each side, raised his chasuble in the back to keep it from brushing the ground. The effect to me was comical: two men keeping another man's skirt from being defiled. How is this edifying for worshipers? More importantly, how does it glorify God?

Father Dennis Kolinski of St. John's told me that the church sees "more young people coming of their own accord—singles, families, couples." Something at St. John Cantius is attracting them, he observes. He says the church has been "flooded" with calls from priests and dioceses around the country seeking to imitate their liturgy.

Reese, however, doubts that interest in the Tridentine Mass is very widespread. "We Jesuits have some thirty colleges and universities around this country, and we don't see any great hunger among students for this."

Jews have expressed concern that the revival of the Latin Mass will revive an ancient prayer calling for the conversion of the Jews. But John Paul II had already changed the prayer so that it expresses the hope that Jews will "continue to grow in love of [God's] name and in faithfulness to his covenant."

Haynes did not allay all of my concerns. In speaking of the power of cloistered nuns to effect miraculous change, he referred to how a single prayer of St. Teresa of Ávila had "converted ten thousand heretics." For a sixteenth-century Spanish nun like Teresa, I realized, the heretics in question were Protestants.

Dare to Discipline?
John Kerry and Communion[1]

"IS THERE ANYTHING LAYPEOPLE can do to get themselves kicked out of the United Methodist Church?" My question stumped the speaker, expert on Methodist church law though he was. He had just delivered a detailed list of offenses that could get Methodist ministers cast into outer darkness. Wanting to democratize the misery a bit, I wondered if the church disciplined anyone other than ministers.

He thought hard, then replied, "I think there's something in the Book of Discipline about not being able to belong to a hate group."

That's it! As long as you don't join the Ku Klux Klan, you can be a Methodist. It is hard to imagine setting the bar any lower.

From this perspective, Roman Catholic efforts to discipline John Kerry because of his support of abortion rights look singularly odd. Kerry is not a minister in his church, nor is he a theologian. Yet some Catholics want him barred from communion.

To some extent, the effort reeks of partisan politics, not religious fidelity. Catholic politicians have been running on pro-choice platforms for years without this degree of angst. Why the concern now? And why just for Kerry? Other Catholic politicians may be targets, but they seem an afterthought compared to the focus on a candidate for the highest office in the land.

Deal Hudson, editor of the Catholic magazine *Crisis* and a consultant to the White House on Catholic issues, has explicitly said the denial of communion should begin and end with Kerry, and not extend to pro-choice Catholic candidates for other offices. Even more strongly, he suggests that priests should denounce Kerry from their pulpits "whenever and wherever

---

1. Copyright © 2004 by *The Christian Century*. "Dare to Discipline? John Kerry and Communion" by Jason Byassee is reprinted by permission from the July 27, 2004 issue of *The Christian Century*.

he campaigns as a Catholic."[2] The focus on Kerry alone—not on other Democratic or Republican candidates—seems blatantly partisan.

It is also contrasts starkly with previous modes of Catholic witness. In 1984, when pro-choice Catholic Geraldine Ferrara was on the Democratic ticket with Walter Mondale, Cardinal Joseph Bernardin articulated a comprehensive Catholic perspective: "Our moral, political, and economic responsibilities do not stop at the moment of birth. Those who defend the right to life of the weakest among us must be equally visible in support of the quality of life of the powerless among us: the old and the young, the hungry and the homeless, the undocumented immigrant and the unemployed worker . . . Consistency means we can't have it both ways."[3]

What has traditionally made Catholic political engagement so interesting is precisely that it could not be reduced to one issue. It has linked opposition to abortion with opposition to the death penalty. Catholic proponents of traditional teaching about sex have also opposed the arms race and have advocated for the poor and the environment. That venerable tradition of Catholic moral teaching is in danger of being reduced to the level of a bumper sticker.

For all of that, it is difficult to disagree with the idea of excommunicating or disciplining a church member in cases of extreme moral failure. The complaint that conservative bishops are "mixing religion with politics" is an odd one for liberal Protestants to take up. After all, liberal Protestants defended church leaders in the civil rights movement when they were charged with mixing religion and politics. And they defended the work of pastors like Desmond Tutu and Peter Storey in fighting apartheid in South Africa. They rightly celebrated the current pope's fight against communism.

My own preaching saddlebag is chock-full of sermon examples in which the church has wielded its political muscle for good in the broader society—Óscar Romero opposing El Salvador's brutal repression of dissidents to the point of his own martyrdom; Dietrich Bonhoeffer working against the Nazi empire to the point of being willing to use violence (and thereby, he feared, risking his own salvation); Christians courageously standing up against American aggression abroad.

The *New York Times* has been apoplectic at the way Kerry's critics are supposedly mixing church and state. But it once praised Cardinal Joseph Francis Rummel of New Orleans when he excommunicated a white supremacist Democratic political boss (cited by Shields).

2. *Washington Post*, May 7, 2004.
3. Quoted by Mark Shield on CNN.com, May 7, 2004.

Dare to Discipline?

The church should not be silent in the face of moral failure in the political sphere—that much is a given in mainline Protestantism. Some United Methodist bishops spoke up when two of its sons, George Bush and Dick Cheney, led the nation into war in Iraq on flimsy evidence and for questionable motives. Bishops signed petitions, took out ads in major national publications, filmed TV commercials—all in an effort to change their leaders' minds and stop an unjust war before it started.

What if they had simply excommunicated them? What if they had said, "Jesus is clearer about violence than about almost anything else in scripture. The burden of proof for going to war has not been met. Please repent before you come back to us."

The move probably would have backfired. Bush would have looked quite the martyr for standing up to a church brazen and foolish enough to mix religion with politics. It would probably have hurt the church in the offering plates. Yet it still might have been the right thing to do. Grace, as Bonhoeffer wrote and then demonstrated, must be costly, and not only to those on the receiving end of such severe discipline.

But if such an exercise of church discipline were to make sense, it would have to be based on concern for Bush's and Cheney's souls. The church has traditionally excommunicated those who arrogantly continue in open and obvious sin without repentance. How could the church do otherwise when souls are in danger? The church responds by making its split with the person public and unmistakable in hopes that the dramatic gesture will return them to grace. Matthew 18 and 1 Corinthians 5 lay out clear guidelines for such a procedure.

Church discipline matters not just for the sake of affecting elections, but for the care of souls and for the holiness of the church "without which no one will see the Lord" (Heb 12:14).

In a sense, what it means to be a mainline Protestant, as opposed to a Catholic or an Anabaptist, is that one cannot be excommunicated for anything (except, apparently, for joining the Klan). While such severe forms of ecclesial discipline are rare in Anabaptist or Catholic circles, and problematic when exercised (as in the case of the Catholic Church barring remarried persons from communion), they remain options that help define those communities. Any gathering of persons requires some sort of boundary to have integrity. How much more so in the case of the church, which seeks to grow in grace and witness to the world.

Perhaps the Klan example is salutary here. We would be right to remove a Klansman from our midst. His soul is in grave danger for his racism. Our fellowship is doing him a disservice to let him think he is a Christian in good standing with the Lord and in communion with the church. He would be "eating the bread and drinking the cup of the Lord in an unworthy manner" (1 Cor 11:29).

Proponents of the movement to excommunicate Kerry point out that abortion differs from such issues as just war and capitol punishment in that Catholic teaching on the issue is unequivocal. Abortion is always and essentially wrong under any circumstance in Catholic morality, whereas the church has made and continues to make exceptions in the cases of war and the death penalty. Mainline Protestants, among others, would make a similarly unequivocal moral claim about racism.

So perhaps the lesson to take from this controversy within the Catholic Church is not about abortion but about church discipline. It is difficult, on theological grounds, to disagree with those who would discipline a politician who strays wantonly from church teaching on a key moral issue. A willingness publicly to excommunicate any member of a church is a risky one. It has terrible potential for abuse; it could turn into a witch hunt in which no one's standing in the community is safe. But it can also be a mark of the integrity of a community. It is a form of costly grace to say to a sister or brother in Christ, "We simply cannot let you think you are a member of our body in good standing if you continue to teach or practice x."

One could undertake such a risky move only with great fear and trembling, hoping it represents a step down the narrow and difficult way that leads to life.

Going Catholic

Six Journeys to Rome[1]

WHEN I RAN INTO a friend from divinity school recently, we asked each other the normal catch-up questions. Then, in the same casual tone, she said, "So are you going to become Catholic?"

It's not that odd a question these days in theological circles. Last year a string of theologians left their Protestant denominations for the church of Rome. The list includes three Lutherans—Reinhard Hütter and Bruce Marshall, theologians at Methodist seminaries (Duke and Southern Methodist), and Mickey Mattox, a Luther scholar at Marquette; two Anglicans—Rusty Reno of Creighton and Douglas Farrow of McGill University; and a Mennonite—Gerald Schlabach of St. Thomas University.

All six have strong connections to mainline institutions, and several were involved in official ecumenical conversation at high levels. They are also relatively young, poised to influence students and congregations for several decades. They more or less fit the description "postliberal" in that they accept such mainline practices as historical criticism and women's ordination while wanting the church to exhibit more robust dogmatic commitments. All of them embrace what Mattox describes as an "evangelical, catholic and orthodox" vision of the church. They could not see a way to be all those things within mainline denominations.

Rusty Reno, who studied with George Lindbeck at Yale, is best known for his book *In the Ruins of the Church: Sustaining Faith in an Age of Diminished Christianity*.[2] He argued that mainline churches like the U.S. Episcopal

---

1. Copyright © 2006 by *The Christian Century*. "Going Catholic: Six Journeys to Rome" by Jason Byassee is reprinted by permission from the August 22, 2006 issue of *The Christian Century*.

2. R. R. Reno, *In the Ruins of the Church: Sustaining Faith in an Age of Diminished Christianity* (Grand Rapids: Brazos, 2002).

Church are in disarray because of their inattention to church teaching and scripture and because they accept modernity's relegation of religion to the private realm of feeling. But in making this argument in 2002, Reno maintained that orthodox believers should not leave their home churches. The proper scriptural response to living in ruins, he said, is to follow the example of Nehemiah, who dedicated himself to living in a devastated city. To flee institutions in search of something supposedly better elsewhere would be to simply replicate the modern tendency to favor a posture of ironic distance over one of dogged commitment.

In a February 2005 article in *First Things*, aptly titled "Out of the Ruins," Reno announced that he had changed his mind. He had left the denomination that he had long seen as a "smugly self-satisfied member of the liberal Protestant club." What had changed? Reno writes that his defense of staying in the Episcopal Church had become more a theory to him than a full-blooded commitment. And he had come to agree with John Henry Newman, the archetype for any Anglican converting to Rome, that the Anglican *via media*, its prizing of the middle path between extremes, is a mistake. After all, in the fourth century it was the backers of the *homoiousion* term in the Nicene Creed who were the via media party, with the claim that Christ became God. The backers of *homoousion*, with their claim that Christ is eternally God, were the extremists—though eventually the church determined them to be right.

More important, Reno wrote, his feelings had changed. "I may have wanted to return to the ruins of the Church with Nehemiah's devotion, but in reality I was thinking bitter thoughts as I sat in my pew. The most innocuous diversions from the Prayer Book made me angry. The sermons of my quite faithful rector were subjected to an uncharitable scrutiny.... The good people of my parish lost their individuality and were absorbed into my mental picture of 'Episcopalians,' people to whom I would be heroically but lovelessly loyal."

It's unclear how Reno made this move without indulging the modernist temptations—listening to one's feelings, being impatient with institutions, believing things are better elsewhere—that he describes so well in *In the Ruins*. He claims that having taught at a liberal Jesuit school, Creighton, he is "not naive about how insouciant about orthodoxy priests can be." In an allusion to recent Catholic sexual-abuse scandals he says simply, "I do read newspapers." But he does not fully explain how the Roman Catholic Church is any less "in the ruins" than the church he has left behind.

Mickey Mattox, trained at Duke, served as a consultant to the Lutheran World Federation in dialogues with the Orthodox and the Anglicans. He credits the work of Jaroslav Pelikan and Richard John Neuhaus (Lutherans who converted to Orthodoxy and Catholicism, respectively), among others, for making him both "evangelical and catholic." In a letter to friends and family upon his conversion, Mattox, previously a member of the Evangelical Lutheran Church in America, wrote that "the pull" of Catholicism was stronger that "the push" away from Lutheranism. Yet he worries that "the Lutheran center no longer holds, as insistent voices from the left and right dilute our catholic liturgical, catechetical, and theological traditions to much the same effect." As for the pull, he wrote: "We as a family want to venerate the Blessed Virgin Mary, and to unite our prayers with and to the holy martyrs and saints. We want the holy icons, the rosaries, the religious orders, yes the relics too . . . and to practice and experience the real presence of Christ in the Eucharistic meal while retaining the bond of love and fellowship in communion with the bishop of Rome."

Mattox also has an argument particular to the Lutheran-Catholic conversation. He thinks the Joint Declaration on the Doctrine of Justification (JDDJ) should have worked. Once both Catholics and Lutherans concluded that they have no substantial disagreements on the doctrine of justification—the doctrine on which Lutherans have long said the church stands or falls—then there is no reason why they should not reunite under the bishop of Rome. Mattox thinks the problem lies with the ELCA: "There is an institutional intransigence, I believe, on our Lutheran side, and a cultural captivity to hyper-Protestant ways of understanding the church that stymies even the best efforts to overcome the visible breach of the sixteenth century."

Bruce Marshall held a similar vision of evangelical and catholic Lutheranism that he caught while studying with Lindbeck at Yale, a vision in which the Reformation is viewed as an attempt to restore genuine catholicity to the church. He has written widely on the Trinity, on Aquinas and Luther, and on the church's relationship with Israel. He was also involved in Lutheran-Orthodox dialogue.

Marshall says he long ago came to the conclusion that "there is no doctrinal reason why a Christian of the Augsburg Confession cannot be a Roman Catholic." So there was no doctrinal change of mind needed for his reception into the Catholic Church. He admits that this evangelical and catholic vision of the Lutheran church is "a minority position"—indeed, with Mattox, Marshall, and Hütter converting, it is even more so. As with Mattox, the Catholic "extras" were not a barrier to conversion, but a bonus: "I would rather—far rather—live with the possibility of excess that accompanies Catholic understanding of Mary and the Church's teaching authority than with the complete absence of the former—and, it now generally seems, of the latter—in Protestantism."

He insists there was no "push" factor for him: "If disenchantment with my denomination had been the decisive issue, I would have stayed where I

Part 4: Searching for Jesus among Roman Catholics

was." Indeed, he says, "I could not see that I had any right to leave the community in which I was baptized, in which I learned to believe the catholic faith from the heart, and in which I had my theological vocation."

After a pause he adds, "except that right which Christ alone can give—and did." He clarifies that "entry into the Roman Catholic Church was Christ's way of drawing me closer to himself, and mercifully granting me the fulfillment of my baptismal vocation." He adds that his wife's decision to foreswear the Anglican ordination she had been seeking was critical (in all of these cases family matters are crucial, idiosyncratic, and difficult to talk about on the record).

Reinhard Hütter is even more reticent to speak about himself. He was educated at Erlangen in his native Germany before teaching theological ethics at the Lutheran Theological School in Chicago and then systematic theology at Duke. The church has long been central to Hütter's theological vision, and he has called himself a member of the "Catholic church of the Augsburg Confession." In writing and teaching he has used what Luther called the seven marks of the church—preaching, baptism, the Lord's Supper, church discipline, ordination, catechesis, and discipleship—to help discern order amid the chaos of divided church life. Hütter calls these the "constitutive practices" of the church that allow us to glimpse the Spirit's presence and work.

Hütter has written extensively about the work of Karl Barth, John Howard Yoder, and Stanley Hauerwas on the one hand, and on the Roman Catholic moral and dogmatic tradition on the other—especially on papal encyclicals. It seems that the appeal of the latter finally won the day. In a forthcoming essay on "The Christian Life" for the *Oxford Handbook of Systematic Theology*,[3] Hütter focuses on the classic disagreement between Protestants and Catholics over the nature of the law and the freedom of the will. Are humans free to do the good, as Erasmus of Rotterdam insisted in his famous argument with Luther (and as liberal Protestants today maintain), or is it necessary for God to override our sinful nature and enable us to do the good that we do (as per more classic Lutheranism)?

In Hütter's view, the alternatives were wrongly stated by Luther and Erasmus, and the dispute was actually solved beforehand by Thomas Aquinas, who manages to capture the strength of both positions while avoiding their weaknesses. For Aquinas, God's transcendence is such that God's action is never in competition with human action—humans can act with complete freedom, yet God's sovereignty is not compromised. Hütter says

3. "The Christian Life," in *The Oxford Handbook of Systematic Theology*, ed. John Webster, Kathryn Tanner, and Iain Torrance (Oxford: Oxford University Press, 2007) 285–305.

Going Catholic

that in Catholic theology the Holy Spirit "affects the human being tangibly, first and foremost by way of the sacraments—in ways that . . . constitute a journey toward the goal of perfect union in charity with the blessed Trinity."

It was as a Lutheran that Hütter developed his theology of the church and his appreciation of Aquinas. Was a conversion necessary? Hütter has always been interested in the inseparability of ideas and practices, so perhaps it is not surprising that his deep appreciation for Catholic theology and practice became a way into the Catholic Church itself.

None of the figures mentioned so far have directly addressed the churches' various tumults over homosexuality in recent years. Douglas Farrow has. He was a strong opponent of the decision by the Anglican Church of Canada to bless same-sex unions. He criticized the Anglican Church's recent Windsor Report and its effort to navigate a middle ground on the homosexuality question among Anglicans, insisting that a definitive decision on homosexuality "may be the one process that really matters." Farrow also opposed Canada's move to permit same-sex marriage on a national level. Farrow testified before a Canadian parliamentary committee, arguing that a vote for the proposal to allow gay marriage was "in fact a vote for tyranny" and, ratcheting up the religious rhetoric, that the proposal "has ten horns on its head."

But Farrow is not simply a conservative malcontent. He has written that the description *conservative evangelical* is an oxymoron—for the gospel upsets conventional notions of morality, it does not conserve them. He has chastised conservative Christians for merely playing chaplain to the conservative subculture. He is also a renowned theologian who did his doctoral work at King's College in London and taught at Regent College in Vancouver before coming to McGill. His book *Ascension and Ecclesia*[4] has been hailed as an important treatise on Jesus' ascension. Ellen Charry of Princeton called it "nothing less than a theological breakthrough."

Farrow's rationale for his claims about homosexuality are more interesting than mere culture-war rehash. He asks why the government, in permitting gay marriage, felt the need to promise religious groups that they would remain free to "refuse to perform marriages that are not in accordance with their religious beliefs." Just by raising the issue, Farrow suggested, the state was indicating that it could, if it wished, require ministers to perform rites against their will. "What has happened in Canada that suddenly we are forced to contemplate such a thing?"

Theologically, Farrow takes issue with the Anglican proposal to "affirm the integrity and sanctity of committed adult same-sex relationships," for the

---

4. *Ascension and Ecclesia: On the Significance of the Doctrine of the Ascension for Ecclesiology and Christian Cosmology* (Edinburgh: T. & T. Clark, 1999).

wording suggests that persons can be "already pleasing to God, requiring no redemption in Christ." Such marginalization of Christ's redemptive work in favor of approval of what people innately "are" would give up "what cannot be conceded without denying the gospel itself." Finally, Farrow wrote in *First Things* about the oddity of the Anglican primates criticizing conservatives for poaching on the dioceses of liberal bishops in forming the Anglican Mission in America—a conservative network of parishes that have defected from the EC-USA to submit to mostly African primates. For is not Anglican existence in a place like Montreal (where Farrow teaches) a relic of a previous poaching effort into Roman Catholic land? "If Episcopal disunity and competition is wrong between Anglicans, it is wrong full stop." Farrow concluded that essay of January 2005 with a hint of his pending departure: "Perhaps the crew of the good ship Anglican needs to put in at the nearest Roman harbor."

Unlike the other converts, Gerald Schlabach does not come from a magisterial Protestant tradition of state churches—though some other Anabaptists, like Yoder, have argued that the Mennonites also pursue a catholic (small *c*) vision of the church. Also unlike the others, he studied at a Catholic institution (Notre Dame). He has written widely in church history and theology, especially on Augustine. In a statement about his reception into the Catholic Church posted on his personal Web site, Schlabach insists he is a "Mennonite Catholic"—before, he had been a "Catholic Mennonite." He refers to his experience with Bridgefolk, a Catholic-Mennonite dialogue. He affirms the gifts of the Mennonite tradition of enduring persecution and speaking out for nonviolence when the rest of the church is too cozy with imperial power. He says, "God always intends such witness to help transform the whole (catholic) body, not to cement an eternal split."

Like Mattox, Schlabach worries that Protestant churches have become ends in themselves rather than reform movements dedicated to the church universal. Schlabach sees the Catholic Church as the best hope for a reunion of "liberal" and "conservative," "protestant" and "catholic" visions of the church: "Imagine a church ... that could not sing without feeding the poor, nor feed the poor without nourishment from the Eucharist, nor pass the peace without living peaceably in the world, nor be peacemakers without depending on prayer, nor pray without joining in robust song."

What do these conversions mean? Perhaps nothing beyond the significance of these six personal journeys. Yet for each of these stories there are many similar ones involving graduate students and lesser-known theologians.

Carl Braaten, one of the key figures in the "evangelical catholic" movement and founder of the journals *Dialog* and *Pro Ecclesia*, recently wrote an open letter to the ELCA's presiding bishop in which he cited some of these conversions and lamented a "brain drain" in the church. He contended that

Going Catholic

the ELCA is driving out its best and brightest theologians—not because it is too Lutheran, but because it has become just another "liberal Protestant denomination." By *liberal* Braaten means the theological liberalism that Karl Barth spoke of as a "heresy"—the view that Christian language for God represents universal human feeling writ large on the cosmos rather than God's address to humanity in a Word that disrupts preexisting categories. Braaten concluded that all that is left of the Lutheran heritage in the ELCA is the "aroma of an empty bottle."

Another engaged observer of these conversions is Ephraim Radner, an Episcopal priest in Colorado (and another student of Lindbeck's) who has been just as critical of the mainline church as Braaten or Reno. He more explicitly takes up the arguments of liberals within the mainline church who suggest that conservative histrionics over the inclusion of homosexuals are no different from the resistance to racial or gender inclusiveness or to revision to the Book of Common Prayer (indeed, conservatives on the issue of homosexuality are in some regrettable company in recent history). The issue of homosexuality is different, Radner insists. He says that the Episcopal Church's "revisionary teachings on sexual behavior is unique in our church's development," and that appeals to "justice" and "love" over the particular and defined words and actions of scripture suggest that a general principle has become more important than the lordship of Christ. He also laments liberals' "chilling" indifference to the protests of more conservative Anglicans in the Third World.

But Radner has also developed an argument for why it is important to stay in what he sees as a deeply flawed church. "God has allowed us to come to faith and to practice our faith within divided Christian communities so that, forced to follow Jesus where we have been placed, we might learn repentance." Radner offers a figural scriptural argument: though Israel was divided because of human sin and divine punishment, "No Jew . . . is ever asked by God to 'choose' between Israel and Judah." Jewish writers of scripture did not even consider such a move—rather they stayed where they were and tried to help the people be more faithful to the law of the Lord.

Radner sharpens this argument with a christological coup de grace: in the face of infidelity, Jesus himself stays put and dies for his enemies. He does not flee for greener pastures. "It is facile and ultimately misleading for orthodox Christians to identify, face, and respond to their churches' errors by saying 'repudiate and separate' . . . for the simple reason that this is not the shape of Israel's history—which must ultimately be our own—because it is not the shape of Jesus' own life. There is no other standard."

A significant figure hovering over this discussion is Hütter's Duke colleague Stanley Hauerwas, who over the years has encouraged his students to engage Catholic theology and the teachings of the Catholic magisterium. "When John Paul II confessed the sin of the Reformation on the part of Catholicism, I thought, 'That's really significant—who would do that in Protestantism'?" He suggests that perhaps the Reformation *worked*—Catholics now hear more scripture in Mass and in preaching than do many Protestants. And with its teaching office, monastic orders and other practices, Catholics have gifts that Protestants lack: "Catholicism has maintained the integrity of being the church of the poor in a way that we Protestants don't have a clue about."

So why not join the Catholics? His answer is partly personal. While raising his son, Hauerwas found that the Methodists were good at shaping young people in faith. He also prefers loyalty to one's church of origin: "I feel like you need to stay with the people that harmed you." At the theological level, Hauerwas cites the remark by Cardinal Walter Kasper, the Vatican's chief ecumenical officer, that "the ecumenical aim is not a simple return of the other into the fold of the Roman Catholic Church nor the conversion of individuals, even if this must obviously be mutually acknowledged when based on conscience. In the ecumenical movement the question is conversion to Christ. In him we move closer to one another." Hauerwas hopes that his work contributes to a catholic unity that all Christians should seek. He is sympathetic with friends and students who become Catholic, but at the same time he wants to say to them, "Don't do it. We need you!"

These converts have all been captivated by a catholic vision of the church—a vision they have come to believe is best realized in the Catholic Church. Braaten worries that "the very persons who ought to be troubled by this phenomenon will say to themselves (perhaps not out loud), 'Good riddance, we won't be bothered by those dissenting voices anymore. We wish more of their ilk will leave.'" A more widespread response might be that genuine catholicity is best promoted by the approach that Hauerwas describes, in which one refuses to despair over the church of one's baptism, believing that the Spirit can always renew the church. Still others might argue that a more influential and long-term movement in the church catholic is the trend of people leaving the Catholic Church because it will not ordain women or allow priests to marry. Nevertheless, for those in mainline churches these converts raise in a pointed way the question of what it means to be evangelical, catholic, and orthodox.

Fathers and Sons at the Beach[1]

My kids mastered the beach for the first time this year. They waded out into the water and stood there while waves broke over them. And they didn't always get knocked down. "Knees bent!" I'd yell over the surf. "Lean in if there's an especially big one. And remember the rule: there's always another wave coming."

That last part is especially key. If you're under the water, about to come up, and find yourself thinking, "Hmm, I wonder if there's another wave coming," the answer is always yes. And if you forget that rule, you'll come up to gulp a blast of refreshing air and end up with a lung full of saltwater. Saltwater tastes good on your lips. It feels good on your face at the end of the day. But you do not want that water in your larynx, trust me.

I watched this happen with my six-year-old. He went underwater to look at a crab. He came up and smiled at me, a huge, melt-your-parents' heart sort of smile. He wasn't looking at the mammoth wave coming behind him.

"Jack!"

And down he went. I watched his blond curls tumble as the wave spun him over like a towel in the dryer. He ran from the water, sobbing.

"I hate the beach! I never want to come back!"

I explained to him what had just happened. "You've been trashed. You're in. It'll happen again. It's even fun in a weird way. Just hold your breath and it'll be fine."

He nodded, tearfully, and rejoined the ocean.

How do you teach children to respect and love the ocean without terrifying them? If we told them the whole truth, we'd tell them about the kinds of riptides that drowned my brother's guitar teacher in high school. When they asked about the sharks and the whales, we wouldn't say they're way out on the horizon, past where we can see. We'd admit that such creatures could

---

1. Copyright © 2010 by *The Other Journal*. "Fathers and Sons at the Beach" by Jason Byassee is reprinted by permission from the October 2010 issue of *The Other Journal*.

Part 4: Searching for Jesus among Roman Catholics

come closer. Yet if you relax, if you ease in, if you respect the water, it will bear you up, it will sustain you, it will become a place of refuge.

My other son, Sam, is more of a daredevil. He followed my instructions maximally, keen student that he is. He bent his knees, stretched his arms toward the waves, and shouted over the din, "I have this mastered!" His arms gestured toward the threatening waves in a sort of parody of me—all the more funny because it was out of admiration, not satire. And sure enough, when the biggest wave of the day came, he was not trashed. He was covered up, like Moses's burning bush, and was not consumed.

And I felt gratified. My advice was followed and the dutiful son was rewarded. What about later, when I don't have advice? When I'm not nearby to go running to when they get trashed? When they have to make it up as they go? What about when I give advice that they follow and suffer for it? Why bring children into this thicket of risk?

My Sam was on my lap once while I checked e-mail. In the twinkling of an eye, he was gone, tumbling from my lap, his head hitting the computer, a gap opened up between two sides of a wound, blood pooling on his blanket, his face contorted with sadness and confusion. We went to the emergency room, Sam clutching his bloody blanket and sucking his thumb, the ER people asking me over and over, "You say he hurt himself while you were e-mailing?"

They stitched him up while he watched *Finding Nemo*. In this case I knew how to help him—this is the ER, we have health insurance for this, here's how you operate in a hospital. But I hurt him.

"This won't hurt," they said, and they meant it—needle technology has improved, he was numb before the thing even went in, and he was too unaware of what was coming to be afraid. But he cried out, and he was brave, and it was my fault.

Amid small talk, the ER doctor told me about the local beaches. "Oh, yes, people do surf on Lake Michigan. There are waves up toward Wisconsin that make North Carolina waves look small."

Back at the beach, my third son, Will, sat in my lap in the surf. It took two waves and cries from Will for me to see that I was essentially waterboarding him. My body created a sort of dam that kept the wave from going past and shot its current up in the air, into his face, into his nose and mouth. He sputtered and roared. Am I even safe with these guys now?

My brothers and I went to the beach with my father when his father died. Freud said that the most important day in a man's life is the day his father dies. I don't know what Freud meant by that, but I know my dad had lost his final chance to talk to a father who never took time to talk to him. We walked on the beach at Sarasota, Florida, famous for white sand and retirees. I asked my dad if we would ever come back.

"No, I can't see why we would," he said. And he started sobbing, crouched down in the sand, as if something deep down in him couldn't get out. I didn't know what it was at first. None of us did. And then we covered him with our arms and let him heave.

A year later, a patient of his had a dream. She dreamed that an old man with old man's glasses was sitting on a bed looking sad. She proceeded to describe my grandfather, whom she'd never met, in detail she couldn't possibly know. In her dream, she asked the man why he was sad.

He said, "My boy Jimmy is sad, because of me, and I can't do anything about it now." She cried with him, prayed with him, and woke up. At her next appointment, the patient didn't remember the dream. My dad thinks his dad was sending him a message, saying, "I'm sorry" in the way an altar-call-going, full-immersion-dunked Baptist could do—through a psychic in a dream Freud would love. Do with that what you will.

Another time I went to the beach with friends. I went not because I wanted to be with friends but because I wanted to be at the beach. I left them at the house and walked to the sand; I fell on my side and plopped down, face first, and slept. It was the end of a first-year internship in seminary and I was not only exhausted—I was "she's-not-going-to-marry-me-and-I-don't-want-this-life" exhausted. So I had a little bit going on.

Some college boys stopped by me. The sorts of college boys who make your life hard at the beach by staying up too late, being too loud, making you wonder if you should play the asshole grown-up and call the cops or not.

"Dude, you all right?"

I realized I looked like a fellow college brat who'd OD'd. I sat up, blinking.

"Yeah, sure, fine," I said, lying to reassure them.

"All right, man, cool." They moved on.

I brushed the sand from my face, careful not to get it in my eye, and walked down to the water—I dove into the first wave I saw, and floated there, like a flounder, flat on the bottom, hopeful the next bite of food wasn't a hook on a worm.

I was back on another North Carolina beach not two years later. There was another girl now, one who loved me and wanted life with me and wanted it to start as soon as possible. We both knew what was coming. We had bought the ring together. There was no surprise about when I would give it to her. We would be on the beach, on a blanket, the wine drunk, the small talk over, and it would be time.

"I'm so excited I want to give you this thing now," I said. We were in the car line snaking around the Biscuitville.

"Really? You want to propose to me in the Biscuitville line?" she asked. She has not let me forget this.

"No, I don't. I just want to get this over with."

So then there we were, on the beach, wine drunk, small talk over. It was time. I had done this before once. Offered my heart to someone and had it stomped. Even worse, she had said yes before she said no. I would at least ask the question differently this time. Before, I had asked, "Will you marry me?" in a forest, at the same spot we had met at as preteens, years ago. It was a romantic story, one she could tell to all her friends, but we only told a few people before it was over.

This time I would ask, "Would you be my wife?"

Right before it was time to ask I saw a flock of pelicans. Pelicans are ancient Christian symbols for Jesus. It was believed that mother pelicans would slay their young and then pour their blood on the young to revive them. Augustine doubted the zoological accuracy, but that was not the point. Christ has a motherly love for her church, he wrote. His presence is one that includes death to self and life for another. Do not be afraid. Marry the girl. I'll be with you. It'll be okay.

She said yes too. And she went on saying yes.

The reassuring pelicans were right. Good things require the risk of heartache, sacrifice, death even. And our Pelican God raises the dead to new life.

<center>~~~</center>

What is it about the ocean, about sheer masses of water, that brings up primal things?

St. Catherine of Sienna compared the beatific vision to the ocean—ever changing, ever the same, ever beautiful, ever new. This is a vision of God himself, who kills and gives life. God, who spills his own blood. God, who demands our affection like a needy child and gives humanity new life as a needy child himself.

I saw Catherine once. Her head is preserved above the altar at a side chapel in Sienna, Italy. Her nose is gone, but for being 650 years old, she looks pretty good: her eyes are wide open, blazing blue, as if she's seeing the beatific vision right now, as if all we have to do is look in the same direction as her.

Fathers and Sons at the Beach

"Does it look like the sea?" I wanted to ask. "Were you right?"

She couldn't have answered—she had no trachea—but someday she will, and we'll have all the time we need to talk about it.

I want my ashes scattered at the beach, Emerald Isle preferably, where the successful proposal happened. Some Christians in the communion of God's saints would find this blasphemous, I know. They want us whole-body buried, feet toward Jerusalem, ready to pop up on the last day and face our savior. I wonder if they're not a little paranoid. God blew life into us from the beginning, when we were dirt. Surely God can blow life back into the dirt we become when we're ash. Surely cremation can witness to the resurrection of the body as sure as whole-body burial can.

Ancient skeptics used to wonder about sailors who fall off boats and are eaten by fish, which are then eaten by bigger fish—how will God gather you back into one whole body? You're missing the point, Gregory of Nyssa would say. You've seen quicksilver, right? God made creation so that it could be rolled back up into one piece, even if it splits and separates by miles and miles. If God could do that with weak creaturely material stuff, what do you imagine God can do with a creation as strong as it was originally meant to be? With eighth-day-of-creation resurrectional stuff, so infused with grace that the dead will rise and never die again?

Not clear? Good. It's a mystery. We don't understand it. The point is God does, and we trust God, and all will be well. Really.

And that brings us back to parenting in light of the resurrection of the body.

I'm told I'm going to have to let them go. Make their own mistakes. Incur their own injuries. They'll get in touch sometime, too much probably, for money or advice or, increasingly in the Facebook age, constant chatter. But mostly they'll be gone. And then one day I'll be gone. And I hope they're there, combing gray hair as they get ready to spread me on that beach together. I'll tell them not to worry. Getting trashed is sort of fun. Plus, I'll be ashes. It really won't bother me. And when they lean into life, I hope they'll think of me.

One member of a church I pastored in Zebulon County, North Carolina, was ninety-three years old when I last saw her. When she goes to the beach, she makes a point of walking right out to the sand, holding her arms up and shouting, "Glory!" It's not a bad response.

Part 5

Searching for Jesus in Popular Culture

THE ESSAYS IN THIS section were partly born out of my aspiration to be a slacker. Lebowski is a patron saint of sorts for my generation and those younger. As I argue in that essay, he can be described as a practitioner of *apatheia* rather than of sloth. He's not going to care about what "the man" thinks of him, he's not even particularly thoughtful, he just wants to bowl. By contrast, if I have a few minutes to spare I feel like I should do something productive. Not something prayerful, attentive, loving of others, or just nothing.

    I started reviewing movies because I loved the idea of sitting in a theater and having someone pay me for it. The very possibility got me my job at *The Christian Century*—I heard David Heim, executive editor, lament at a conference he couldn't find writers to review for him. People who knew about movies didn't know anything about God, and vice versa. I volunteered, figuring I watched enough of them, and hoping at least to make it profitable. As it turned out I mostly wrote on other things for him, but my best days may have been in the theater, on the hunt for God. Hollywood has both traded on faith (*The Ten Commandments, The Passion of the Christ*) and grossed billions. It has also lampooned faith. Now it mostly ignores it, which is what makes sightings of God in the movies so much fun. They're not aware they're looking for God, but they are—we all are—often disastrously wrongly, but often surprisingly fruitfully. The church has never been hesitant to recognize "our" truth outside "our" walls—to do so is to plunder the Egyptians, as the biblical Israelites did, it is to recognize that the source of all wisdom rains gifts on all creatures, it is to see secular parables even far outside our bounds. Ancient Christians were justifying their use of Plato, I'm justifying mine of Lebowski. It's the same thing, really.

This does open the question of piety for those who look for God in popular culture. I remember reviewing a popular movie positively and one of my pastoral mentors renting it and being scandalized at its contents. I can't recommend movies to my church that contain material they wouldn't want their kids to watch. Why? They're watching them anyway, for the most part. Yet something still keeps me from lending them my imprimatur. I think this is right in a way. Our culture is far too revelatory of the flesh on film. We Christians hold that such unveiling is part of God's intention for us in marriage. What we imagine shapes us, and once we see an image we cannot un-see it. Yet simply being a prude seems no answer. Somehow what we Christians offer to the world should be more sensual, more body-affirming, more "sexy," even, than those who show us the live act of sex and call it entertainment. It interests me that ancient Christians were baptized nude (likely with curtains, but bear with me) and took public baths, while we act as though Jesus came and died and rose among us to shield our eyes from naughtiness. Clearly I don't know how to balance all these concerns. I do know we should be there on Mars Hill (Acts 17), noticing when our neighbors worship an unknown God, testifying in their midst to Jesus, more fascinated by his beauty and holiness than we are scandalized by how the pagans worship and entertain themselves.

More of these pieces deal with music than with film, and with live music rather than recorded. Something of the concert evokes worship. I remember Scott Bader-Saye first writing on the Emerging Church Movement that they have a point—a U2 concert is far more like worship than most of church most of the time. And these are instances where I glimpsed something of God in people coming to sing together songs they love. The point is not to bash the church or even exhort it (marriage is not "awesome" all the time either, yet its very ordinariness is what makes it worth living into). The point is to thank the God who makes us all sing, on the way to leading all the world in praising the God fleshed in Jesus, poured out on the church in the power of the Holy Spirit.

What You're Looking For
Worship at the U2charist[1]

A CHURCH SERVICE CALLED the U2charist would seem like liberal Protestantism at its worst: take music from a band that was cutting-edge over two decades ago, sprinkle some religiosity on top, and try to reach hip younger people. I went expecting the worst.

My dread increased when I arrived for a staging of the event at Fourth Presbyterian Church in Chicago. The crowd was mostly folks in their midthirties who had listened to U2 as kids. Many had brought their own youngsters with them. Not a few church youth groups had been dragged in for the event from the suburbs. Seeing them, I remembered my youth group's reaction when U2 was featured at the 2001 Super Bowl: "Who are these guys?"

The music by a U2 tribute band called Elevation was so loud that the tunes were unintelligible, let alone the lyrics. Elevation imitates U2 slavishly. Its lead singer is even named "Danno," after U2's Bono. Danno wore his hair, clothes, and shades to resemble his idol, and even donned the leather jacket with the American-flag liner that Bono wore for U2's Super Bowl performance. Watching him bounce around in a fully lit gothic sanctuary in front of people sitting in pews was, at first, downright painful.

The widespread press coverage of U2charists has followed a familiar trope: "Stuffy old church updates for new day." Episcopal liturgist and well-known blogger Sarah Dylan Breuer devised the U2charist in 2004 to pair the Irish rock band's passion for God and social justice with the sacrament of Christian worship. The band allows its lyrics and name to be used as long as any proceeds go toward organizations working to further the UN's Millennium Development Goals.

---

1. Copyright © 2007 by *The Christian Century*. "What You're Looking For: Worship at the U2charist" by Jason Byassee is reprinted by permission from the November 27, 2007 issue of *The Christian Century*.

Part 4: Searching for Jesus in Popular Culture

The UN's Millennium Goals are certainly laudable: eradicate poverty, promote gender equality, reduce child mortality and so on. But with this kind of focus, God's good news in Christ can be easily reduced to do-gooderism. At best this kind of event offers social justice without obvious religious content; at worst, it touches on Pelagianism, reducing faith to the sum total of our impressive good deeds. Tack on what Bono calls U2's tendency to be "painfully, insufferably earnest," and a liturgical disaster was ready to unfold.

But then Elevation lit into the guitar riff that precedes U2's great song of religious longing, "I Still Haven't Found What I'm Looking For." Something in me changed. I started to groove. So did the thirtysomethings and their kids around me. It takes a lot to get Presbyterians up in their pews and dancing, but it happened. The parents didn't just mouth these lyrics, they shouted them, as they doubtless had thousands of times before. Their children smiled at their parents and danced in the pews beside them. Suddenly it worked.

"Still Haven't Found" is the sort of song that led Breuer to write the U2charist liturgy in the first place: "You broke the bonds and you loosed the chains, carried the cross of my shame." They're lyrics that almost demand to be sung in church. Loudly. When the song finished and we stood, rather formally, for a typical high-church responsive reading, our shouting voices were ready, and we bellowed with the psalmist, "Sing to the Lord, all the earth!"

Later in the service Danno asked for help. He had the church bulletin in front of him—not a normal part of Elevation's performances, to be sure. "Uh, okay, I guess we're supposed to sing the Doxology now. You all are going to have to help me." And he began, a cappella: "Praise God from whom all blessings flow." These were church people, good Presbyterians, and their voices were warmed up.

We lingered as the last note, sung in harmony, wafted by the carved wooden angels in the top of the nave. Somehow, between Danno's charming hesitation and the congregation's confident response, the Doxology had never been more beautiful.

It all may have worked in the end because of U2's ability to capture the tensions of the city. Bono often speaks and sings of the religiously inspired violence in Northern Ireland. U2's great song "Where the Streets Have No Name" is an eschatological plea for a time when we can't tell who's Catholic and who's Protestant, who's friend or enemy, based on address or surname. It's a lament, full of longing, but finally hopeful.

Singing that song in the midst of Chicago, a city with great beauty but also huge social problems, somehow seemed right. As visitors wandered into the church from the street to see what was going on, it felt like the church was serving them well—it was making space both for U2's passionate love for humanity and for its fury at how we treat one another. The church was speaking about a merciful God not perched above the fray but down here in the mess with us.

Maybe this service actually represented the mainline church at its best. It was about worshiping a God who is too passionate to allow for cynicism, a God ready to bless our best and curse our worst, eager to bring the kingdom, but not before we turn to God in freedom.

Sure, the show would've been better if staged by Willow Creek. The music would have been better if performed by U2 itself. But earnestness ain't all bad: "One life, but we're not the same, we get to carry each other, carry each other, one, one."

Saint Lebowski[1]

I've tried this theory out on university and ecclesial superiors and they've not been impressed. So let me try you, gentle reader, and see what you think.

I think slacker movies are a profoundly Christian thing. What looks simply like escapist nonsense or celebration of nihilism has a great deal to do with ancient Christian wisdom on the good life.

Exhibit A is *The Big Lebowski*, the cult favorite put out by the Coen brothers.[2] Jeff Bridges' character, "The Dude," bops from scene to scene in his life, smoking dope, bowling, and working hard not to care about anything.[3] His proudest accomplishment is that he wrote the "Port Huron statement. The first draft, not the compromised second version." He was part of the "Seattle Seven," in a great caricature of '60s radicalism. But he's proudly unemployed now. Rarely a scene passes in the film in which he's without his favorite drink, a White Russian (as a bruiser pushes him into a car in one scene, he protests: "Hey, careful man, there's a beverage here!"). And he spouts pearls of wisdom like a modern-day Buddha on Ritalin: "Well, that's, just, like, your opinion, man" (fellow Lebowski lovers, please insert your favorite line here).

The Dude also happens to be the patron saint for my generation. Baby Boomers: be very afraid. We'll choose your retirement homes and executive your living wills soon.

But this, as I say, is a sign of hope.

---

1. This essay was first published on December 15, 2010, as a post to *Call & Response*, a blog on the Web site of *Faith & Leadership*, the online magazine of Leadership Education at Duke University.

2. For a sensitive theological reading of the entire Coen oeuvre, see Cathleen Faslani, *The Dude Abides: The Gospel according to the Coen Brothers* (Grand Rapids: Zondervan, 2009).

3. Except his rug, of course!

Saint Lebowski

The desert fathers and mothers of the ancient church warned against despair. The demon usually strikes in the early afternoon, asking if all we're working to achieve is worth anything and whether we're not better off dead. The ancient Greek word the monks and nuns used was *acedia*, and contemporary spiritual writers have also fingered it as a crucial obstacle to the spiritual life. Mother Teresa, with her now-famous multi-decade struggle with the silence of God, is a sterling example of the power of this demon. One of the holiest people of our age felt that *acedia* got the better of her most of the time.

Needless to say, The Dude was not afflicted by this particular imp. That's because The Dude is the perfect exemplar of *apatheia*. Careful now, there's a false cognate to this word. *Apatheia* in the ancient church meant refusal to be acted upon by the desires that play us. For the monks it meant to act, actively, out of love of God and neighbor. The Dude seems, in one way, apathetic indeed in our English-language sense of not caring. The Big Lebowski, a millionaire who shares The Dude's given name, accuses him of simply being a ne'er-do-well. "The revolution's over! The bums lost!" he bellows. But The Dude actually cares about a lot of things. He cares about bowling and his friends and his vices. He's willing to risk his life for his friends or even a job he's been asked to do. He's just not willing to care about what people like the millionaire want him to care about. He's not pursuing career, money, relationship, fatherhood. In short, he's rejected advancement. Ladder climbing. Success. The very things most of us chase so vehemently they threaten to compete with our pursuit of the true God, fleshed in Jesus.

The ancient monks and nuns rejected those things—especially money, sex, and power—as competitors for their devotion to God. Most of us have not rejected them outright. Just so, they endanger us more than they did our monastic brethren, for we hesitate to name them as potential idols. But their power as good gifts of the Creator God tempts us deeply to worship them, to arrange our lives around them, to die for them even. The monastic witness of rejecting them outright is an important one to keep alive (and this is done exemplarily in the new monastic movement, an example of traditioned innovation if there ever was one).

The Dude rejects wealth and power too. They simply don't hold sway over him the way they do over most of us. Even his non-rejection of sex is interesting, for what he actually rejects is fatherhood. Peter Brown has shown that the ancient Christian rejection of sex is actually rejection of building a family empire, of having children to carry on the family name and passing on multigenerational wealth in a desire for secular immortality. The Dude is not interested in any of that either. He just wants to roll.

And, just so, he's an appropriate patron saint for Gen X. He's a friend, a bowler, a slacker, someone willing to tell a hard truth to a friend, and someone passionately devoted to avoiding achievement. Those of us with the hammer down in avid pursuit of achievement do well to take note.

Message of Light
An Interview with Seth Avett[1]

THE AVETT BROTHERS HAVE been described as "grunge grass," "punk grass," and "Robert E. Lee playing with the Ramones." Their high-energy performances have scandalized bluegrass purists but delighted fans: they were identified by *Rolling Stone* as a band to watch in 2009 and have appeared this year on David Letterman's and Jimmy Kimmel's shows. They recently released *Live, Volume 3*, which contains many of their most popular songs.

The four-man ensemble includes the two actual Avett brothers, Scott and Seth, as well as bassist Bob Crawford and cellist Joe Kwon.

Kwon and the Avetts all grew up in small United Methodist churches in North Carolina. Clegg Avett, the Avetts' grandfather, was a Methodist minister in western North Carolina. Growing up in the church, with its "ongoing message of light," has been a powerful influence on the band members and their music.

In live performances they throw themselves around the stage, as *Esquire* magazine says, "in the best campfire, hootenanny sing-along tradition." Yet their songwriting has the delicacy and truth of the very best sermons.

I've heard that a key determiner in whether children attend church once grown is found in whether their father sang the hymns. It pains me to look out on Sundays and see dads standing there stiffly, not singing, not worshiping, bodily present, mind anywhere else. Their kids will be gone soon too. The Avett Brothers' dad sang loud in church. And while they're not exactly in it, they're not exactly out either, and the result is a lot like worship.

---

1. This interview was first published on November 15, 2010, as a post to *Call & Response*, a blog on the Web site of *Faith & Leadership*, the online magazine of Leadership Education at Duke University.

Part 4: Searching for Jesus in Popular Culture

Q: What's the significance of your church upbringing?

Growing up in church for us was about more than hearing about God and memorizing the Apostles' Creed. It introduced to us an example of community that was based upon principles and beliefs, a group of people that came together not necessarily because they had to but because they wanted and possibly needed to.

It also was a place where we heard a sermon, a weekly speech that was articulate yet relatively understandable, on some level, even for a child. Youth group was a place where we learned about the Bible but also learned how to get along with our young peers (and, oddly enough, to ski).

Of course, we learned hymns too, and our dad always sang very clearly and loudly. Sometimes he sang the lead, sometimes the harmony. I think the main point I'm trying to make (and consequently the relevant impact here) is that church presented an ongoing message of light and positivity in the routine of our lives. That message has undoubtedly played a role in who we are as grown men.

Q: How do you approach faith with clarity and criticism at the same time?

Well, it seems that no matter how you go about life, the error is always a human one. Faith itself is of course a beautiful thing, a spiritual possession without which we are lost. I guess our criticism is more for ourselves and our failure to have faith consistently. We all lose faith sometimes. I think it is important to remember that it doesn't make you a bad person to stumble and to lose faith or hope. It happens to every last one of us.

In our songwriting I would like it to come through that we know about falling and about failing, but falling can be a great thing if you can learn even just a little from it. With enough perspective, it can even be funny.

Q: There's a quote from your grandfather online in which he says that he doesn't mind that he was in multi-point charges his whole ministry career and not at a high-steeple church. Has that attitude toward success affected you?

I'll take any comparison to our grandfather I can get. I never had the honor of meeting him, as he died four years before I was born, but from all I've heard from those who knew him and by reading his sermons, Clegg had a lot of wisdom and clarity to offer. The older members in our church still will tell me how soft-spoken and well-read and intelligent he was. Humility and modesty were apparently among his more admirable traits, and I do hope those traits were passed down to Scott and me.

We certainly don't feel as though we are made any more important by a growing popularity, the spreading of our name or the spreading of our songs. If anything, we are more and more humbled by the appreciation we have been so fortunate to receive.

Q: What about your parents? How did they influence you and your brother?

Our dad ran a welding crew for thirty-five years, building bridges throughout the Southeast for the bulk of that time. Construction is no place for lazy folks. We saw him work hard without excuses throughout our childhood. Our mother dealt with us three children while Dad traveled with the crew. She made 90 percent of our meals, washed and patched our clothes, and worked extremely hard to keep us healthy and growing well. When we were old enough, Mom went back to school and studied to become a teacher, which she still is today. I never saw my parents rise after me in the morning. They didn't tell us we should work hard; we just knew it was the right thing to do, because we saw how they did it.

[Our parents] are and always have been big readers. There were always a ton of books in the house, piled in the living room, filling the shelves, in little stacks on nightstands. That accessibility was key in the early years of my life. We were never a big TV family. The older I get, the more I realize that my vocabulary is much stronger when I'm actively reading a couple books. . . . I've always been affected by great words, and I suppose I've just stayed on a path to find more.

Q: Tell me how you view success.

It helps that we have received this attention in a gradual way. I have said before that I am skeptical towards how I would have reacted to it had we received it ten years ago (when the band started). I am thirty years old now, and I am confident that I can make a living one way or another.

I don't have that view because we've been on TV or have sold a few records. I have it because my parents let me know from an early age that I am a capable person with a lot to offer. Success can be defined in an infinite number of ways. It is true that professionally we have experienced some great milestones, and I am very thankful for those experiences.

But it would be inaccurate to say that those events are any more important or worthy of attention than the triumphs of anyone else: another sober day for a recovering alcoholic, or a machinist getting a raise, or a child passing the fifth grade. Every single person has a growing line of successes and failures. I think the trick is appreciating what you've done and having the right kind of pride for it, as the wrong kind will have you thinking that you're somehow above your neighbor, which is a silly and potentially dangerous notion.

Q: Your music is deeply rooted in Appalachia, and yet it reaches out from there into lots of other genres. How do you hold tradition and innovation together?

I believe it would be not only a shame but unnatural to operate, almost in any capacity, without considering one's whereabouts and present environment/landscape. Tradition exists because it has been tested and proven to work for whatever reason. I believe the fundamentals of tradition should be focused upon, rather than its stylistic frills.

With music, in our case (and keep in mind, we are songwriters, not musical historians) it makes sense to draw upon the songs and melodies that have inspired us over the years, regardless of seemingly opposing genres. So while an Americana-based tradition may dictate that we use the banjo in a certain traditional, predetermined, and established way, we feel that it is largely unimportant for us to be rigid in our delivery of that instrument. Scott should play the banjo as he plays it, with his own unique personality showing through. The fundamental element is that we use the talents we were given, to the best of our ability.

Innovation is sometimes a product of just the good old condition of being yourself. If we are seen as innovators, that's purely accidental on our part. We've just attempted to be ourselves and to let the songs do the talking.

Q: Talk about place in your music. You're deeply rooted in one way, but in another you've moved far beyond North Carolina.

Roots are imperative. We have been around the world in the last decade (and in the last six months!), and traveling in such an intense way has been incredibly educational and exciting.

Without a home to come back to, though, I doubt I would be able to appreciate the traveling as much. I have never had a great desire to up and move to Europe. But I certainly have always wanted to see it.

Thanks to the music, I have been able to see some of it, and maybe will get a chance to see more. No matter what, though, the beautiful state of North Carolina is my home. It is always my honor to return whenever possible. I would encourage anyone to travel if they can, when they can, because it has a way of opening your eyes on a few things that you thought you had figured out. It challenges you, and then gives you the reward of meeting those challenges.

Then, when you return home, you can maybe see a bit more of the beauty in the place you're coming from.

Q: How do you manage to approach such serious topics (love, loss, shame, death, delight) with such a gleam in your eye?

We have been humbled many times, personally and collectively, professionally. I believe the older you grow, if you are able to move past your own failures and tragedies, you'll gain a perspective that reveals a commonality among all people.

Love and loss, shame, delight, and death are just a few of the thousands of states/conditions that we all find ourselves in sooner or later, if we live long enough. I think our approach to songwriting allows for a certain measure of (hopefully) candid speech, with an eye on the responsibility that is somewhat inseparable from the fact that people will hear what we are saying in our songs.

That said, I think that music can be fun to listen to but not disposable. Scott and I take what we do pretty seriously, aesthetically and thematically, but I don't think a desire for artistic integrity should get in the way of the sheer joy of it.

Q: You don't hold back as you perform. What can other kinds of leaders learn from the way you give yourselves to your performance?

I hope that it is clear in what we do and how we do it that we are not interested in a halfhearted effort. I have yet to encounter anything in my life that could be done well without a formidable investment of time and care. It will come through to an audience, if you fully believe in what you are presenting.

And that doesn't mean you have to juggle chain saws or command a pride of lions to get attention. Truth, genuine intent and simplicity, in these times, is plenty when considering the presentation of a message to a group of people.

Q: How do you understand your appeal across generations? (My seven-year-old wants me to ask, "Why do you rock out so much?")

We can only hope to bring a quality sound and a sincere message with our songs. If we are able to do that, then it may be relatable not to just one small corner of society but to a broader landscape of people.

We have been blessed with an audience of great variety, this is true. But we did not go out intending to write songs that would gather attention from all sorts of people. We have just been telling our story and learning that our story is not just our own but one of a somewhat common human experience.

Oh, and tell your young one that rocking out is a part of life. And if the rockin' bug gets you, don't deny it! Most of the time it's best to just dance it out . . .

The Banjo Lesson
The Carolina Chocolate Drops[1]

1. This essay was first published on October 27, 2009, as a post to *Call & Response*, a blog on the Web site of *Faith & Leadership*, the online magazine of Leadership Education at Duke University.

Part 4: Searching for Jesus in Popular Culture

I'VE ALWAYS LOVED THIS painting, *The Banjo Lesson*, as an image for teaching—we can apply it also to leadership. The old man is sitting patiently, providing a physical frame for the boy in his lap to learn his way around the strings. He is also holding up the neck of the instrument for a boy not big enough to bear the weight himself. The goal is to make space for the child to love the instrument, for his fingers to learn his way around it, to have him grow into love for music and the joy it will bring for the rest of boy's life.

We here in Durham recently got to hear an outdoor concert of the Carolina Chocolate Drops, a trio of twentysomethings playing old-time African-American string band music for a new generation. It was striking to watch a crowd of all races get up and dance unabashedly in a rain-soaked field to instruments their grandparents, black and white, left behind as antiquated—the jug, the banjo, the fiddle, the kazoo.

A review of the concert in the local newspaper described how the Chocolate Drops got into this sort of music. They had their own banjo lesson, of sorts (a fiddle lesson really). They met a man named Joe Thompson, a ninety-year-old fiddler, one of the last of a generation that played old time African-American music from several generations ago. After first meeting one another at a festival called Black Banjo in the North Carolina mountains (institutions like festivals are clearly incubators of new creativity), the three—Rhiannon Giddens, Justin Robinson, and Dom Flemons—started visiting Thompson at his home in Mebane. They got to know the man, studied under him and learned his repertoire, playing backup to him. Thompson is from an age that doesn't dole out compliments freely. But the band knew he approved of them because he kept inviting them back to play. He took to calling CCD "my band." And his effect is obvious—these three play with old souls and make strangers want to hop up and dance with one another.

What a gift Mr. Thompson has given to the members of the Carolina Chocolate Drops. He made a frame for them, a space, to grow into. He passed on wisdom from his own childhood (he was twenty in 1940!)—wisdom that would have been lost otherwise. And their relationship yielded fruit in the form of new creativity gobbled up by a willing audience.

The challenges of mentorship are obvious: communicating across generations that may not inherently understand each other, the difficulty of any collaboration between creative people, the sheer need for time amidst other demands. But the payoff is beautiful and the rest of us dance.

The Difficulty and Glory of Collaboration[1]

SIMONE DINNERSTEIN, A CELEBRATED American classical pianist, apologized to the audience for *not* bowing when the show opened, contrary to classical convention. Her collaborator for the evening, Tift Merritt, the folksy singer-songwriter, explained that *she* had suggested they not do so: "We haven't *done* anything yet!"

The two were performing together at Duke as a sort of experiment. Can a classical musician most renowned for her performances of Bach and a crooner whose voice makes hearts ache in smoky bars and honky-tonks from Texas to North Carolina make each other better? Or would they simply row in different directions?

I attended the concert thinking of collaboration among Christian institutional leaders and came away with several observations:

1. The two musicians met when Merritt interviewed Dinnerstein for *The Spark with Tift Merritt*, a radio show she hosts for a public radio station in Marfa, Texas, a tiny South Texas hamlet with a penchant for down-home music. The two women hit it off, became friends, and started to wonder what it would be like to play together.

   What would it be like for Christian institutional leaders to go out of their way to seek creative partnerships with people similar enough to pursue shared ends but different enough to make one another better?

2. Collaboration can be difficult, even awkward. At times these two joked about it: Tift tried to launch into a song directly after a Dinnerstein solo, and had to stop. "My guitar's out of tune," she explained. "So much for the smooth transition we planned." In some ways, playing together made *less* of each musician. Tift is used to playing with a

---

1. This essay was first published on February 2, 2011, as a post to *Call & Response*, a blog on the Web site of *Faith & Leadership*, the online magazine of Leadership Education at Duke University.

Part 4: Searching for Jesus in Popular Culture

whole band. Yet here she provided her own percussion in the form of stomping her high-heeled boots.

The best way to deal with such difference is with as much grace as we can muster. Tift made a joke at one point at Coach K's expense (she's a Carolina grad, poor thing). Then she looked over at Simone and apologized: her counterpart had no idea what she was talking about. They recalled rehearsing together when Dinnerstein asked Merritt whether she was employing a certain vocal technique. She named it with an Italian word known to classical singers. Merritt responded, after an awkward pause, "sure"—making clear she had no idea what Dinnerstein was talking about.

Real difference means, well, real difference. And the best way to negotiate is probably self-deprecating humor.

3. Collaboration culminates in making one another better. As Tift played a handful of solos, she explained that "Simone sweetly convinced me to play my newer stuff tonight." After one opera piece on which Dinnerstein played and Merritt sang, Simone explained, "I always imagined a voice like Tift's singing that part." Safe to say most don't imagine opera in a voice that sounds like it's from down the holler. After another duet Tift thanked Simone for letting her *not* sing in German. I imagine if one partner *doesn't* have to say "uncle" at least a few times, the other isn't pushing hard enough.

This seems to be the greatest benefit of collaboration: pushing each party to be their best, and better than they thought they could be before they got together.

4. One of the highlights for me was watching each musician take turns as a member of the audience. When Tift first walked out on the stage, she waved and sat down and watched Simone open the show. As Tift played her music, Simone looked on with admiration. Each took turns showing us how to listen—with attention, appreciation, and even love.

Working together requires us to appreciate one another and model for others how to listen deeply.

5. The payoff for collaboration is harmony and delight. At one point, Simone was playing an elegant piece, when Tift bent down and came up playing . . . a harmonica. Not a normal accompaniment to classical piano, yet it worked. Their concluding song was the cover band mainstay "I Can See Clearly Now." Tift crooned and tapped her guitar

The Difficulty and Glory of Collaboration

while Simone played . . . Beethoven. Neither could perform this way without the other.

Individually these two are great in their own worlds. Yet together they could do things that neither could do alone.

In such collaboration we can see the wisdom of ancient Christian accounts of music. To make music is not to invent anything. It's to discover something that's already there, to which we only rarely have access. A musician gives access to something, a holy of holies to which we rarely get admittance—the harmony of the Father, Son, and Holy Spirit in world-creating mutual embrace.

Little wonder that echoes of such harmony come more often by way of collaboration than by way of individual performance.

Part 6

Searching for Jesus in Sports

I KNOW PRECISELY WHY I write. Because it's fun. I know some writers agonize over their prose, freeze before the blank screen, and I've been there. But mostly writing is a delight. I'm less interested in what the work does after its over than I am in creating it. Self-indulgent, to be sure, but there we are.

If writing is fun, these pieces were downright delicious, a party on the page. I've grown up a Duke basketball fan—we moved to Chapel Hill when I was a kid because the schools were "better" but my dad worked at Duke. I attended my first Duke basketball game as an eight year old when Mike Krzyzewski had his first good team, in the 1983–84 season. Johnny Dawkins, K's first great, was a sophomore, effusing delight and dropping left-handed rainbows over helpless defenses when he wasn't dunking backwards over (literally) would-be defenders. It was fun to catch the Duke basketball wave as it was rising, to stand out counterculturally in Chapel Hill, and to live and die with the mini-dramas on the court. My most prized memory of my late mother is when she went with me to sneak into a Duke-Carolina game in Cameron. She was just crazy enough to agree to such a thing. God bless her memory.

I love sports for the same reason most of the millions of loafers on their recliners worldwide—the mini-dramas, the character stories, the suspense, all things that should be present in our lives as Christian disciples but often are not. But I don't love sports generically. I love Duke basketball, and could

Part 6: Searching for Jesus in Sports

hardly bring myself to write about basketball in general. I'm attracted more to obscure players too. These essays are the fruit of studying Duke entirely too meticulously for entirely too long. I wish I could replace the memory power represented here with some kind of more virtuous data. Failing that I just write about it. Duke football is an entirely different species—what God gives us Dukies to keep us humble during the basketball off-season. I've attended Duke's last three bowl games (in 1989 and 1994) and plan to be at the next one, if Jesus doesn't come back first. Even bad teams and programs have good players and moments and better people, and we had one in Chris Combs, profiled here.

My own athletic career is a bit less glamorous than those in royal blue. I failed to make the basketball team in tenth grade—a grave injustice I shall avenge someday—but only then could I start leading in our school's campus Christian group, which met at the same time basketball practice would have been. It seems providential, and whatever kind of writer or preacher I am, I would have been no kind of basketball player—even if I *was* the best guard at my high school (is there no justice?).

Running, later in life, was more of an attempt at health than one I pursued as a sports fan. I was lured in by friendship and stayed for the runner's high. And I couldn't help finding myself drawing parallels and conclusions for Christian leadership. I was working for Leadership Education at Duke Divinity at the time, but it's more than that. We reach for the sports metaphors for a reason, and running seems particularly rife with them. I was proud to run a marathon, however slowly (I remember people passing me while I was still "running" who were, in fact, walking), and I'm glad my day job benefited a little.

As a writer, I felt almost giddy when I could connect sports, the early church fathers, and Christian institutional leadership—like a triple jump in checkers, entirely too much fun for one blog post. As much fun as these pieces were to write, they're also deeply serious in a way. Some of my favorite theological insights happen in these pages. I love Augustine's pelican more than I can express. I cherish Chris Combs turning a sports "failure" into a lifelong source of humble grace. And I love that attending to sports can make for better insights than the hackneyed clichés and faulty analogies that usually come from athletics or leadership manuals. More interesting observations come when we pay attention to specific people and story lines and to surprising points of connection with other fields. I remember a friend in graduate school once called basketball "aesthetically pleasing." I should have slugged him. It's *fun*, it doesn't have to be turned into an obfuscating dissertation title. And like all genuine delight it's also serious—in (I hope) a lighthearted yet strenuous way.

Holy Hoops

The Quasi-religious Basketball Rivalry between Duke and North Carolina[1]

THE AIR HAS TURNED. The heat is gone, cool is here, cold is coming. This can only mean one thing: college basketball is on its way.

In advance of this quasi-liturgical season (at least for those reared in North Carolina, Kentucky, Indiana, and other enlightened places) let us ponder matters metaphysical. I have evidence for the existence of a merciful God. Proof, almost: Duke and North Carolina have never met in a men's basketball Final Four. How could heaven compare to the joy of winning such an apocalyptic contest, or hell to losing it? If bonfires and naked revelry erupt when the two meet in *regular season* games, what manner of destruction and mayhem would accompany a title game between the two?

They almost met in 1991, but God sent an ill spirit upon Carolina star Rick Fox's shooting touch, and the eschaton-inducing title match was averted. God used me to bring this about actually. I was in a video arcade on Franklin Street in my native Chapel Hill (video arcades were just barely still cool, or even open) when Fox appeared behind me at the pop-a-shot game. I had a stack of quarters, so just to get to play he challenged me. This was an error. Whatever advantage he held in height or athleticism evaporated when the goal was six feet high and five feet away. Surely the humiliation of this defeat at the hands of a teenager wearing a Duke shirt was responsible for Fox's personal debacle in the Final Four.

The Carolina/Duke rivalry is always personal. One would think that only sports fans, or just basketball fans, or more narrowly still Duke or Carolina fans, would care about a book on the history of this rivalry. Even a very good sports book like Art Chansky's *Blue Blood* suggests as much by its

---

1. Copyright © 2007 by *Books & Culture*. "Holy Hoops: The Quasi-religious Basketball Rivalry between Duke and North Carolina" by Jason Byassee is reprinted by permission from the September/October 2007 issue of *Books & Culture*.

Part 6: Searching for Jesus in Sports

subtitle: *Inside the Most Storied Rivalry in College Hoops.*[2] But Will Blythe's wonderful title truthfully announces how much more widely applicable his work is: *To Hate Like This Is to Be Happy Forever: A Thoroughly Obsessive, Intermittently Uplifting, and Occasionally Unbiased Account of the Duke-North Carolina Basketball Rivalry.*[3] Here is Blythe, a grown man, a successful writer for *Esquire* and the *New Yorker*, among other esteemed publications, who still shouts at the TV when these two lock up. What do these lingering childhood neuroses mean? And *can* he or we even get rid of them?

The delight in the book is Blythe's hand as a wordsmith. Interestingly (from this Dukie's perspective) some of his greatest phrases come in begrudging praise of Duke players past and present. A crucial three-pointer fired in crunch time by Ichabod Crane lookalike Mike Dunleavy brought this delightful curse: "If the shot didn't fall cleanly through the hoop and stab me in the heart like the sneakiest cheatin' girlfriend." Bobby Hurley was a "New Jersey white kid" who used to "blaze up and down the court like a Chevy Camaro about to throw a rod." And more recent Duke great J. J. Redick would weave his "ceaseless figure eights around the court, rubbing defenders off big men down low, darting for the cover of successive screens like a roach desperately seeking a hiding place." It's only natural that his greatest turns of phrase come in praise of his mortal enemy. For the hatred has become second nature to him—he *needs* to hate Duke—and when he spends a year following players and coaches from both teams, he finds himself disconcerted to be liking some of the dark minions. Just a little.

But Blythe wields a powerful pen praising the Tar Heels as well. Shooter Joe Forte could launch jump shots that fell "into the net like groceries plopped into a bag by a pimply checkout boy." When all-time great Michael Jordan dunked the ball, he would "throw it down as if punishing it for insubordination." And when Sean May almost single-handedly defeated Illinois for the national title, he did so by "fouling out every big man in the state of Illinois, including ones not yet born." The gentle giant had magnificent hands: "Watching him shoot was akin to watching a bear dine on salmon with a knife and fork—such unexpected refinement captured one's notice."

But it's not just great sports writing with applications to other spheres of life that make this book jump off the shelf. As a southerner himself (and a Chapel Hill native like me), he can't escape religion. He's tried—he lives in New York City, where worship of hoops and God are both very much

---

2. *Blue Blood: Duke-Carolina: Inside the Most Storied Rivalry in College Hoops* (New York: St. Martin's, 2006).

3. *To Hate Like This Is to Be Happy Forever: A Thoroughly Obsessive, Intermittently Uplifting, and Occasionally Unbiased Account of the Duke-North Carolina Basketball Rivalry* (New York: HarperCollins, 2006).

optional. But neither is optional back home. And Blythe's sports-watching habits have had an impact on his particular blend of not-quite-faith, raising the troubling question of whether they do for the rest of us. As he stands in the receiving line in the Presbyterian Church fellowship hall after his father's funeral, the pastor sidles up beside him to whisper this nugget of compassion amidst grief: "UCLA by ten. But it's early." Blythe reflects, "If only all parsons ministered to their flocks like this, I might still be a churchgoer."

Blythe's mother "tried to placate the New England God of her youth, that stern Congregationalist who frowned upon too much celebration." So she didn't celebrate wins too much. Blythe, on the other hand, asked hard questions about the providence of God and prayer for sports victories: "It was clear to my eleven-year-old mind that if God didn't care about who won the basketball game, then who was to say He gave a shit about an individual sparrow falling from the sky?" His front-row seat for a year of Tobacco Road basketball yields this observation about one of the culture war's verbal grenades: "'Hate is not a family value.' That depended on whose family you were talking about."

One family not at all built on hate that Blythe follows most closely is that of Melvin Scott. He'd been an urban basketball legend in Baltimore, and that was his ticket out of a risky neighborhood. He'd had decent success at Carolina early on, but in the year Blythe writes of, 2004–2005 (in which the Heels eventually won the national title), Scott's role on the team steadily declined. His friends back home in Baltimore told him to shoot more, take charge more, like he did back in the day. But Chapel Hill's caramel drawls and kind strangers and palatial basketball life had softened him, melting the chip right off his shoulder. Nevertheless, he graduated from a great state university (loathe as I am to call it that), and forms the warm heartbeat amidst the book's rollicking humor.

Blythe even finds humanity in Duke's coach, Mike Krzyzewski, "the dark prince" or "the rat," as he likes to call him (the latter an unkind reflection on K's visage). He is wary the rat will charm him. Dictators and fiends are often charming: "The killer in his cell was so gracious, so mannerly, so calm. It was hard to believe that he had eaten an entire family of Icelandic farmers." Even so he *is* charmed. Coach K comes from a Polish immigrant family in Chicago, so he can take the state of North Carolina's disdain for his élitis*e* school, all the while smiling that he makes them learn how to spell the very name his father once anglicized. Pretty soon the author and the rat are crying about their respective mothers during their interview. "The world was too damned complicated. Man, this hatred gig was tough."

Still, Blythe manages to sustain it against all odds, coming full circle back to the view that Duke is the domain of self-righteous, egotistical rich

Part 6: Searching for Jesus in Sports

kids whom Carolina fans are fully in their rights to despise. So he'll hang onto the "eternal-toddler" manner of sports. Where else can an erstwhile Presbyterian cut loose? Sports fans, especially Christian ones, will love watching him do precisely that in these pages.

Duke Basketball

You Are What You Do Regularly, Excellently[1]

THE CLICHÉ THAT "PRACTICE makes perfect" is, of course, wrong. Yet practice can habituate to the point that we're more rather than less likely to do the right thing. And good practice means we don't have to think about what to do.

I saw this recently at an open practice of the Duke basketball team, offered as part of Coach Mike Krzyzewski's leadership seminar. You may recall last spring that my Blue Devils had a bit of athletic success on the hardwood. In the last moment of the title game against upstart Butler, Duke was on defense, up a mere point, with the seemingly unstoppable Gordon Hayward primed to play the hero. He slipped past his man and had what looked like a clear lane to the basket. Until, that is, Duke's 7'1" big man Brian Zoubek leaped out at him and altered his path and his shot. Hayward missed long by inches and Zoubek grabbed the rebound.

It was a simple, unglamorous, and glorious play.

Afterwards Zoubek was remarkably unimpressed with himself. He attributed his heroics to a play the Blue Devils run every day in practice called "closeout." The moment when the national title was on the line and Hayward saw his way clear to the basket, Zoubek didn't have to think. His body *knew* what to do. He stretched himself out and forced Hayward to take a tougher shot than he would have liked. Hayward swore later the shot felt like it was good.

At practice, I got to see the drill for myself. Four defenders go up against five offensive players who are charged to pass until one has an open shot. The defenders' role is to scramble as best they can to guard the

---

1. This essay was first published on November 2, 2010, as a post to *Call & Response*, a blog on the Web site of *Faith & Leadership*, the online magazine of Leadership Education at Duke University.

shooter—simulating helping against an opponent who's just beaten his man. Just like Hayward beat his man last spring with the game on the line.

The drill's glory is its very ordinariness. Close out on the open shooter? Cut down nets on a Monday night in April? Yeah, we do that here.

Another point of practice that impressed me was the players' talking. The five hundred or so in the stands weren't nearly as loud as the ten on the floor. To hear K tell it, talking is the most important thing the players learn how to do in practice. "We can't call a timeout every time we're in trouble," he said. "They've got to figure out their problems on the court." Here K made the clear connection to the organizations represented at the conference—the teams in our (less athletic) organizations also have to learn how to trust each other to talk through our problems on the fly.

I was struck by how the practicing Dukies could run a play perfectly, and K or one of his assistants might still fuss at them for failing to talk. As soon as they broke into a new drill or scrimmage, the players broke out in song-like unison, chattering, encouraging, shouting, cajoling, demanding excellence from one another. "Mason! Andre!" K called out to two sophomores at one point—both of whom made contributions last year, and from whom more will be expected this year. "Kyle and Nolan [the team captains] are down there. *You guys* have got to talk." Mason Plumlee and Andre Dawkins did nothing but dunk and rain threes all day. But it wasn't good enough if these budding floor leaders didn't talk.

Maybe that's what leadership, what excellence, is: knowing when to talk and when not to. Zoubek didn't talk up his heroics after the championship. But this basketball program—which K often calls a family—insists on talking nonstop in practice and in games. K is a great coach. But the greatest coach never leaves the sideline. When games are on the line next spring, he won't be out there hunting for that next title. The players will. And you can bet they'll be talking. And closing out.

And winning titles? Yeah, maybe that, too.

Invisible, Sticky Leaders[1]

Athletes, coaches, and fans of all sports know that not every player on a team can be a superstar. No matter how many scorers you have on a basketball team, there's only one ball. Someone has to play defense, rebound, and dive to the floor to keep the thing from going out of bounds.

To stay with basketball for a moment—and go local—no one outside of Duke Nation is likely to remember David McClure, a player who graduated in 2009. He never showed up on *SportsCenter* with thunderous dunks or dagger-in-the-heart three-pointers. Reporters rarely gave him the honor of being the postgame interviewee; television commentators seldom or never named him MVP. He did score a game-winning shot once as a junior against Clemson—but even then, appropriately, the credit went to the player who threw him the dazzling pass (and a certain controversy with the clock that we Dukies choose to forget).

All McClure did most of the time was guard the other team's best player, rebound like a fiend, and do the dirty work to set up his teammates to shine. In short, his play was largely invisible, except to his coaches and teammates and their counterparts on the other bench who knew he helped Duke win. Don't be surprised if Duke is a worse team this year without him—or if the commentators struggle to explain why.

McClure was a "glue guy": he held the team together by grit and tenacity without being noticed for his own sake. To continue the metaphor, he was sticky, getting his hands on loose balls he shouldn't have and binding his teammates to one another. He was a leader who was barely noticed even as he led.

To risk blasphemy, he was a bit like the Holy Spirit. The patristics scholar Joseph Lienhard wrote an essay years ago about St. Augustine's interest in the odd biblical word *glue*.[2] When Augustine hears the word in the psalter (they

---

1. This essay was first published on October 15, 2009, as a post to *Call & Response*, a blog on the Web site of *Faith & Leadership*, the online magazine of Leadership Education at Duke University.

2. "'The Glue Itself Is Charity': Ps. 62:9 in Augustine's Thought," in *Augustine:*

mostly read Scripture aloud in the ancient world rather than read it silently), he thinks immediately of the Holy Spirit. In Augustine's theology, the Spirit is the glue, or the love, between the Father and the Son. Likewise, the Spirit is the One who glues us creatures to the Son and so to the Father.

This glue work is not easy. Augustine argues against what we might call "charismatic" opponents who think salvation does not require participation in the church: "For charity itself, which holds people together in a knot of unity, would not have a means of infusing souls and almost mixing them together if people could teach nothing to people." The very difficulty of arguing over the meaning of Scripture in church becomes, by God's grace, the glue that binds us together, the pitch and tar that seal us to one another as surely as the glue in Augustine's world. We need glue because of the brokenness between us in this age of human sin and frailty, and thanks be to God that the Spirit glues the shards of our life back together even as we sinners go on smashing things.

Glue people are leaders. Even if we cannot see them lead most of the time. The Eastern Orthodox theological tradition speaks of the Spirit as the shy member of the Trinity; she points not to herself but to Christ. David McClure, and the glue people in all of our organizations, could not agree more.

Presbyter Factus Sum, ed. E. C. Muller, R. J. Teske, and Joseph T. Lienhard (New York: Peter Lang, 1993) 375–84.

The Last Guy on the Bench

Casey Peters[1]

ONE ADVANTAGE OF WRITING about the goodness of *institutional* leaders is that we can attend to those not usually in the limelight. There is no transformative leader who is not nurtured in a vibrant institution before giving life to other vibrant institutions. Leadership literature often falls prey to fascination with the great woman or man, forgetting that any genuine greatness is communal and enabled by people whose faces the public rarely sees.

I saw this anew recently at the Duke basketball banquet commemorating the 2011 season. The stars of the show were justifiably graduating senior All-Americans Nolan Smith and Kyle Singler. But the most surprising star was their fellow senior, former walk-on Casey Peters. Nolan and Kyle won a national championship, turned in two of the great athletic careers in the history of the Atlantic Coast Conference, and will be drafted into the NBA soon. The event program had to scrounge for Peters' on-court accomplishments: one rebound in a game his junior year. He had the ball in his hands as time expired against UNC once. Casey Peters never scored a point in his Duke career.

But Peters has long been a crowd favorite at Duke, partly because he appeared only at the end of blowout victories ("Casey Peters!" chants, pleading with Coach K to put him in, echoed in Cameron at the end of such games).

I'd learned a little more about Peters recently when I toured the team's weight room and saw its posting of individual players' athletic accomplishments. I expected some of what I saw there: the top vertical leapers on the team are the Plumlee brothers, skinny Kyrie Irving isn't a weightlifting champ, etc. But at the top of several of the athletic lists is one Casey Peters: fastest mile, top bench press weight, most times benching 185 pounds.

---

1. This essay was first published on May 3, 2011, as a post to *Call & Response*, a blog on the Web site of *Faith & Leadership*, the online magazine of Leadership Education at Duke University.

Part 6: Searching for Jesus in Sports

Peters isn't Rudy, a fan favorite because he's a runt. That guy's a beast in the weight room and on the track.

Both Kyle and Nolan wept as they thanked Peters, their classmate and Kyle's roommate. It's touching enough to see twenty-one-year-old men weepily profess their love for one another (with no liquid courage involved). What was more impressive was Peters' tribute back to them: equally weepy, but more revealing.

Peters spoke of how hard he worked to make the Duke team. He arrived from a good, not great, high school career in New Jersey and went to work for Duke as a manager. He was good enough in pickup games to be considered for the team, but selection was far from automatic. So he worked in that weight room and on that court. In his farewell speech, Peters thanked the weight coach for working extra time with him every day to make the team. Nolan Smith praised Peters for taking extra shots before and after practice—this for a player who would *never once* shoot in a game in his Duke career. And when he made the team, Peters said through tears, Nolan Smith, Duke's public face and national player of the year candidate, sobbed with joy over his triumph. Peters then went from walk-on to the ultimate pinnacle: a scholarship player.

"I think of myself as a hard worker," Smith said, "but Casey works harder." Then he turned from his speaking notes on the podium and looked at his friend: "Casey, you made me better."

This is a remarkable statement from the team's heartbeat and leader, the one who always takes the big shot and gets the media attention: a walk-on few outside of Durham have heard of made him, and so the whole team, better.

That's how you lead in an institution as vibrant as Duke basketball: work hard, make others better, have fun, love your friends, inspire others, set goals so big they're nearly impossible, achieve them, and then pay no mind to the public anonymity. Those who know, know you matter.

Duke Football
How to React to a Failure that's Not Your Fault?[1]

CHRIS COMBS WAS A star defensive lineman for the Duke football team in the late 1990s. He holds the school record in tackles-for-losses, was first-team all-conference twice, and went on to play in the NFL for four seasons. Yet Combs has the misfortune of being remembered for a game-changing penalty more than anything else.

It was third and long as Duke held on to a tenuous lead at archrival Virginia in Charlottesville. UVA was right on the edge of field goal range. A big play here likely tips the outcome in Duke's favor. It would be a huge win for a victory-starved Duke over star-studded and bowl-bound Virginia. Combs, a Virginia native, was determined to make that big play in front of his many friends and family members who were in the stands. As he did so often in his career, he tore through the opponent's offensive line and sacked the quarterback. Combs leapt up and saluted his personal cheering section as it went wild for him.

The ref threw his flag: unsportsmanlike conduct for excessive celebration, fifteen yards for Virginia and a first down. The referee had effectively taken the game out of the hands of the players and decided it himself. Even today, ten years later, when Combs attends alumni or fan club events, he is greeted with salutes or serenaded with the name "Sarge." He takes it in good humor. But it clearly still bothers him.

When we met recently, I too asked this ACC football great about his moment of undeserved failure rather than his twenty moments of greatness (career sacks) or years with the Pittsburgh Steelers and Jacksonville Jaguars. A serious Christian, Combs now looks back at that career-marking play with a theological frame.

---

1. This essay was first published on December 2, 2009, as a post to *Call & Response*, a blog on the Web site of *Faith & Leadership*, the online magazine of Leadership Education at Duke University.

One, the ref repented. Two weeks later, before another game, he approached Combs to apologize. "I'm really sorry I had to throw that flag," he said. Even now Combs is not sure exactly what sort of apology this was. "That's okay, sir," he said at the time, biting his tongue. Reflecting back on the conversation now, Combs reflects that he "never was much to challenge adults."

Two, Combs sure dialed down his celebrating. After a sack in the NFL, he just walked back to the huddle. His teammates ribbed him for not celebrating. Jacksonville's star quarterback Mark Brunell dubbed him "Five-State Combs," saying his serious demeanor forecasted a five-state killing spree. A UVA grad on the Jaguars piped up. "I can tell you why Combs doesn't celebrate," he said, and passed on the story.

Combs' larger reaction is more faith-filled. "Football was an idol to me," he said. It sure isn't now. "If you value anything more than God, that's an idol."

Combs may be too hard on his old, less-Christian self here. He was just a driven football player, as all successful people are driven. An assistant coach saw him as a rookie and called him "a blind dog in a meat factory"—all motor and no smarts. So he told Combs he "had a chance" to play in the NFL. That glimpse of hope was enough, and Combs became a dedicated student of the game. He watched film and lifted weights maniacally. When teammates spent spring break in Cancun, he'd travel to work all week with a personal trainer. His position coach taught him to be a master at noticing the small things: "When offensive linemen are heavy in their stance it's a running play. At least in college. They're too big not to tell the play in advance." By his senior year he was so in the groove of the game he could see what was going to happen before the offense snapped the ball.

The hard and smart work paid off personally for Combs, even if his team in college won very infrequently. Combs stepped away from any potential idolatry for good when he stopped being Duke's strength and conditioning coach two years ago. He wanted to have control over his schedule (his former boss, ex-Duke head coach Ted Roof, once coached at four different schools in thirteen months). He has a young child now, and so works for the gentler taskmaster of Merrill Lynch.

The experience of losing so often at Duke has been helpful for this relatively new investor. "Just look at the economy we're in," he said. It taught him to worry about what he could control rather than what he couldn't. Combs is used to working hard even if the result, for now, is a loss. If you can't stop a ref throwing an idiotic flag, or an economy from tanking, you sure can work harder and smarter than everyone else, and get better on every play.

And you can win in the game of life. Even if you didn't as much as you deserved to on the football field.

Marathons

Straining toward Holiness. Together.[1]

THERE ARE MANY VERSIONS of Christianity that hold the faith to be merely a matter of belief. We might ask, "Can you swallow that the world was created by a good God who sustains it in existence?" And maybe potential believers can. But such questions don't require us to do much more than hold those beliefs in the space between our temples.

Jesus often demands more than beliefs. For example, in Luke 12, Jesus wants us to act. "Sell your possessions, give alms, be ready for the end." These are the sorts of demands that can set us to intellectual dissembling: "He didn't really mean . . ." Or: "Viewed in its historical context . . ."

I wonder instead whether life built on the strength of community could make some of this discipline seem . . . doable.

In the last few months a friend and I have tried to train for a marathon. We each have some pounds to lose. Or dozens. We're Methodist ministers, we go to potlucks; it's not easy, okay?

The first few times we tried to run, the spirit was willing, but the flesh was weak. The alarm would go off at 6 a.m., and I would rejoice to see that it was raining outside. Can't possibly run today. Anything to avoid the date with soreness and sleepiness.

Then something happened. I realized that whether I made it out there or not, my friend would be there. If I didn't show up, he'd run alone in the dark. Suddenly the decision of whether or not to run wasn't just about me. It was about my friend, who, if I failed to get up, would be left alone. I started showing up more.

As we ran, we got to listening to one another's stories differently. Something happens as you crawl toward 26.2. It takes us hours. We've taken

---

1. This essay was first published on June 30, 2010, as a post to *Call & Response*, a blog on the Web site of *Faith & Leadership*, the online magazine of Leadership Education at Duke University.

to calling each other "cellmate." We're beginning to finish each other's sentences and to ask for retellings of stories about each other's cousins.

This is how relationships are supposed to work. You can't cram it all into a power lunch. You have to have long stretches of unstructured time where you've both long since run out of things to say.

Something else happened: our bodies started to change. We'd run for hours and feel great all day—energized, like we're flying. We pressed through injuries so that weak muscles and joints went from wounded to better to strong. We made progress through friendship to health. Now we wouldn't *not* run.

This is how the early Methodists pursued God. They banded together in small groups to ask one another how their pursuit of God had gone: "So, did anyone sin this week?" They also had to do works of mercy like visiting in prisons and feeding the hungry. And they had to give financially to the group to support mission.

Notice: all these acts are public, bodily, externally verifiable—done together, never alone. A relationship between me and Jesus was never enough.

People who work in public health know that you can't correct a public malady with individual solutions alone. Want to stamp out smoking? You don't just pass out information and trade on guilt. You also tax the bejeezus out of cigarettes. You make smoking illegal in many places. And you build a culture of disapproval around it. You have to change a whole ecology of behavior.

So too with holiness. Ancient Methodists knew that you would need friends, communities, churches, and eventually whole societies to pursue holiness if you wanted individuals to do the same. It's no accident my friend and I are running. We're in a town that's built running trails. Our culture increasingly frowns on fatness. In fact, our culture's banging of the drum of health runs the risk of substituting for faith—are we seeking eternal life as we bound around the track?

My friend and I are only halfway to twenty-six miles. But I'll bet we'll get there. Not because either one of us can do it alone, but because (and only because) we've done it together. And that's how to pursue selling possessions, giving alms, and waiting actively for Jesus' return.

And how to avoid the doughnut shop.

Marathons as Grace or Heresy?[1]

I LOVE SARAH COAKLEY's comparison between our culture's obsession with bodily health and the ancient Christian heresy of Pelagianism. For Coakley, efforts to make the body infinitely pliable, to keep it "jogging on (literally) for as long as possible," amounts to a new version of the old teaching Augustine rejected. The Pelagians taught that if we worked hard enough on holiness we could earn our favor with God. Coakley and Augustine both insist that God grants favor out of sheer goodness and mercy. Salvation is God's doing; all that's left for us is to give thanks.

Having just run a marathon—the Outer Banks Marathon, from Kitty Hawk to Manteo, North Carolina—I'm more interested in Coakley's comparison than ever.

People keep asking me why I did it. I don't actually know. I've written before about how training with someone gets you going farther than you ever could by yourself. True enough. But 26.2?!

Part of the allure is the danger. People do die running these things. There is a sort of epic struggle trying to max out what the body can do. Sure enough, my running partner had tendinitis flare up in his shin and couldn't run after mile thirteen. Around mile twenty-something my right arm got very cold. Odd. But the extreme exertion is part of the point. Where else in our culture do we put ourselves in danger for some worthy goal?

A recent documentary about the growing enthusiasm for marathons described another part of the allure. These races are populated by two kinds of runners: those who compete and those who just want to complete. My friends and I were decidedly in the latter camp. Yet we ran "with" those who finished in less than three hours. Imagine playing on the same court as Michael Jordan or studying at the same library desk with Cornel West.

---

1. This essay was first published on December 8, 2010, as a post to *Call & Response*, a blog on the Web site of *Faith & Leadership*, the online magazine of Leadership Education at Duke University.

Part 6: Searching for Jesus in Sports

When we arrived for the race I saw the attraction even more. There were not only thousands of runners. There were also thousands of fans. Apparently in a tourist area like the Outer Banks, locals are delighted to have visitors in a down economy, especially in the off-season. Every mile, cheering strangers shouted words of encouragement that were almost as helpful as their Gatorade and Gu. I made a point to look them in the eye and say thanks (until mile twenty, when I could no longer speak out loud. Then I mouthed it). It reminded me of a time when I was in Cameron Indoor Stadium with a friend when Mike Krzyzewski walked in just before tipoff. The building rose in applause. My friend turned to me, "What would it be like to get a standing ovation just for showing up to work?" Truth is, most of us could use such recognition. In a marathon you get it twenty-six times.

The main reason I ran has to be theological. I don't mean to be trite: the martyrs are the first theologians, their work written in their blood, and millions of persecuted Christians are out there now (in fact, the popularity of extreme exercise may be a reaction to hyper-modernity's noxious safety). But bear with me. This will take telling some details of the race.

After I left my training partner at mile eight I did nothing but pass people until twenty-one. I was in a groove, feeling great. But at twenty-one that fell apart. The last five miles for me were all want-to. I drank and ate and stretched as much as I could and just soldiered on.

Somewhere around mile twenty-two I found myself crying. I didn't mean to, and I'm not a person who cries frequently. But I realized I was going to make it. I'd worked for this goal for over a year, I was in the homestretch, and it was going to happen. The finish was anticlimactic compared to this realization: I'd set out a goal and here I was fulfilling it.

Sounds like Coakley's heretical "sweaty Pelagianism," doesn't it?

Then at twenty-four I began crying again (so much for my claim about being a rare cryer). This time it wasn't about my success. I'd seen a pelican soaring over the water. A common sight at the beach, sure. But pelicans, according to St. Augustine, are Christ symbols. He'd heard stories of mother pelicans slaying their young, then wounding themselves and pouring their blood on their young, reviving them. To his credit he's not sure it's true biologically! But if it *is*, what a great image it would be of the savior who wounds us and himself in order to save.

When I saw the pelican, I saw Jesus, who wounds himself to save us. And suddenly all human effort to achieve, all desire for danger for the sake of some greater good, all community in which Jesus' beloved creatures cheer on one another to greater deeds, all of it made sense. It's odd to pound out 26.2 miles in order to see the very Jesus you can see in your Bible, your church down on the corner, your own heart. But no one ever said marathoners are anything other than odd.

Part 7

Searching for Jesus in Christian Institutions

A FRIEND RECENTLY SAID in passing, while discussing a potential job change, "I believe in institutions. They're not necessary evils. They're positive goods." She couldn't have been more right. Many of the best goods in my life have been mediated by institutions: Davidson College, Duke University, *The Christian Century*, the United Methodist Church. We could go back further: preschool, sports leagues, hospitals, bookstores, whoever built this computer. It's hard to think of a single good humans pass on to one another that is not institutionally mediated. And Christians, who meet Jesus only because he sent his Spirit upon the church, should know that more deeply than anyone.

Of course we don't. A current rap video making the rounds (for another Internet-mediated meme of twenty-seven or so seconds) pillories the church and celebrates Jesus. For a medium that trades on the moment, this distinction is a good half millennium old at the very least. We've been trying to get the goods of institutions without their ills forever. It doesn't work. Institutions are as corrupt and as glorious as we human beings are, mired in sin and made in the image of God, being repaired by the Spirit on the way to the renewal of all things. Why we're shocked when they fail or when they succeed is beyond me.

The problem with our institutions is that our rhetoric hasn't caught up with them. We still sound like we live in the 1960s when we speak of them (Individuals good! Institutions bad!)—oblivious, contemptuous, ignorant

Part 7: Searching for Jesus in Christian Institutions

in the profound sense of the goods made possible in our lives that would not be there otherwise. Greg Jones of Duke taught me that the church in Africa doesn't lack dynamic, inventive, creative geniuses. What they lack is functioning institutions: hospitals, banks, universities, governments, denominations, businesses. Christians there do not mock, lampoon, or pillory institutions. They need them. So do we. We just take their presence for granted and so snidely dismiss them. Try getting that rap video made without the institutions that build the Web, the computer, the camera, the traditions that gave birth to rap, or, in fact, the institutions that pass on the tradition of church-bashing.

These institutions are ones I love or have come to love by getting to know them. Often friends work there and share the goods of their lives made possible by so working. Other times they invited me to spend time with them and I learned about the particular shape of the gospel over time in that place, forged by that mission, tended to on that patch of ground. No doubt I received a flattering portrait of each place in one way. But as Hugh Heclo points out in *On Thinking Institutionally*,[1] our capacity to be outraged by an institution suggests we still expect them to behave honorably and improve our lives.

I've come to think of institutions on two analogies: the pregnant Mary and the eucharistic chalice. Just as both hold our salvation, but are not themselves it, so too institutions bear grace to us but can themselves fail, often miserably, precisely because what they bear is so precious. I hope some of these pieces about particular places give some sense of how those analogies hold.

Seminarians often pause before entering ordained ministry these days. They say a version of this: "The United Methodist Church may not be around for my whole career; why should I do all the work to give myself to it in ordination?" It's a sobering question. Indeed the UMC may vanish and the church universal would worship on. What's striking is this—where else will they give themselves in ministry? If they go on their own, they'll effectively be starting a new institution. That can work grandly; we Methodists did that too once. Yet why do they think that the institution they found will be any less fragile, or any more grace-bearing, than the one they opt out of? Just as no one can be Christian alone, no one can worship Jesus without an institution—namely, the church.

---

1. *On Thinking Institutionally* (Boulder, CO: Paradigm, 2008).

Hierarchy of Holiness[1]

ONE OF THE GREATEST gifts of the modern West is our insistence on the equal dignity of all human beings. Yet every gift has a concomitant challenge: We find it enormously difficult to justify distinguishing one person as higher than another.

It's true that all too often, hierarchy is simply about the exercise of domination. Like a game of "king of the hill," the strongest hurls the others off the peak until shoved off by someone even stronger.

Yet it is difficult to get rid of hierarchies and get people to accomplish anything. So we continue to institute them, even while those not at the top grumble and those who are at the top watch for challenges to their reign.

Is There Any Other Way?

I think of the line from "Ye Watchers and Ye Holy Ones": "Higher than the cherubim and more glorious by far than the seraphim." This line does not appear in many Protestant hymnals. That's because it is about Mary, mother of Jesus, toward whom we Protestants tend to blow cold. But think with our Catholic and Orthodox brethren for a moment: If there is a hierarchy of holiness in the world, Mary is at the top. And not because she has hurled anyone else down. It's because she is holding out a way for all others to climb up.

Given our contemporary, Western difficulty in thinking well of hierarchy I went looking in Orthodoxy for some help. Eastern Orthodox Christianity's gift is that it claims to steward the treasures of ancient theology unchanged from their origins to today. And I found it in the work of Vladimir Lossky, one of the great generation of Russian émigré theologians who

---

1. This essay was first published on June 30, 2010, by *Faith & Leadership*, the online magazine of Leadership Education at Duke University.

Part 7: Searching for Jesus in Christian Institutions

fled the Bolsheviks (another group who was against hierarchy in principle and yet was maniacally hierarchical in practice).

Lossky writes of the way the Holy Spirit is present to all people. Quoting from the sixth-century church father Maximus the Confessor, Lossky writes the Spirit is even more "particularly present in all those who have the law," meaning among the Jews, who received God's revelation at Sinai. And, naturally, the Spirit is present in Christians, whom God draws into union as sons and daughters.

It's (unfortunately) not surprising that Maximus draws distinctions with Christians at the top. But he goes on: all baptized people may have a portion of the Spirit, but not everyone has the gift of wisdom—"Only in those who have understanding," who by "struggles and labors" have that additional gift. And yet another distinction crops up: the saints, who have the deepest gift of understanding so as to enter into full union with God.

Lossky comments, "In relation to union with God, the universe is arranged in concentric circles." Or, he might have said, in hierarchies.

It is true that many of our worst moments in history as Christians have come when we have identified ourselves as better than others, as Maximus does here. Yet what impresses me about Maximus is the concentric circle at the innermost point: the saints. The ultimate grace-filled hierarchy is one of holiness. And most of us who look in the mirror, spiritually speaking, are aware that we belong nowhere near the top of that.

But some do. Think of the holiest person you've known. One to whom you could sit and listen all day. One who breathed in and exhaled a grace that made you want to stand closer. And one whose presence showed you that God regards you as more precious than you ever thought. Such a person is like Mary, extending down to you the grace given to her.

I witnessed that in Jean Vanier, founder of L'Arche, who visited Duke Divinity School last year. L'Arche is a series of small intentional communities where able-bodied people live in community with adults with disabilities. Vanier is in the winter of his life, and rarely leaves the house he started in France in 1964.

When it was time for Vanier to go to the airport, Stanley Hauerwas, my teacher whom Vanier came to see and argue against and write with, leaned over and kissed him on the forehead. For me, it was a glimpse of the meeting of theology (Hauerwas) and practice (Vanier), of dialectical rigor and holiness, of a white-hot intellect and a blazing fire of grace. I felt like I should take off my shoes—that's what you do when "righteousness and peace kiss," as the psalmist says (Ps 85:10).

Each man has used his position of authority in a hierarchy—one as founder of an institution, the other as a university professor. They have reached down from their place to pull others up. Vanier has made space for the disabled to live with dignity and the able-bodied to learn their fear in the face of weakness. Hauerwas has introduced students to the joyful discipline of academic theology. Both delight in having helped others be better than they were. They are not at the top to fling others down, but to fling them up.

If you asked them where that holiness came from they'd likely deny it, or turn attention back to you, or to God. That's holiness—fascinated with God and the other, uninterested in the self. That's the center of the concentric circles of grace in Maximus' and Lossky's thought.

And that's hierarchy, of a sort. Not bishops or rectors or presidents at the top, though each has his or her place. In this life we cannot regularize holiness, and someone has to take the lead in running an organization. But such people do not rule, ultimately. Only saints do.

It is good news that Mary is not only higher than the cherubim, but more glorious "by far" than the seraphim. She's working to pull them, and all of us, up to where she is and all of us long to be: with God.

Outrageous Ambition in East Africa[1]

"THIS WAS A TOTAL accident. We had no master plan."

So says one of the wisest and warmest-hearted leaders I've ever met: Zablon N'Thamburi. Formerly the presiding bishop of the Methodist Church in Kenya, N'Thamburi until recently directed external relations for Kenya Methodist University (KeMU). Born out of the Methodist Training Institute in 1997, KeMU had from its founding a vibrant, liberal-arts style campus in Meru, several hours from Kenya's capital, Nairobi. Like most missionary churches, now indigenous, the Methodists built their university far from the bustle of the city where students could study serenely.

Then something happened.

The school had modest plans to expand to Nairobi. They were going to offer extension courses to a few dozen students on the city's outskirts. At the last second their location fell through. They scrambled, and the best they could come up with was a high-rise on a busy roundabout at the heart of the capital, one of East Africa's busiest banking hubs. It was, in short, anything but serene.

Little did they know, it was also perfect. Being on that site gave them visibility to downtown commuters—"middle-class people," N'Thamburi says, those who work day jobs in the city and want to take classes in the evenings. In Kenya, the very elite students are admitted to public schools such as the University of Nairobi and granted full scholarships. For everyone else, private schools are the only option, and as a result, KeMU has a certain "of the people" quality. For KeMu, the expansion from Meru to Nairobi worked. Suddenly KeMU couldn't offer enough courses in business and management. KeMU opened its Nairobi campus in 2007 and already has more than five thousand students. In just three years! The university

---

1. This essay was first published on September 28, 2010, as a post to *Call & Response*, a blog on the Web site of *Faith & Leadership*, the online magazine of Leadership Education at Duke University.

Outrageous Ambition in East Africa

has used the income generated by that expansion to open new campuses elsewhere in Kenya: in Nyeri, Nakuru, and Mombasa, and plans to open a campus in Juba, Southern Sudan, later this year.

You might wonder if anything is still Methodist about KeMU. One of the two high-rises it occupies (one it owns, the other rented) has an enormous photo of a headscarf-clad Muslim student, appropriately enough in a country with a large Muslim minority. Offering so many business classes to all comers is an effort to be attentive to the context in Nairobi, N'Thamburi told me. The original campus in Meru has many more theology offerings since so many pastors are trained there. The new campus envisioned for Juba will offer what the Sudanese are telling KeMU they want: health sciences, education, and yes, business. That's just to kick things off. "We'll get to know the people on the ground and then hear their interest," N'Thamburi said. This is a missional approach to education: gauge what the setting needs in both religious and secular leadership and then offer education that meets and surpasses those needs. Further, students at KeMU all have to take a course in Christian belief, and many participate in student-led worship.

I love both halves of this story: the accidental nature of KeMU's blowing up big in Nairobi, and then its eagerness to double down on that growth and expand elsewhere. Who can say where we'll bump into opportunity, totally unplanned, even by accident? KeMU showed that there's a hunger for education in downtown Nairobi—and now competitors (most church-based) have sprung up on every corner not already occupied by KeMU. I also love the haste with which they've tried to replicate that growth. No multi-decade plan here, no endowment carefully in place in advance—they're just opening new campuses, offering what they hear is needed and going for it. Here at Duke we think of ourselves as the upstart university, much younger than the Ivy's with our 1920s founding, willing therefore to have "outrageous ambition" and take risks. Clearly we have a thing or two to learn about risk and ambition from our sister university in East Africa.

Clearly vibrant institutions have to do as KeMU has done and seize a surprising opportunity even when it comes from an unexpected quarter. And then they have to be willing to pour energy and resources into expanding that opportunity. This has to be done in a missionally savvy way, faithful to the institution's heritage yet doing a new thing.

And lo and behold they'll come.

Campuses of the Kingdom[1]

IT IS HUMBLING TO contemplate how many vitally important institutions were created by the church. The hospital (early church). The university (medieval). The social service organization (early twentieth century). Habitat for Humanity (late twentieth). All trace their roots back to the church.

Yet, even though specific institutions might start out Christian, many have had a difficult time remaining Christian in any way other than name. However thriving and vibrant it might be, a Baptist hospital or a Methodist university, for example, over time might become more generic or secular, its Christian roots remaining only in a token way.

All the more reason, then, that the church should give thanks for colleges and universities that promote the ends of the reign of God. Last fall, I became better acquainted with two such schools that are as dramatically different from one another as can be imagined. The first is tiny Berea College, in Kentucky, founded by an abolitionist Christian community in 1855 and still avowedly Christian.

The other—believe it or not—is the University of Virginia, one of the oldest public universities in the United States, specifically founded as a secular institution. Though still as secular as its founder, Thomas Jefferson, intended, UVA is today the home of one of the most vibrant religion departments anywhere, a rich center of theological thought. Together, these schools show us the extreme lengths to which God will go to help the church love God with our minds.

Located in the Appalachian Mountains in eastern Kentucky, Berea was founded after the Second Great Awakening by converts coming from revivals held by the likes of Charles G. Finney. It was created as a work college, with a vision for serving rich and poor alike, committed to making students work with their hands as well as their minds. Yes, Berea admitted men *and*

1. This essay was first published on March 16, 2010, by *Faith & Leadership*, the online magazine of Leadership Education at Duke University.

women. In keeping with the egalitarian spirit of revivalist preaching (*all have sinned, Christ died for all, all can be saved*), Berea was coeducational from the beginning. Even more impressive—a miracle, really—Berea took that "all" to include African Americans. This was in a slave state. In 1855.

The college maintains these same commitments today. It is still a Christian work college with a mission to educate poor kids from the mountains. Its motto is the same as in the beginning, taken from the book of Acts: "God has made of one blood all peoples of the earth." As Shannon Wilson notes in *Berea College: An Illustrated History*,[2] few institutions—educational or otherwise—can claim to have pursued that vision in the South for so long.

The rationale for that vision—and the way in which it was executed—is breathtaking. Berea would be "antislavery, anti-caste, anti-rum, anti-sin," insisted its founder, John Fee. The school was modeled after Oberlin College, an institution founded in Ohio by a pair of Presbyterian ministers, refugees from a battle over race at Lane Seminary in Cincinnati. The link to Oberlin shows how remarkable Berea is; Oberlin is still an elite liberal arts college, one of the nation's best, but any Christian commitment is long gone.

"What Is Right Is Also Practicable"

Convinced that Jesus' gospel is a "gospel of impartial love," Fee intended to create in Berea an institution that demonstrated and furthered this conviction. The school's third president, William Frost, put the rationale beautifully. Berea, he said, "stands as an object lesson to the world—a demonstration that what is right is also practicable."

What is right is also practicable! How radical is that? So many of our beliefs remain abstract, distant, unpracticed. We believe the demanding words of the gospel: Christians should give up their possessions, love their enemies to the point of a cross, join with despised outsiders in a society with neither "Jew nor Greek, slave nor free, male nor female." But we have all sorts of sophisticated rationales for why these things can't be fully practiced.

By contrast, people who were converted in a revival more than 150 years ago believed the gospel so deeply that they founded an institution to show its truth—a college that has blessed its region and maintained its mission through all these years. There have been setbacks, of course. Early debates over doctrine hurt the school. Berea today wrestles with its Christian heritage in an age when colleges must be open to all faiths and none. For much of the twentieth century, until the 1950s, a state law

---

2. *Berea College: An Illustrated History* (Lexington: University Press of Kentucky, 2006).

prohibited the school from admitting black students. But when that law was overturned, only Berea could claim that it was *returning* to a heritage of interracial education. Other schools had to begin one. Only those with high ideals can actually fall short.

Remarkably, Berea's ideals didn't remain ideal. What would happen if we founded institutions to show that what is "right" is also "practicable"? Examples abound among social entrepreneurs: Muhammad Yunus, who pioneered the use of microcredit as founder of the Grameen Bank, showed that poor people could be good credit risks and so helped millions of women and their families in Bangladesh; Kiva, an online lending site, has built upon Yunus' insights, using the Web to recruit millions of microlenders; Teach for America has shown that young people in this country still want risky, demanding, low-reward (materially speaking) vocations.

What about the church? Where are we now founding institutions to show that our radical beliefs are also "practicable"?

An Accidental Theology Department

Few colleges or universities can claim a founder as radical as the University of Virginia's Thomas Jefferson. Today, his statues stand triumphant over the campus he "fathered," as his tombstone says. Apparently, for Jefferson, being president of the United States was a lesser distinction, so insignificant he had the carver leave it off the stone.

You can understand why when you visit UVA, a place where history lives and breathes. The beauty of the Appalachian foothills is still stimulating, just as Jefferson intended. One of Jefferson's dreams was that his school would be an "academical village" where faculty and students lived and worked together. Some students still live in housing Jefferson designed on the Old Grounds, in rooms still heated as they were in Jefferson's day, by firewood. Even a few professors still live in housing with students, including Chuck Mathewes, my host on a visit to the campus last fall. He and his wife, Jennifer Geddes, also a UVA professor, are co-principals of a residential college. They and their children live with undergraduates in a house where James Monroe lived for a decade before the university was founded. The academical village still lives.

It's not surprising that UVA is both beautiful and historic. Many state universities are. What *is* surprising is that it boasts a world-class theology department, though it's not called that. Technically, it's a religious studies department. But with world-class thinkers like Mathewes, Jamie Ferreira, Charles Marsh, Judith Kovacs, Kevin Hart, and Jim Childress, and faculty alumni like Robert Wilken, Eugene Rogers, and John Milbank, it is most certainly a center of theological thought and inquiry.

If you know anything about Jefferson, you know how odd this is. The hyper-rationalist was not content to lead the United States, birth a state university, write the Declaration of Independence, and define separation of church and state. He also wanted to update Christianity for a new age. Taking scissors to the New Testament, he cut out all but the non-miraculous, figuring he had updated the faith for a new day and allowed it to survive. Today, Jefferson's Bible is a literary oddity. Biblical Christianity, meanwhile, is alive and well.

So how did it happen that Mr. Jefferson's university would be home to a thriving theology department rooted in historic orthodoxy? The answer is counterintuitive: "It's because non-Christian religions led," Mathewes told me. "We backed into it more than anything." Early on, UVA hired a leading Buddhist scholar and translator of the Dalai Lama. Buddhists are nonthreatening to Western secularists. They pose no danger of taking over the United States and running things. Later, Virginia hired Abdulaziz Sachedina, a leading Shi'a scholar. Peter Ochs and Vanessa Ochs are great thinkers and practitioners of Judaism. If Virginia had set out to build a solely Christian department of religious studies, it would, and should, have failed. Instead, the department offered up full-throated theology, non-defensively and always open to challenge from other perspectives. And it worked. Students loved the courses.

Bursting at the Seams

By aggressively courting and hiring scholars of faiths other than Appalachia's predominant Christianity, the department cleared the necessary space to allow it also to hire top-notch Christian faculty. Once it did, those faculty naturally attracted top-notch graduate students. Now the department is bursting at the seams, literally. Two massive trailers flank its current building as the department awaits the completion of a new edifice to house its growing faculty and programs. It competes with the very best programs for PhD students and often wins. Its PhD graduates, including Duke's own Jay Carter, make its name great elsewhere.

This status is fragile, of course. Virginia will still need to hire non-Christian faculty and recruit graduate students for them, as many as or more than the Christians have. More power to them. We can't have too many excellent institutions of theological training. The University of Virginia won't be the only one who benefits. As UVA's religious studies graduates go out into the world, the church will be made smarter, more faithful, more like the biblical Christ. All, ironically enough, because of Mr. Jefferson's university.

The lesson for leadership is also counterintuitive: If we are to clear the space for a more forthright profession of Christian faith, then maybe we need first to clear more space for the forthright profession of other faiths. Long may great Buddhist and Muslim scholars inhabit the halls of "The University" (as the school presumptuously calls itself). The church is better off for it.

Second, a thriving community, on Christian grounds, can pop up in unexpected places. Truth be told, a Christian department is probably what Jefferson would have had in mind for religion. It just would have been a Christianity ruled by the Enlightenment's vision of a rationalism on the warpath against superstition. It may be a surprise that something much different has taken root and grown at UVA. But Jesus, who told us the parable about a farmer slinging seed willy-nilly and gaining an unbelievable crop, has a way of surprising his people.

Note how dissimilar Berea and Virginia are. One is a story of dogged determination in the face of overwhelming opposition, dedication to a principle and eventual vindication. Another is a completely unplanned department—a side effect of hiring great non-Christian scholars. Both institutions are to be celebrated and to be mined for lessons. And both should give us pause. God will have God's way with God's people. We should do all we can to help. But often as not, it happens despite us and not because of us.

Cells in the Body of Christ[1]

WHEATON COLLEGE IS THE rare case of a school founded by zealous evangelicals that can still claim the ideals of its founders without embarrassment. Jonathan Blanchard was an abolitionist preacher, an end-times visionary, and an institution-building educator. He founded Wheaton, he said, because the Lord "had need" of it, "to aid in preparing the way for His coming." Wheaton would be part of the education and evangelization of not only what was then (in 1860) "the West," but via the international hub of Chicago, the entire world. And then Christ would come back and inaugurate the kingdom. In the meantime, the college was a stop on the Underground Railroad. Radical politics wed to eschatological zeal—may Blanchard's tribe increase.

There was another sort of inauguration recently, this one of the eighth president of Wheaton. This "Harvard of the evangelicals" is now a three-thousand-student Christian liberal arts college with fantastic departments of English, philosophy, and political science, among others, and boasts a gleaming new science building. Its department of Bible and theology is fast becoming one of the best places in this country to study the "queen of the sciences." The place has a decidedly conservative bent—pity the Bible scholar of the last quarter century with designs on a Wheaton job who wanted to stand up for historical criticism or was unsure about a "literal" Adam and Eve. Yet it's a thriving institution in the best sense. Wheaton's difference from other places makes it a crucial contributor to the ecology of both faith and learning.

Newly minted president Philip Ryken was almost ancillary to the inauguration's proceedings. Scholars from several hundred schools processed in academic regalia. I sat next to alums from Holy Cross and of the quite different Wheaton College in Massachusetts. Noticing the representative

---

1. This essay was first published on October 27, 2010, as a post to *Call & Response*, a blog on the Web site of *Faith & Leadership*, the online magazine of Leadership Education at Duke University.

Part 7: Searching for Jesus in Christian Institutions

from Butler, Duke's opponent the year before in basketball's national title game, I wondered if I should challenge him to a game of rock, paper, scissors. Evangelical schools and seminaries, more in Wheaton's institutional orbit, sent their brass. There were enough presidential medallions to rival the bling in the average rap video.

Why all the colorful gowns? Like most academic events, this inauguration continues medieval traditions of Christendom. In that day, newly installed leaders of academic institutions would be visited by other leaders—bishops and deans—as a sign that what would be taught there was the faith of the one Catholic Church. A school was a cell in the larger body of Christ, not inventing its own knowledge or packaging it for sale but passing on the faith once delivered to the saints, and occasionally breaking new ground in scholarly endeavors.

There were two moments in the inauguration that moved me. One was a blessing and prayer sent from Wheaton's most famous and influential alumnus: Billy Graham. A representative read a note from Graham expressing his wish that he could have visited his alma mater one last time. Graham wrote of his affection for the institution before praying God's blessing on Ryken and Wheaton. It was like hearing a missive from Augustine or Wesley, only the man yet lives and prays for the school he loves (perhaps—forgive me evangelicals—Augustine and Wesley too still live and pray for Wheaton!).

The other was the charge from the now-former president, Duane Litfin, to his successor Ryken. Litfin's reputation is not that of a sunny executive. The president of Wheaton will always be to the right of its faculty and to the left of its donor base. One might have expected Litfin to charge his successor to be on guard against the acids of liberalism.

Instead, Litfin charged Ryken to see his presidency as a labor of love. Then he read 1 Corinthians 13. I had never noticed how perfectly "the love chapter," normally intoned in clichéd ways at weddings, could work in an academic context: "Love . . . does not insist on its own way; it is not irritable or resentful; it does not rejoice in wrongdoing, but rejoices in the truth" (13:4–6). What more perfect word could there be from and to an academic community?

Visiting Wheaton as a representative of Duke—as one cell of the body of Christ recognizing another—I saw anew the need for events like these, with all their pageantry and pretense. They can bring out the best in us, from one president to another, one school to another, one thriving institution to another, from the dead to the living to generations yet unborn. God bless Wheaton, and so, all of us.

Luring a Campus into the Faith[1]

How DOES A COLLEGE or university stay Christian?
Most schools in this country gave up long ago. Harvard began as a school to train ministers, then left that behind, so Yale was founded to keep the faith, then left that behind, and Andover Newton was founded to keep the faith, then . . .
But what if a school doesn't want to leave faith behind? One possibility for those that choose this narrower road is to mandate that all faculty or even all students be Christian. This is a venerable choice, but it's hard to enforce and can lend to narrowness or resentment.
What else? A school *can* make Christianity a robust possibility, but not a mandate. It can offer top-flight worship. It can ask faculty across the board to respect the historic Christian mission of the school. And in that way, it can create room for possibility, hopefully to lure, woo, *entice* students and faculty into more faithful Christian life.
I've written before about schools that have chosen this latter path. (Mt. Olive, DePaul, Hope, North Park). Another is St. Olaf College in Northfield, Minnesota. The Lutheran liberal arts college is a serious Christian school in a day when it's hard to put that adjective and that noun together. How do the Oles do it?
One, they have a bang-up chaplaincy team. Bruce Benson, the college pastor, has spent more than thirty winters on the campus. A personality that makes him a celebrity on campus doesn't hurt: "My atheist friends are like, 'Hey, there goes Bruce, he's awesome!'" Elizabeth Clark, a recent graduate, told me. Jennifer Koenig, Benson's associate, has intentionally bucked the trend of using associate jobs as a quick trampoline to some other job. She starts year fourteen this fall. "It took six years to feel like I knew what I was

---

1. This essay was first published on August 25, 2010, as a post to *Call & Response*, a blog on the Web site of *Faith & Leadership*, the online magazine of Leadership Education at Duke University.

doing in this job," Koenig, a former dancer, told me. "The school expects us to give liturgical structure to events," she said, and not only to the occasional awkward hymn or prayer other schools still tolerate. St. Olaf has chapel every weekday at a time when no classes are scheduled, and Sunday worship that draws five hundred on a campus of only twenty-four hundred or so.

Two, St. Olaf doesn't twin Christianity with some other political or cultural agenda. Sure, there are vestiges of a burlier sort of Christendom at St. Olaf: the eleventh-century death of one (not actually so saintly) King Olaf is memorialized in stained glass in Boe Chapel. The campus motto, "Fram! Fram! Kristmenn, Krossmenn" ("Forward! Forward! Men of Christ, Men of the Cross") perhaps works only because it's in Old Norse and so seems quaint rather than bellicose. I loved seeing Harry Potter translated into Norwegian on the bookstore shelves (you know, just in case). More seriously, the Scandinavian heritage makes for scholarly excellence: its top-notch Kierkegaard Library was the home for the Dane's translation into English.

But St. Olaf has never had a retrograde political agenda. It admitted women in its very first undergraduate class. A towering windmill provides a third of campus energy (part of a virtuous rivalry with crosstown Carleton College over whose power is greener), and food comes from local sources. Some seventy foreign flags fly beside Old Glory in Boe Chapel, representing a surprising number of international students for a school so small.

One reason that so many internationals come is a third element in how St. Olaf has stayed Christian: be devoted to a traditional craft, in the Oles' case, music. Renowned student choirs tour the nation. Undergraduate music courses train organists and conductors and others. A biannual conference on worship, theology, and the arts (why I got to know the place) gathers world-class church musicians ("Bach's church in Leipzig was pretty great," the organist in the van beside me answered when I asked where the best place he'd played was).

"Ninety-five percent of the music we play is sacred," John Ferguson, music professor, chapel organist, and campus icon, told me. "Music can pack the field house, but basketball is lucky to get five hundred." An annual Christmas concert not only sells out. Its waiting list is as frozen as the Minnesota winter. Although the great scholar Martin Marty was once acting president of St. Olaf and longtime regent (trustee), he never got tickets during the four years his son attended the school.

The music strikes me as particularly clever. Pack in students and professors for studied excellence at a rigorous task, and at least a little Jesus is communicated, whether musician or listener intends it or not. "St. Olaf is understated," Enuma Okoro, a'94 Ole, told me of the place where she converted and felt a call to ministry. "It allows students to see and embrace Christ through ordinary yet beautiful ways. But embracing is left up to the students to decide."

Who was it who said, "Let the one with ears, hear"?

Academic Diversity through Church Affiliation[1]

IT'S HARD FOR A church-related college to maintain its ecclesial ties and welcome all comers. Most schools have shed their churchly trappings in anything but a token way as they pursue liberal arts excellence. It's a move James Burtchaell described brilliantly (if somewhat hyperbolically) in the title of his book, *The Dying of the Light*.[2] This shedding of church ties is, contrary to its proponents' intentions, a blow *against* diversity. Who could possibly think that the best way to have a diverse variety of schools across the country would be to make them all equally secular? The slogan "Let's be like everyone else!" is hardly good news for diversity generally.

Actually, it's not impossible for a college to maintain an ecclesial heritage. Evangelical schools like Gordon, Westmont, Wheaton, and many more show their secular peers that a Christian school can be both academically rigorous and culturally rich. I've lectured at Hope College in Holland, Michigan, taught at North Park University in Chicago, and recently preached at Mount Olive College here in North Carolina. Each has managed to maintain its churchly ties while growing in profile regionally and nationally.

The newly minted president of Mount Olive, Philip Kerstetter, was previously president of Kansas Wesleyan University in Salinas, Kansas. He told me Mount Olive has a more robust relationship with the Original Free Will Baptist Church than Kansas Wesleyan ever did with the United Methodist Church. The Original Free Will Baptists still choose 60 percent of the school's trustees, and the current trustees sign off on any new ones. Yet the Mount Olive trustees don't meddle in academic freedom or go playing politics with the school.

---

1. This essay was first published on June 9, 2010, as a post to *Call & Response*, a blog on the Web site of *Faith & Leadership*, the online magazine of Leadership Education at Duke University.

2. *The Dying of the Light: The Disengagement of Colleges and Universities from Their Christian Churches* (Grand Rapids: Eerdmans, 1998).

Academic Diversity through Church Affiliation

How has Mount Olive maintained this strong tie? Money is a prime reason. Congregations give Mount Olive nearly twenty-five times as much as my fellow United Methodists gave to Kerstetter's previous institutions. But Kerstetter is quick to point out that money alone is not enough to keep the church-college relationship strong: "There have to be important, significant ways that the college reaches out to the church and the church reaches out to the college."

Mount Olive also boasts a hallmark of strong religious colleges: campus worship, virtually a prerequisite for maintaining a churchly tie. Having chapel, though, can be tricky. At Wheaton, chapel is required—you get kicked out if you miss too much—and yet students openly show their disdain by putting their feet up, reading the paper, and generally not paying attention. At Hope, chapel is *not* required, yet the preaching and programming is so good that nearly a thousand kids come each week. At Mount Olive, chapel is not required, just encouraged. Officially encouraged. Student IDs are scanned on the way in, like at the cafeteria. Being present has very real, tangible benefits: extra credit in a required course that encourages students to experience fully the school's opportunities for fellowship, fine arts, and scholarship. As I preached, I could tell who was there under duress (most everyone) and who was genuinely interested (hopefully more of these by the end of my sermon).

One more striking thing about some of the schools I've mentioned: North Park, Hope, and Mount Olive don't have to jostle for attention in their denominations. North Park is the Evangelical Covenant Church's only college, and the denomination's three hundred thousand (and still growing) members are proud of the school. Pastors send their kids there, Evangelical Covenant academics consider it their Notre Dame, and the church supports it. This doesn't make it an exclusively churchy place—far from it. Some years ago the school slashed its tuition in hopes of luring more Chicago kids to go to college there, and it worked. Flush with cash for a while, it built building after building.

Similarly, Hope is one of only three schools of the Reformed Church in America, another relatively small denomination with a third of a million members or so. Again, members take pride in the school, clergy send their kids, and the church supports the place. And Mount Olive is the Original Free Will Baptists' only school. Kansas Wesleyan, on the other hand, is one of three United Methodist schools *just in western Kansas*. No wonder that conference can't afford to support it other than in a token way.

But if churches offer only token support for their schools then they can't be surprised when those schools have only token support for the church and its mission. Even today, it is still possible for a college—an institution created for the life of the mind—to be a specifically Christian ministry. Difficult, but possible.

Just like all ministry.

Part 8

Searching for Jesus Amidst the Task of Writing

EVERY PASTOR IS A writer. Sermons may have a short shelf life, but they are a creation of the written word, requiring time, attention, finesse, wisdom, humor, lots of grace. I'm struck now that I'm in the parish how hard it is to write anything else (like this). Another deadline is looming, and the Sabbath recurs with remarkably consistent regularity, what seems like every three days.

Writing grows out of reading. I didn't care about reading till I became a Christian. Then out of desire to follow Jesus I was reading the Bible before school for an hour or so per day, memorizing scripture, trying to apply God's word to my life. I wish those halcyon days had remained in some ways. But then something surprising happened—my schoolwork ticked up in quality, I was qualifying for honors classes, and a general desire to learn was born out of a desire to learn about God.

Everybody writes for much of his or her life in school, and for some of us nerds, school continues longer than usual. This can hurt our ability to write: graduate school famously rewards sentences that obfuscate rather than clarify, the desired goal being, it seems, the reaction "the writer is really smart" rather than "that subject is so much clearer now." The good it does is to force students into a disciplined pattern of reading on the way to evaluation. Without that no one would read as manically as doctoral students do.

Part 8: Searching for Jesus Amidst the Task of Writing

I've heard those with academic degrees swearing they would write a new dissertation before they would take their comprehensive exams over.

All that reading does little to sharpen the intellect without writing. Good thing graduate school requires us to write then. And that writing should send us back to the desk for more reading as we discover holes, grow new curiosities, need to learn more. Reading and writing can create a kind of virtuous circle—one encourages the other. Reading without writing anything can be simply self-indulgent, making us consumers of words only and not creators. Writing without reading can leave us foisting our stuff on the unsuspecting reader, therapy without co-pay. Reading and writing together can be a form of worship, twin disciplines of seeking God and telling others what we find. That's the process I try to describe in these essays.

The thing that strikes me about writing is the friendships it allows. Friends who also write are crucial to check ideas, to inspire and be inspired, to get proofreading, help with places to publish, the works. It's a sort of closed fraternity (I heard a popular writer say recently, "The first rule of Write Club is don't talk about Write Club"!). It can breed insecurity and envy—even writers more accomplished than I seem jealous of more minor successes of mine. But it can also create and sustain friendships we would not otherwise have. The conjunction of writing and pastoral ministry is a rich one, possibly because they trade off the same skills: paying attention to God, the scriptures, each other, the world. Praying for each, drawing truth from each, speaking as much truth as we have to each. For this kind of writing there is always more work to be done. One can get published every Sunday. And the reward of faithfulness among God's people (please Jesus) is a richly undeserved, but delightful, royalty.

Why Religious Journalism Is Boring[1]

PICK UP ANY MAJOR American newspaper, turn to the religion section (if there is one), and with few exceptions you will immediately discover just how boring religious journalism is. The energy level on the religion pages is so much lower than anywhere else. Not only can you guess the contents of the entire article from the lead, you could guess before you even turned to the page in question.

Peter Steinfels, then of the *New York Times*, wrote in 1993 that there were basically six different religion stories written for newspapers:

1. Religious leader reveals feet of clay (or turns out to be a scoundrel)
2. Ancient faith struggles to adjust to modern times
3. Scholars challenge long-standing beliefs
4. Interfaith harmony overcomes inherited enmity
5. New translation of Scripture sounds funny
6. Devoted members of a zealous religious group turn out to be warm, ordinary folks[2]

Steinfels confessed, "Sometimes I think that computer programs could be devised, leaving all the necessary blank spaces. Reporters could simply insert the names of the denomination or clergy, and the specific issue, supply quotes from critics, and fill in splashes of color."[3]

Since 1993 things haven't changed as much as one might think. Religion writers still naturally gravitate toward conflict and contention. This is a problem theologically. Steinfels quotes Paul Moses, writing in *America*,

---

1. Copyright © 2007 by *Theology Today*. "Why Religious Journalism Is Boring" by Jason Byassee is reprinted by permission from the October 2007 issue of *Theology Today*.

2. "Constraints of the Religion Reporter," *Nieman Reports* (Summer 1993) 3–5, 55.

3. Ibid., 4.

Part 8: Searching for Jesus Amidst the Task of Writing

a liberal Catholic magazine: "Religion coverage focuses on the continuing culture war over such topics as homosexuality, abortion, AIDS, and contraception (and dissent from church authorities on these issues). This is like covering major league baseball only when there is a dispute about allowing women to be umpires."[4] Most of religion—mine anyway—is predictable. We show up at the same time with the same people every week, do the same sort of stuff, and then leave. If you're looking for a hot news item on Sunday morning, you're not likely to find it at First United Methodist, unless there's some sort of fight. But the ordinary, uninteresting stuff is the *very stuff of faith*. Still, preaching, sacraments, good works—the church's very life—won't sell magazines or newspapers.

James Alison is a Catholic theologian who has written that Mass is *supposed* to be boring: "At the center of a typical act of creation of the sacred there is a sacrifice, a murder, and those of us around it get excited—we derive from it meaning, scandal, satisfaction, *Schadenfreude* and so on. The Mass is exactly the reverse of this. It is about our learning to be approached by our Victim, who is forgiving us, moving toward us, nudging us out of our excitements and false identities into the quiet, gentle bliss of recognizing ourselves as loved and of loving our neighbors as ourselves."[5] Alison works on atonement and desire with help from René Girard. For both Alison and Girard, Jesus' atoning work is not about satisfaction of a debt to God, paid by Jesus in our stead. It is rather about the undoing of our wrongful desire for a scapegoat. Like all societies we get our social cohesion by banding together to exclude one of our number—Jews throughout Christian history, blacks in the American South for hundreds of years, and gay people or Muslims often in America today. These are ritualistically excluded and often murdered in an act of religious sacrifice in which we all participate, looking over our shoulder to be sure that we are doing it right, and others approve of us for kicking out the trash.

In Christ, God himself enters into this demonic process of religious scapegoating *as* the scapegoat. We glance on the crucified Christ then not so much as an icon of our salvation but as a sign of our sin—the way we run outsiders out of town on a rail, or string them up on a cross, to give our world purpose and our community cohesion. In worship we slowly unlearn our habit of sacrifice. In church that wrong desire is picked apart, moment by moment, as we unlearn violence and learn

---

4. Ibid., 3.

5. "Violence Undone," an interview with James Alison, *Christian Century* 123.18 (September 5, 2006) 30–35, here 33. See his more extensive treatment of this theme in "Contemplation in a World of Violence," in *On Being Liked* (New York: Crossroad, 2003) 1–16.

contemplation—wondering about a God who appears to us as a victim at our hands offering forgiveness instead of violence.

Alison is interesting not just because he is a gay Catholic who has seen this scapegoating firsthand but because of his view of church as that which teaches us to be bored rather than to froth with sacrificial excitement. Don't feel like getting up this week for the same people all over again? Good—you're starting to get the hang of this—now go. So too with religious writing—some of it is boring because, well, religion at its best is boring. The stories Steinfels describes are perennial stories, rooted in religious observance itself. Mark Silk, in his book *Unsecular Media,* argues that these religious *topoi* are themselves religious.[6] Silk agreed with Steinfels' *topoi* but traces their origin not to the Enlightenment, as Steinfels does, but to the New Testament. "Religious leader reveals feet of clay (or turns out to be a scoundrel)" sounds like Jesus' warnings about the hypocrisy of the Pharisees. "Interfaith harmony overcomes inherited enmity"—Orthodox and evangelicals embrace over the environment or whatever sounds like the Christian hope "that they would be one, that the world might believe," as Jesus prays in John 17. That is not to excuse bad writing or unimaginative framing of religious journalism! It is just to say that a turn from the front of the paper to the back might coincide with realizing that the slow, patient work of faith is crucial to unlearning the excitement of the front page and being drawn into the plodding, patient life of God.

I have tried to let this commitment guide my own journalistic work for *The Christian Century.* Still, I have noticed that some of my work has been just plain boring. I wrote a cover feature on Benedict XVI's first year.[7] I praised his theological acumen, criticized him on women and liberation theology, then sat back and waited for what I was sure would be a thunderous response. None came. The article was like dropping a stone down a bottomless well. It was boring. What else would a liberal Protestant magazine do than praise the pope for speaking lots of languages and criticize him on identity politics? My article, though, was the *bad* kind of boring: it was predictable.

I had another cover feature on the so-called new monasticism, about evangelicals rediscovering the Gospels' rigorous calls for divestment of property, communal living, gardening, nonviolence, and obedience to a rule.[8] In one way that piece wasn't very sexy—some Christians have always remembered poverty, chastity, and obedience. In another way, viewed doxo-

---

6. *Unsecular Media: Making News of Religion in America* (Urbana: University of Illinois Press, 1995).

7. "Being Benedict: The Pope's First Year," *Christian Century* 123.8 (April 18, 2006) 22–25.

8. "The New Monastics," *Christian Century* 122.21 (October 18, 2005) 38–47.

logically, those folks are the vanguard of the kingdom, a sign that God has not abandoned creation, that the Spirit is still active and may well lay hold of lives and transform them. It was the good kind of boring.

I learned of James Alison from reading Rowan Williams, whose enthronement as archbishop of Canterbury was not a promotion. You can hear it as he describes his day in *Where God Happens*:

> I have signed the fifteenth letter of the morning and made the fourth uncomfortable phone call. I have emerged from a meeting about next year's budget, and I am getting ready for a session with our investment advisors after lunch. After which I have to go and take an afternoon's school assembly. Probably in the evening I'll have to institute a new parish priest somewhere.... "Was it all for this?" The only thing I find that helps is to let myself be drawn into the present moment . . . putting my hands on the arms of a chair and feeling the fabric. And breathing, saying, "Well, here I am. This is what I must do next. All I can say is, 'God is in this moment.'"[9]

Williams' beloved desert fathers constantly reminded each other, "Stay in your cell, and your cell will teach you everything." Only by pressing through boredom can one finally listen in the silence for God. Or, in Williams' words, "You learn how to face the boredom without terror."[10] Stunning description. So too, I suggest, with religious journalism—it would be helped by slowing down and patiently listening for God, even when to do so is dull. Some time in front of the reserve sacrament would serve every religion writer well. After it, we might be able to notice a detail we would have missed, something gentle and elegant that deserves praise in our writing.

In other words, I am a better journalist when I have spent more time at prayer. Prayer, Simone Weil taught us, is primarily about paying attention.[11] It is not sentimentality, or warm, religious feelings, or asking God for stuff, but about attending to the depth of things. In her great essay "Reflections on the Right Use of School Studies with a View to the Love of God," Weil suggests that education is not primarily about making good grades or passing standardized tests but about learning to pay attention. It is especially important then that students work hard at subjects they dislike, "because all of them develop that faculty of attention which, directed toward God, is the very substance of prayer." When we struggle with something we're not

---

9. *Where God Happens: Discovering Christ in One Another* (Boston: New Seeds, 2005) 97.

10. Ibid.

11. *Waiting for God*, trans. Emma Cruafurd (New York: Putnam, 1951) 105–16.

good at we learn humility, or as Weil puts it, "a sense of our mediocrity is borne in upon us with irresistible evidence. No knowledge is more to be desired." Weil again: "Writing is like giving birth: we cannot help making the supreme effort. I need have no fear of not making the supreme effort provided only that I am honest with myself and that I pay attention."[12] I think my best writing has come when I didn't have the story written before I made the first phone call or read the first book, but when I asked open questions, paid attention to what I was told, noticed the crevices beneath the surfaces that don't show up in sensationalist accounts in daily newspapers.

This is hardly to say that one has to pray to be a good journalist! The best of this sort of writing often happens in secular publications such as *The Atlantic* or *Harper's*, or in Christian ones that aren't mainline Protestant, such as *Books & Culture* or *Commonweal*. Sociologist Steven Brint calls this sort of writing "particularizing refinement."[13] John Schmalzbauer, a historian of both religion and journalism, elaborates: "Instead of emphasizing explicit ideological claims, intellectual refinement focuses on bringing out the nuances and ambiguities of a debate, debunking established interpretations, and dissecting the logic of arguments."[14] So learning to see, to pay attention to the workings of human desire, especially at their most twisted, is hardly something you have to be Christian to do—it looks like the world does it better than us, in fact. But it is what Christian prayer is *designed* to do—to teach us to see more clearly all created things illuminated with wisdom and truth.

An extra burden is placed on a specifically Christian vision of journalism. We cannot just offer intellectual refinement; we have to speak from and to the church. As I write, I try to help opposing political factions in the church learn to discern the face of Christ in the other, to see the other not as a political or theological antagonist but as a fellow member of the body of Christ. There is a specific face I look for when I write or interview or take stock of a story—the face of Jesus, which will be present here too, even if in surprising form. To learn to contemplate that face takes time. You have to sit in patience with the face of Christ, and with the faces of others, to see them both in their particularity and in their universality, and to learn to express the one to the other.

I have suggested that journalism, or at least journalism informed by Christian theology, must be mindful of the human desire to scapegoat victims, as we did with Jesus, and so often continue to do. It must practice

---

12. *Gravity and Grace*, trans. Arthur Wills (New York: Putnam, 1952) 108.

13. Brint, quoted in John Schmalzbauer, *People of Faith: Religious Conviction in American Journalism and Higher Education* (Ithaca: Cornell University Press, 2003) 55.

14. Schmalzbauer, *People of Faith*, 55–56.

Part 8: Searching for Jesus Amidst the Task of Writing

paying attention, press through boredom, and see what is glorious with a second look. It must practice paying attention, taking time, when it would rather not. And with what I do, speaking from and to the church, it must attend to the face of Christ for the sake of those who would rather only see an adversary. I am aware of how far I am from journalism as objective observation of events, providing the five *W*'s, not passing judgment, quoting a liberal riposte and an academic, hitting spell-check, and sending it in. But I am also aware of how far most secular journalists are from those rote lessons. Postmodernism has taught us that we are all interested parties, not mere observers but agents as we talk, think, and write. Despite our interestedness, it is right to say that we can strive to be fair to all parties. My hope is that specifically Christian resources can help us not only to be fair but to pay the sort of attention that closely resembles prayer—to do journalism with a minister's sense of vocation for the upbuilding of the body of Christ. If you can't join me in this sort of "boring" work, I at least implore you to see that it can be of value both to the church and the world.

Paying Attention[1]

NICHOLAS LASH, THEOLOGIAN EMERITUS from Cambridge, speaks of language as the first casualty of original sin. Adam eats and pretty soon we have terms like "collateral damage," "WMD," and "rendition"—technical speech that quickly becomes acceptable and hides outrage. So Lash speaks of the church as an academy of word care, a place where we learn to take care of language and where slowly, by a divine gift not of our doing, we learn from each other to tell the truth.

As a preacher you learn to treasure words. They are all you've got. There aren't any other tools, not much political power, certainly little financial power, and our ability to coerce our parishioners is at an all-time low, thank God. All you have are words, persuasion, rhetoric. You get to throw those words around like the sower in the parable and hope something lands and takes root. We're charged to become, as AME Bishop Charles Hurst Adams calls us, "wordsmiths." As workers whose trade is crafting things from words, we have to notice what makes a word right, as a carpenter notices the grain in a piece of wood. Adams recommends writing down words that interest us, looking them up, and finding excuses to use them. Not fancy words, not ones that put distance between us and our parishioners, but ones that build bridges, that open folks up to us and us to them.

Frank McCourt, author of *Angela's Ashes*, talks about the first time he read Shakespeare: "The words were like jewels in my mouth." Speaking for the mostly young members of what I call the "whatever" generation, we are not known for our care of words, so taking care of words is where we can be most radically countercultural. Speak clearly, creatively, passionately. Though it is now a cliché, avoid clichés. Read the beautiful sentences at least twice. Care for words is a way of paying attention.

---

1. Copyright © 2009 by *Theology Today*. "Paying Attention" by Jason Byassee is reprinted by permission from the April 2009 issue of *Theology Today*.

Part 8: Searching for Jesus Amidst the Task of Writing

Theology itself is a matter of learning the right habits of attention. Above all, we have to learn to pay attention rightly to the Scriptures. Old Testament scholar Ellen Davis shows what I mean in her book *Wondrous Depth*.[2] Davis has made a career of showing contemporary biblical scholars that the rabbis, the church fathers, the medievals, and the Anglican divines may teach us something about how we interpret Scripture—that however good we are with languages and manuscripts and historical reconstruction, when we endeavor to plumb the "wondrous depth" of Scripture, we will never arrive at the bottom. There is always more to see. Davis writes of an art instructor who teaches not future artists with talent, but future amateurs without talent. The goal is not to make them good artists; it won't happen. It is to teach them to pay attention—to the particular texture of light, of surfaces, of depths—to learn to notice how one could draw a particular landscape or building or corner of the room. It is, in the words of the art instructor, "to teach them how never to be bored again."[3] If you look at things in their depths, there is always more of their creator to marvel at. So too with Scripture—there is always more there to wonder about. Davis suggests biblical readers read like "mushroom hunters"—plodding along slowly, unwilling to miss the tiniest detail.[4] Pay attention when you read Scripture—you will see something there that applies directly to your parishioner's needs at the moment, if you have also been paying attention to their pastoral care.

Annie Dillard shows this as much as she tells it in her writing. There is no one better for a quote or a vignette, for she writes elegantly about things most of us don't pay attention to. She wanders into the woods and watches as a water bug stabs a frog and sucks its insides out, leaving its skin to float helplessly downriver. Dillard had been taught as a good church kid to look for God in nature. And when she looked, she saw *savagery* in creation. Paying attention, then, is not merely a matter of seeing the world as God is remaking it—it is a matter of seeing the world clearly as it is right now, as a bloody place where cruelty is rewarded and the just suffer.[5]

But reading Dillard in chunks takes patience, for nothing really happens. She is trying not just to talk *about* the slow, painful process of learning to see. She is trying to seduce you into it. Something similar happens as we learn to read Scripture with the church's tradition. In both cases we learn

---

2. *Wondrous Depth: Preaching the Old Testament* (Louisville: Westminster John Knox, 2005).

3. Ibid., xiii.

4. Ellen F. Davis, "Reading the Bible Confessionally in the Church," *Anglican Theological Review* 84.1 (2002) 27.

5. See Annie Dillard, *Pilgrim at Tinker Creek* (San Francisco: HarperPerennial, 2007), and *Holy the Firm* (San Francisco: HarperPerennial, 1988).

how to pay attention. But there *is* a key difference. Dillard wanders into the woods and pays attention to whatever comes. In the church, we know what we are paying attention to: Jesus. The question is how to pay attention in this particular instance. The children's sermon story is often told of a teacher who asks the kids, "What's gray and furry?" And the kids all shout, "Jesus!" One of them mumbles, "But it sure sounds like a squirrel." In the church, the answer is always Jesus. Now we have to shape our questions—our habits of paying attention—to that answer.

I learned in graduate school how to pay attention to doctrine from Lewis Ayres, a patristics scholar recently at Emory and now at Durham University in Britain. Ayres has written of how ancient Christian theology was a matter of learning to discern Christ in odd forms, of how to pay attention, despite difficulty, to Jesus. Theology in the patristic age was a matter of discerning what Ayres calls "persistent patterns of signification" in the pages of the Scriptures, through the Creed.[6] The church learns the Creed from the literally clear portions of Scripture. Then we go on discerning the depths, the substance of that teaching, by seeing it oddly related in other parts of Scripture. We learn the Creed from, say, the Gospel of John; then we go on and discern the same teaching, with more difficulty, from Leviticus. Theology is a matter of learning to discern the face of Christ throughout the Scriptures, in some places more clearly, in others with more difficulty. As we do so our minds are repaired from their fallen nature, our desire is inflamed to love God and neighbor, and our bodies are aligned with the grace given to the church.

Allegory—that much-derided patristic and medieval practice of looking for Christ under every scriptural rock—is simply a matter of paying attention to Christ in a variety of scriptural ways. Christians believe that God is drawing all things to himself. We in the church are learning to see the form of Christ, the shape of redemption in all creation, not least on the pages of Scripture. It was actually then the pinnacle of theological attention in the patristic age to find Christ in odd forms like the pages of the Old Testament, in the natural order in animals and plants, and even in the difficult neighbor. Our travails in life are a matter of the Spirit groaning within us. Our glories are a foretaste of the eschaton; our much more common moments are often ones of boredom. Christ is then working out our salvation by teaching us that we need not be entertained all the time.

Let me give a particular example from Augustine's own biblical exegesis. Augustine's *Enarrationes in Psalmos* may be his greatest work.[7] It

---

6. See especially Lewis Ayres, "On the Practice and Teaching of Christian Doctrine," *Gregorianum* 80 (1999) 33-94.

7. For more on this, see Jason Byassee, *Praise Seeking Understanding: Reading the Psalms with Augustine* (Grand Rapids: Eerdmans, 2007).

Part 8: Searching for Jesus Amidst the Task of Writing

is certainly his greatest work that no one reads. The whole work together is twice as long as the *City of God*. It is made up of sermons preached to laypeople during morning prayer when they would stop on their way to work and hear their bishop exposit a psalm in the light of Christ. Augustine made tremendous intellectual demands on laypeople who were largely illiterate, but they kept coming back. (Do you ever wonder why our people keep coming back?)

In one sermon, Augustine comes to the line in the 101st Psalm, "I have become like the pelican that lives in solitary places." It is a lament psalm—our 102nd. It read well right after 9/11, and it reads well at times of grief generally. But to say it is a lament psalm that expresses grief is not to say enough for Christian preaching. Anyone can see that. Specifically Christian preaching has to show how these words bear witness to Christ, and so how they draw hearers to love God and neighbor better. Robert Wilken argues that allegory is reading in reverse.[8] We usually look to the words and try to figure out the meaning from them. With allegory we already know the meaning (Jesus). Now we are trying to figure out how these words mean that meaning. For Augustine the meaning is always Jesus. So the game of allegory is figuring out how these words refer to that meaning. Now about that pelican . . .

Augustine's heard about pelicans. They don't live in his part of the world, but he knows some myths about them. He has heard that a mother pelican will kill her young in the nest, then wound herself and pour her blood on the young, which then revive. The christological image is clear in the pouring out of life-giving blood. Christ has a motherly love for her church. Even the mother pelican's wounding of her young makes biblical sense, for as Deuteronomy declares, "I will kill and I will give life, I will strike and I will heal." Saul had to be wounded before he could be converted. Few of us are without a significant wound from which we do ministry, as Henri Nouwen taught us all.[9] Augustine is aware that the myth of the pelican may be just that, a myth, but it almost doesn't matter: "This report may be true or false, but if it is true, observe how apt a symbol it is of him who gave us life by his own blood."[10]

Allegory gives no new information. You cannot find anything allegorically in Scripture that is not also present in a clear literal way elsewhere (those who allegorize to find what they want are called Gnostics). The point is to

---

8. Robert Wilken, "In Defense of Allegory," *Modern Theology* 14 (1998) 197–212.

9. *The Wounded Healer: Ministry in Contemporary Society* (Garden City, NY: Image, 1979).

10. Augustine, *Expositions of the Psalms*, ed. John E. Rotelle, trans. Maria Boulding, Works of Saint Augustine: A Translation for the 21st Century (Hyde Park, NY: New City, 2003) 5:53.

see what you already know illumined in a new way, to take fresh delight in knowledge you already have. Allegory is a preacher's art, if you will. It is for preachers who have seen their parishioners drop off to sleep too many times, who need to give them something more than the basic "old, old story." So they tell that old story in a new way—with pelicans. Once it is told in that new way, the pelican changes. We come to see pelicans themselves as signs of Christ.

Notice these people I have mentioned: Augustine, Annie Dillard, and Ellen Davis are all masterful writers. This is because they have paid attention. When they read Scripture, they show us something we didn't see there when we looked. But now, when we look, we can no longer miss what they have pointed out. Similarly, when they also speak of their interior lives, they make us reflect, "I've felt that. I'm not the only one." When they comment on world affairs or churchly goings-on, they say something the local paper cannot say. And when they speak of Jesus, we start to imagine a world stitched back together, as whole as our Creator intended. They have a vision of the whole, within which they attend to the particulars.

With similar imagination, Thomas Aquinas once addressed Jesus in prayer as "Oh, Pelican Divine." At Garrett-Evangelical Theological Seminary in Evanston, Illinois, where I previously taught, there are pelicans over its main doors. Those in the know see Jesus there. More personally, when I was trying to work up the courage to ask the woman who is now my wife to marry me, we were on the beach, the wine was poured, and I was terrified—until I saw a flock of pelicans and read them as a sign of Christ's reassurance. Pelicans cannot be the same anymore. They are Christ-markers, as all creation is—if we just pay attention.

Abounding in Hope[1]

WE'RE ALWAYS OVEREAGER TO know characteristics of whole generations. Sweeping generalizations can be dangerous if taken too seriously. Nevertheless, I will venture one: the next generation coming into the ordained ministry is reason for the rest of us to hope.

I was privileged recently to speak to a gathering of young ministers, mostly twentysomethings in their first churches, gathered by the Lilly Endowment in its Transition into Ministry program. At the conclusion I was asked to give my reflections on young ministers half a generation younger than I.

I was impressed by their almost total lack of cynicism. If I had scratched hard enough I would have found it, to be sure. But in contrast to most gatherings of pastors, this one's lack of world-weariness was enormously refreshing. They think the gospel might change the world and might be worth giving their life for it. Their conviction, their blessed naiveté, is enough to make the rest of us believe they might be right.

By contrast, a colleague of mine teaches at a seminary where she is unhappy. She goes out of her way to insist as often as she can that she doesn't care what happens at her institution. But she says this so much I once asked around what her deal was. I was told she was at one time a passionate person, but then she was wounded in a few institutional fights she lost. So she's trying to shut out any feeling, keep her head down, and wait to collect a full pension. Whether she is a conservative at a liberal seminary or the reverse hardly matters. Tenure keeps her in a place that she was once foolish enough to care about.

I spend most of my time with professors, seminary administrators, and journalists. This is a good source of gallows humor. "How many millions have to come out of your budget?" "Fire anyone today?" "Easy to get

---

1. Copyright © 2010 by *Theology Today*. "Abounding in Hope" by Jason Byassee is reprinted by permission from the January 2010 issue of *Theology Today*.

Abounding in Hope

the good cubes in the newsroom now, isn't it?" These years of economic difficulty will be remembered as a golden age of morose humor.

Among these young ministers, however, I found a different kind of humor—a raucous kind, one that suggests Jesus has indeed been raised, and wherever we look we're willing to be surprised by his presence even there. One of the participants compared this to the Eastern Orthodox tradition of the Sunday of holy laughter—when after Easter the liturgy directs worshipers to laugh with deep hilarity at the devil. The devil, you see, can take anything except being made light of. He has to be deadly serious all the time. The Sunday of holy laughter reminds us that Christ's victory is the greatest joke in history.

These young people see, and show, this sort of humor in their ministries—even if a politician from a political party we don't much like shows up at our first Sunday Eucharist, or if a liberal gets sent to a place commonly known as "the Republican party at prayer," or if an evangelical is sent among people who aren't sure about the literal sense of Scripture or the bodily resurrection of Jesus (all stories these young ministers told me). In such surprising places—places in the church where we've been conditioned to think we *can't* expect faithfulness—even there we find the risen Lord. Maybe he is "going ahead" of us (Mark 16:7) and is not simply captive to our little base of partisan power in the church.

Another sign of hope is the posture of these young ministers toward institutions. Many of my former seminary classmates left the ministry after they tried to fix things at warp speed. They tried to make the whole church pacifist. Or inerrantist. Or as inclusive as they are in their enlightened, tolerant state. All in a year or two. They wrote some articles, served a church or two, went to some conferences, and it just didn't work. So they became Latin Mass Catholics, for whom Pope Benedict XVI is a dangerous liberal with too compromising a posture vis-à-vis the modern world. Or they became bicycling, farmer's market–shopping crusaders against carbon-based fuels. Now they look at people like us and are puzzled: "Why are you still messing around with *church* and those same old pitiful problems?"

In their impatience they fail to see that God chooses to save corporately, through institutions. If the 1960s taught us not to trust anyone over thirty, the 2000s are asking why those under thirty think they can trust *themselves*. God saves by *Israel* and the *church* after all—it should be no surprise to anyone who's even glanced at the Bible or church history that institutions are often corrupt. And as the young ministers often showed me, institutions are the most beautiful thing there is. Andrew Sullivan argued in *The Christian Century* a few years back that institutions make life worth living (this from a gay, Catholic, capitalist Bush critic—from lots of institutions we might expect him to hate). "Institutions are among the most humane things humans beings have created," he said. Their frequent corruption suggests they contain something precious—else who would howl at their waywardness?[2] Hugh Heclo's *On Thinking Institutionally* quotes Katherine Hepburn's character in *The African Queen* that institutions are what we put on earth to help us *rise above* human nature.[3]

I saw in these young ministers not wide-eyed innocence about the harm institutions can do—who could be so naive anymore? I saw eyes opened to their flaws and brows furrowed with determination to lead them for good rather than evil.

The great Jean Vanier, founder of L'Arche, visited Duke Divinity School last year. L'Arche is a series of small intentional communities where able-bodied people live in community with adults with disabilities and so discover together amid weakness and mutual accountability who they really are. This giant of the faith is in the winter of his life and rarely leaves the house he started in France in 1964. He has lived there as his organization has grown to include 135 communities in thirty-three countries.

It was time for Vanier to go to the airport, so Stanley Hauerwas—my teacher at Duke whom Vanier came to see and argue against and write with—leaned over and kissed him on the forehead. I wanted to send up a Pentecostal praise shout. It was a glimpse of the meeting of theology (Hauerwas) and practice (Vanier), of dialectical rigor and holiness, of a white-hot intellect and a blazing spiritual fire. I felt like I should take off my shoes—that's what you do when "righteousness and peace kiss" (Ps 85:10).

Think of all the institutions that made those two men possible. Hauerwas named many of the chapters of his forthcoming memoir after institutions: Southwestern, Yale, Notre Dame, Duke.[4] Vanier was instructed in places as diverse as the Canadian Navy, the Institut Catholique in Paris, and the Catholic Church itself. Now Vanier has L'Arche, which offers lives of grace to those whom the world often rejects, in an institutional ministry that reaches to dozens of countries. This institutional initiative took place originally as a reaction *against* institutions that caged and dehumanized disabled people. That was "institutionalization" in the bad sense. But Vanier created an institution in the beautiful sense—one that lends life where there might have been only death. Institutions bear grace to us not less than Mary bears Christ to us in her body. Without them no salvation becomes visible. It took a certain lack of cynicism in me to see this in two old men parting.

2. Bob Roehr, "Cheap Shots," *Christian Century* 112.26 (September 13, 1995) 837.
3. *On Thinking Institutionally* (London: Paradigm, 2008) 25.
4. *Hannah's Child: A Theologian's Memoir* (Grand Rapids: Eerdmans, 2010).

Abounding in Hope

We want to be guided by lives of holy sacrifice and joy. That is what I saw in the witness of the young pastors transitioning into ministry.

I saw palpably and visibly a word much in vogue in the secular realm: hope. Not optimism—which is crushed in the first major disappointment, when the church fails to ordain them or someone they love, or when money gets misspent. We all know too many stories, both from the newspapers and our personal connections of friends in ministry, or pastors in various bizarre states of trouble. It is inexpressibly important also to tell stories about ministry that abound in hope! Hope is not optimism; neither is it cynicism—that we just do our time until we retire and get left alone and can afford to do what we want, unencumbered by others. No, hope says that Christ has called a kingdom of fools and lovers, and we get to be part of it now. Hope is an *implicated* life—my good is bound up with that of others, and vice versa.[5]

Hope is a little like those who have become "locavores"—those who eat only what grows near them. (The second-largest use of oil after cars is tankers that carry in-season food to places where it's out of season). Many such eaters think our whole oil-based food economy is doomed and that we will all eat local once McDonald's and Wal-Mart collapse. Likewise, the new generation of ministers are ahead of the curve—living now the way the whole world will soon live, whether it wants to or not. Their view of everyone's coming future affects them, cheerfully, now. It's eschatological hope. One day everyone will see and live. We can already get adjusted to the new normal. I saw in these folks the future. Not just in the sense that they'll be leaders in their denominations. That's blazingly obvious—everything they touch will turn to gold. But I saw in them the light of the resurrection and the shine in their eyes of a coming kingdom that you and I can neither engineer nor stop but in light of which we can direct all our attention and energy now.

---

5. This phrase, "an implicated life," is from Nathan Kirkpatrick, a colleague at Leadership Education at Duke Divinity.

Joining the Communion of Saints and Writing the Unwritable Word[1]

WHEN STRANGERS AT A party or on an airplane find out you're in divinity school, they'll want to tell you everything *they* think about God. You're supposed to listen and nod profoundly, and you'd better *not* correct anything they say. You've signed up to be a pastoral counselor, whether you meant to or not. Perhaps you just wanted to study the doctrine of the *communicatio idiomatum* or to reconstruct the community of proto-Q, but suddenly people will call you up when a loved one dies. You've also signed up to be a saint—people will watch how you live, looking for inspiration, hypocrisy, or whatever their own issues cause them to want to see. And most surprising of all, you've signed up to be a writer—perhaps not the chain-smoking types who bounce words around their parents' basements, but a writer nonetheless.[2]

I remember when I was first willing to call myself a "writer." I already had been for four years, working as an editor and writer for *Christian Century* magazine. I was interviewing a marvelous pastor on the West Side of Chicago named Nanette Sawyer. She's the leader of Wicker Park Grace, an emerging church community. She'd worked with several other artists in the church to make these beautiful sculptures of the stations of the cross that the church had displayed at an open gallery show in their neighborhood during holy week. And she'd made them by hand, in a studio, with paint and papier-mâché and wire and all the rest. And she said she still had trouble calling herself an artist. Well, she obviously makes art. It serves a function, proclaiming Christ in one neighborhood and through that neighborhood to all the world, for his pleasure, her delight, and her neighbors' contemplation.

---

1. Copyright © 2011 by *The Other Journal*. "Joining the Communion of Saints and Writing the Unwritable Word" by Jason Byassee is reprinted by permission from the March 7, 2011 issue of *The Other Journal*.

2. This essay is adapted from a lecture I delivered at an orientation for incoming seminary students during my time as Director of Duke Divinity School's writing center.

Joining the Communion of Saints and Writing the Unwritable Word

So we made a deal, I the interviewer and she the interviewee: I'd call myself a writer if she'd call herself an artist.

That's all to say it's hard to call yourself a writer. But think of all the places that a pastor writes. In Marilynne Robinson's novel *Gilead*, the elderly preacher John Ames estimates he's preached 2,250 sermons over his decades in ministry—fifty years, forty-five sermons a year—and this puts him up there, in terms of quantity, with Augustine and Calvin![3] Think of all the newsletters that pastors write—these are often, shall we say, not very artfully done or written with much care. But more people read such newsletters than hear sermons. The sloppy pastoral newsletter is a wasted chance to preach the gospel. With new media, the opportunities to write only grow. I've known more than one pastor who made her life unnecessarily difficult with an e-mail that said too much or too little or forgot the fact that however difficult that parishioner is, he is a child of grace, an image of God, someone for whom Christ died. E-mail, Facebook, Twitter—one could get overwhelmed with all the places you have to write well. A pastor friend called me once to say he was chatting with five parishioners at once on Facebook. He had to be careful. He was juggling souls out there.

The pastoral task of writing means that we ministers are all like the sower in Jesus's parable. You go out, you fling seed everywhere, even on ground that looks unpromising—preaching, teaching, sharing the gospel not only from the pulpit, but in newspapers, magazines, books, blogs. Who knows where the seed will take root? I teach a course on writing in the spring semester, and last semester, a student ran up and gave me a high five when he'd posted his first comment on a blog—that's progress! Proclaiming the truth in public, even if just on a Weblog.

There's still no shortcut in theological education past the hard work of reading, but I want to say that you almost haven't read a book until you've written about it. If you write without reading fresh things you'll end up foisting your psychological stuff on your poor readers. If you read without writing it's almost gratuitous—as a seminary student, it's not just about the assignment in front of you, it's about the parishioners who'll be in front of you in fifty years.

Seminary is largely about learning how to *read*. Dr. Willie Jennings taught me this: reading and writing exist in a virtuous circle. If you read something, really read it, you almost have to write about it. Reading has sparked new things in you that demand to come out, like a fire in the bones, so you write. And if you write something, as you all will do week after week for decade after decade, you constantly realize there are gaps

---

3. *Gilead* (New York: Picador, 2004).

Part 8: Searching for Jesus Amidst the Task of Writing

in your knowledge, so back you go to your study to read more. The best readers I know are writers. And if you write without reading, you'll just bombard your readers and parishioners with the latest theological teaching that you heard when you graduated from seminary—it's often said you can look in a pastor's study and if there are no books after a certain date, you can tell when that pastor's intellect died. The most fulfilled and faithful and successful ministers I know are those who read voraciously and who write prodigiously. They're constantly discovering new things about God and constantly sharing these new things with others.

When I was a seminary student, American Methodist Episcopal Bishop John Hurst Adams told my seminary class we were to become wordsmiths, people who love words with their life. If we learn a new word, we need to pick it up, look it over, turn it around, shine it up, and put it in our pocket to use later. Not to show off vocabulary, but to learn to love language—slowly, bit by bit, like a poet whose ears perk up when she hears something new and doesn't know what it means.

You all will be slogging your way through your reading often enough these next years, and for the rest of your life. But the goal isn't to memorize it all. It's to introduce you to the life of the mind of Christ, to draw you by the hand into new habits of learning to love God with your mind. And it will work best if, occasionally, you stop and notice how beautiful something you read was. Read it twice. Memorize parts of it. Put it on your wall. It won't improve your grade or make you read faster. But learning to love language is the ultimate goal.

And even that might not be enough. For we're putting words to the God who is so ultimately beyond words that his Word took flesh. The best way to get at this is to show both how much and how little words can show. For example, Annie Dillard's book *Teaching a Stone to Talk* describes the experience of a full eclipse of the sun in apocalyptic tones—nine lines of really weird:

> The sun was going, and the world was wrong. The grasses were wrong; they were platinum. Their every detail of stem, head, and blade shone lightless and artificially distinct as an art photographer's platinum print. This color has never been seen on earth. The hues were metallic; their finish was matte. The hillside was a nineteenth-century tinted photograph from which the tints had faded. All the people you see in the photograph, distinct and detailed as their faces look, are now dead. The sky was navy blue. My hands were silver. I was watching a faded color print of a movie filmed in the Middle Ages; I was

Joining the Communion of Saints and Writing the Unwritable Word

standing in it, by some mistake. I missed my own century, the
people I knew, and the real light of day.[4]

When I read this passage recently, it rolled over me like an eclipse. "All those things for which we have no words are lost," Dillard writes. "The mind—the culture—has two little tools, grammar and lexicon: a decorated sand bucket and a matching shovel. With these we bluster about the continents and do all the world's work. With these we try to save our very lives."[5] I put the book down and found myself rapt, in awe, weeping. I'd even read it before, and it never hit me like this.

I wept because I thought of this painting of Mary, Mother of God. The painting is from West Jefferson, North Carolina, in the mountains at St. Mary's Episcopal Church. In the painting, Mary is a good nine months pregnant, feet swollen, ready to bust. And she's pointing up to—you guessed it—an eclipse of the sun.[6]

Why? Why is Mary shown with an eclipse? She's often compared to the moon in artwork, drawing on the book of Revelation. But what is more important is this: Mary is the flesh through whom the unbearable God became bearable. If we can't stand the sight or presence of the physical sun without being consumed, Mary can stand the presence of the Son of God, and she does, and God becomes a howling baby.

Dillard's description of an eclipse is right on—it's a terrible sight, the landscape is transformed, everyone screams (the wall of darkness comes on at some eighteen hundred miles per hour), and nothing can ever be the same. But then everything is the same, and Dillard and her husband are on the same hillside in the Yakima Valley in Washington State. The incarnation is like that—we claim the whole world is different, yet it looks much the same. Now go and explain that.

That's the task of ministry: using words, frail things really, to make sense of the incarnate God who's beyond our sense.

Seminaries, at their best, are strong ecologies of reading and writing. They're about setting students on a course for a ministry of abundant life for the sake of the church's flourishing. They're about helping students and their future flocks inch slightly higher in love of God and neighbor. Saint Basil the Great in the fourth century situated this mission in the context of reading and writing, and he put it really well. In Basil's day, people were arguing over how exactly to describe the relationship between Jesus and the One who sent him,

---

4. *Teaching a Stone to Talk* (New York: Harper & Row, 1982) 16.

5. Ibid., 24.

6. Ben Long, *Mary, Full of Grace*. Long's painting may be viewed online: http://www.benlongfrescotrail.org/stmarys1.html.

Part 8: Searching for Jesus Amidst the Task of Writing

between the Father and the Son—are they the same, different, or sort of both? And there were of course the naysayers, the people who said it didn't matter, who argued that we should be out there helping the poor instead of poring over this esoteric academic nonsense. Basil had an answer:

> Those who are idle in the pursuit of righteousness count theological terminology as secondary, together with attempts to search out the hidden meaning in this phrase or that syllable, but those conscious of the goal of our calling realize that we are to become like God, as far as this is possible for human nature. But we cannot become like God unless we have knowledge of God, and without lessons there will be no knowledge. Instruction begins with the proper use of speech, and syllables and words are the elements of speech. Therefore to scrutinize syllables is not a superfluous task.[7]

Sure, Basil says, those who don't care about holiness don't care about language. But those who want to love God know that our only way to do that is to love language—as theologians, future pastors, and educators, as writers, all we have is words from God to give out to other people. And words are enough.

There's a story that a candidate for ministry before her ordination board footnoted only historical theologians: Augustine, Julian, Wesley. A board member grilled her: why only old sources? Don't you read any theologians who aren't dead? Well, she explained, at Duke Divinity School, where I teach, we're steeped in the thought and practice of the saints, and at Duke, those theologians *aren't* dead. A citation is a tip of the hat to the communion of the saints, and to our borrowing from wisdom outside the church. It's an act of discipleship to point out where we've learned from those before us—so others can go and learn as well.

But the communion of the saints is not a closed club. It's always looking for new members. As much as the church treasures tradition, that treasure is a living thing, and you and I have the terrifying and delightful task of adding to it. Herbert McCabe, the great Dominican theologian, used to say, "We don't know what Christians will believe in the twenty-fourth century, but we know they won't be Arians or Nestorians." Tradition has shown us that those roads are closed off. But the roads we still might take are almost infinite in number. This is the joy of reading and writing: to glean wisdom that is incomplete yet on the way to envisioning God face to face and then to add that wisdom to ourselves and invite others to share in the vision.

---

7. St. Basil the Great, *On the Holy Spirit*, trans. David Anderson (Crestwood, NY: St. Vladimir's Press, 1980) 16.

www.ingramcontent.com/pod-product-compliance
Lightning Source LLC
Chambersburg PA
CBHW031726230426
43669CB00007B/254